D1412112

WARFARE

OF THE 20th CENTURY

Armed Conflicts Outside the Two World Wars

Christopher Chant

CHARTWELL BOOKS, INC.

Photographic acknowledgments

The publishers, and Military Archive & Research Services who undertook the picture research, would like to thank the various archives and agencies who provided material for this book.

BBC Hulton Picture Library, London: 8, 9, 10 top & bottom, 11, 13, 14 top & bottom, 15 bottom, 26, 27 bottom, 28 top, 30, 31, 32, 33, 75 top & bottom, 76 top & bottom, 81 top & bottom, 82, 83, 84, 85, 86 bottom, 87, 89, 91, 164, 165, 166 top & bottom, 167 top & bottom, 168, 169, 170, 171 top & bottom, 172, 173, 175 bottom, 176, 177, 191, 193, 202, 203, 204, 205, 206, 207, 220, 223, 224; Camera Press, London: 152 top & bottom, 153 top & bottom, 154, 156, 157, 158 top & bottom, 159 top & bottom, 162, 190 top & bottom, 196, 197, 198, 201, 208, 213, 216, 217, 225, 226, 227, 228, 234, John Griffiths, London: 247; Imperial War Museum, London: 34 top & bottom; The Mansell Collection, London: 21, 23; Military Archive & Research Services, Lincs: 24 bottom, 25 top, 38b, 41 top, 52 top, 65, 69, 72 top & bottom, 74, 77 top, 78–79, 80 top & bottom, 86 top, 88 top & bottom, 90, 92, 95, 142 top & bottom, 175 top, 178, 192, 194, 199, 200 top & bottom, 240 top & bottom, 241, 242, 248, 249; Novosti Press Agency, London: 12, 15 top, 66, 70, 71, 73, 195; The Photo Source, London: 96, 145, 146, 147, 148, 215, 236; Rex Features, London: 39, 40, 41 bottom, 43 bottom, 44, 47 bottom, 48, 51, 53,

54, 55, 56 top & bottom, 57 top & bottom, 58, 59, 61 top & bottom, 62 top & bottom, 149, 150, 155, 158 bottom, 159 bottom, 184 bottom, 185, 186, 187, 188, 189, 235 top & bottom, 237, 238, 243, 244, 245 top & bottom, 246; The Robert Hunt Library, London: 24 top, 25 bottom, 27 top, 28 bottom, 29, 93, 94, 143, 179, 180; Salamander Books, London: 99, 100 top, 102 top, 103 top, 104, 107, 108, 109 top & bottom, 110 top & bottom, 111, 137 top, 138, 151; Sikorski Institute: 16, 17, 18, 19, 20; Frank Spooner Pictures/Gamma, London: 35, 36, 37, 38 top, 42, 43 top, 45, 46, 47 top, 50 bottom, 52 bottom, 60, 63, 64, 137 bottom, 139, 140 top & bottom, 141, 144, 211 top & bottom, 218, 222 top & bottom, 229, 230, 231, 232, 233; US Air Force/MARS: 105, 106 top, 115 top, 116 top, 120, 121, 131 top & bottom, 135 bottom, US Army/MARS: 100 bottom, 103 bottom, 106 bottom, 112 top & bottom, 113 top & bottom, 122 top & bottom, 126, 127 top & bottom, 128 top, 133 top & bottom, 134; US Marine Corps/ MARS: 101 top & bottom, 114, 117, 118–119, 123, 128 bottom, 129 top & bottom, 130, 136; US Navy/MARS: 50 top, 97, 98, 102 bottom, 115 bottom, 124 top & bottom, 125 top & bottom, 135 top; Victoria & Albert Museum, London: 77 bottom.

Frontispiece: Polisario in Western Sahara (The Photo Source, London)

Prepared by
The Hamlyn Publishing Group Limited
Michelin House, 81 Fulham Road, London SW3 6RB

Copyright © 1988 The Hamlyn Publishing Group Limited

ISBN 1-55521-233-6

This edition published 1988 by
Chartwell Books, Inc.
A division of Book Sales, Inc.
110 Enterprise Avenue
Secaucus, New Jersey 07094

For copyright reasons this edition is
for sale only within the U.S.A.

Printed by Mandarin Offset in Hong Kong

CONTENTS

THE 20th CENTURY: A MILITARY OVERVIEW

The history of the 20th century has been dominated by the two World Wars, cataclysmic events that have shaped the history and emotional climate of the century in a fashion not seen since the religious wars of the early 18th century and the Napoleonic wars at the beginning of the 19th century. But in contrast with these earlier wars (or rather series of wars) World Wars I and II not only completely shattered an established way of life but introduced moral uncertainties of a type not hitherto experienced.

But these wars fall outside the scope of this book: enormous quantities have been written about these two major conflicts, and their natures and effects are moderately well understood to the average reader. The purview of this book is therefore the lesser wars that have peppered the current century and, in their own way, played as decisive a part in the century's history as the two World Wars: this part has often been of a local or regional nature, but just as significant for all that to those involved. And these wars have often been of considerable size by the standards of previous centuries, and thus worthy of examination in the context of the century. However important, these wars have undeniably been overshadowed by the World Wars. This book is an attempt to redress the balance, on a compact scale, so that the reader may come to understand not only what smaller wars were fought around World Wars I and II, but also why, how, and to what cost.

The wars fought up to 1925 are largely related to World War I: those fought before 1914 indicate the stresses the current world order was imposing on nations newly emerging into the political and economic limelight as they sought a role and a niche in the world order; those fought between 1919 and 1925 are attributable largely to the disorder entailed by World War I and the need for countries with a new political order of fresh independence to secure their national and international positions.

Between 1925 and the outbreak of World War II in 1939 there occurred a number of wars in several parts of the world. These were characterized partly by territorial ambition and partly by ideological conflict, the latter coming increasingly to the fore as the strains that ultimately produced World War II began to reach a peak.

The aftermath of World War II can be seen in a light similar to that of World War I: the old order had been disturbed and a number of aftershocks had to be suffered before peace could be established. The trouble lay in the fact that peace did not return, though the threat of nuclear war prevented direct conflict between the superpowers (the USA and USSR) and their primary allies in the European theatre. So the after-shocks of World War II continued as new countries emerged and as an increasing numbers of Third World peoples sought to overthrow the European colonialism in their countries.

Into this already tense overall situation stepped the superpowers who saw in these conflicts the opportunity to further their geopolitical aims by means of proxies: local differences have thus become tainted with rivalry between 'democracy' and 'communism', the injection of superpower influence, capital, and weapons serving to intensify already direct conflicts. And just as malignly, religion has once more raised its head as a primary cause of war, leading to a bitterness just as intense as that fuelled by superpower involvement.

In its most basic terms, therefore, such is the framework into which the lesser wars of the 20th century fall. Remember, though, that 'lesser' is only a comparative term: these wars may have been (and indeed continue to be) smaller than World Wars I and II, but they have been and are fought with equal intensity, and the suffering caused by them is in no way less than that of the World Wars.

Part I

MAJOR WARS

EUROPEAN WARS

THE RUSSIAN CIVIL WAR (1917–22)

On 6/7 November 1917 the Bolsheviks seized power in Petrograd (soon renamed Leningrad) from the Provisional government headed by Aleksandr Kerensky, and the Soviet state came into existence under the leadership of Vladimir Lenin and Leon Trotsky. Beset by internal as well as external problems, the new Soviet leadership was more interested in securing the Bolshevik position than prosecuting the war against Germany and Austria-Hungary, and immediately started talks designed to extract the new state from World War I. An armistice was signed at Brest-Litovsk on 15 December 1917, ending the participation of Russia on the Allied side.

Talks were then initiated towards a full treaty, Germany insisting on independence for Poland, Finland, Estonia, Latvia, Lithuania, and the Ukraine as buffers between itself and the Red state. The Soviets' main negotiator, Trotsky, refused to consider such a diminution of the Soviet state, and it was only when the Germans called his bluff, advancing eastward once more from 18 February 1918, that Trotsky finally signed on 3 March 1918. Germany retained much of western Russia and the Ukraine to secure the arable lands that were feeding Germany in 1918.

The Ukraine was in fact the first of 15 'nations' to have declared independence from Russia after the overthrow of the Tsarist regime in March 1917. A Central Council of Liberation was created on 17 March 1917 and on 20 November 1917 this body declared the independence of the Ukraine. In a tactic typical of his astute political thinking, Lenin organized a Bolshevik shadow government of the Ukraine in Kharkov, where it readied itself for the planned reaccession of the Ukraine to the Soviet state. On 17 December 1917 the shadow government proclaimed the Ukrainian Soviet Republic and called for aid which Lenin was only too eager to grant. So started the Ukrainian War of Independence, rapidly absorbed into the great Russian Civil War.

In mid-1917 Russia was in constant turmoil: this is a street battle outside the Duma (parliament) before the Bolshevik rise to power.

The southern front was the largest single theatre in the Russian Civil War, a vast loop stretching from Odessa on the western side of the Black Sea via Kiev, Orel, Voronezh and Tsaritsyn (now Stalingrad) to Astrakhan on the estuary where the Astrakhan river debouches into the Caspian Sea. The war in this theatre got under way on 9 December 1917 when the Reds seized the lands of the Don Cossacks and thereby provoked an immediate rebellion under General Alekseyev, with General A. M. Kaledin and General Lavr Kornilov as his two field commanders. Under their two leaders the Don Cossacks moved north through the Donbass and the Kuban, defeating extemporized Red militia forces but slowly being checked by the increasing capability of the Red Army raised and trained under the control of Trotsky.

Between 22 April and 26 May 1918 the rebellion in the south spread as the Don Cossacks were joined by Georgia, Armenia and Azerbaijan, which all declared their independence from the Soviet state in growing resentment

A Bolshevik electioneering vehicle in action before the October 1917 elections to the constituent assembly.

of their treatment by Soviet forces tasked with securing the safety of the all-important oil centres in these regions. In November and December of the same year the Ukraine joined the ranks of the Whites, or at least of the anti-Reds: after the withdrawal of the German occupiers on 15 November, the pro-German puppet government was overthrown by a Ukraine socialist coup under

Left: The interventionist forces has many technical superiorities over the Reds, one of the more important being aircraft such as this Short 184.

Bottom: Trotsky flung a wide net for his Red Army, and was more than willing to accept the youngest of 'Komsomol' (Young Communist League) volunteers.

General Semyon Petlyura. Already the Allies had decided that the counter-revolution suited their long-term ambitions, and were supplying the Whites with arms and other necessaries. On 18 December 1918 the French occupied Odessa as the main base for the Allied effort to support the southern Whites.

In the Ukraine the Reds moved more swiftly than the Whites to fill the vacuum left by the retreating Germans, and by 3 February 1919 had taken Kiev as part of the drive to secure the Ukraine for the Red state. The Bug river was the main Soviet axis of advance, with sweeping movements to the west to keep the Ukrainians off balance. By 8 April 1919, the Soviets had retaken Odessa, driving out the French and securing this important port and industrial centre for the revolutionary forces.

Trotsky now turned his attention to the east and decided to secure the oilfields of the Caucasus for the Soviets: fresh troops were pushed into the area during January 1919 and this spurred the local populations to switch from what had been mainly a passive resistance to full-fledged rebellion under General Aleksandr Denikin. One of the abler White generals, Denikin gradually assumed the mantle of overall control in the south as Alekseyev died (September 1918), Kaledin committed suicide (13 February 1919), and Kornilov was killed in action (13 April 1919), with General Piotr N. Krasnov of the Don Cossacks as his deputy. The command structure was more notional than actual, however, and local commanders still did much as they pleased.

By May 1919 the preliminary moves on the southern front were giving way to more formal operations. From west to east the Whites fielded the Kiev, Volunteer, Don, and Caucasus Armies, faced to the north by the 12th, 14th, 13th, 9th, and 10th Red Armies. Trotsky was here faced with a problem, for his limited resources could not sustain offensive operations against all the anti-Soviet forces now in the field against him (Whites in the south, the Baltic states, and western Siberia; and the Allies in the north and in eastern Siberia). The Whites in western Siberia were judged to present the greatest threat and in the south Trotsky ordered a defensive campaign.

The strategic initiative thus rested with Denikin, who launched the White offensive in May 1919 with a northward advance, on diverging axes, by his four armies. The most important tangible result was the recapture of Kiev on 2 September but of greater importance would have been the link-up between General Piotr Wrangel's Caucasus Army and the Whites now pushing forward from western Siberia into Russia proper. This in turn exposed the right flank of Krasnov's Don Army, which had reached and taken Voronezh on 6 October. On 24 October the main Red force, under General Mikhail Tukhachevsky, fell on the Don Army and caused its precipitate retreat, opening the

The advent of the Bolshevik regime witnessed a return to the Russian army of a new vigour, at first in morale and then in capability.

way for Tukhachevsky to continue his westward sweep to tackle the Volunteer Army which had reached Orel on 13 October. The White effort now fell to pieces and Tukhachevsky was able to crown his remarkable achievement by pushing the last of the White forces, the Kiev Army, out of its name city on 17 December. Tukhachevsky could then wheel the axis of his advance south, pressing the disorganized White armies as they pulled back towards the Black Sea.

In March 1920 an Allied naval force managed to extract a fair proportion of the White force from Novorossiysk. This left an army under Wrangel in the Crimea as the only White force in the field on the southern front, and many of the men evacuated from Novorossiysk were shipped in to bolster Wrangel's army. April was used by the Reds to consolidate their position in the Caucasus, Baku being taken on 28 April. Supported by naval forces in the Caspian Sea, the Soviets then moved to occupy much of northern Persia as far south as Enzeli (now Pahlevi) and Resht.

In June 1920, meanwhile, Wrangel had taken the opportunity of the Red invasion of Poland to launch a bold offensive north from the Crimea. But the preparation of his offensive had taken Wrangel too long, and the Reds were in the process of disentangling themselves from the Polish disaster: combat-experienced troops were rapidly switched south to check Wrangel's advance and then drive him back towards the Sea of Azov and the Crimea by 1 November. It was the end of White hopes in the south, and the remnants of Wrangel's army were evacuated by the British. Disunity had cost the Whites any hope they might have had of welding

together an effective southern force.

Resistance to the Red regime in the north-west was like that in the south to the extent that it was fragmented, but unlike it to the extent that it was successful to a limited degree. On 6 December 1917 Finland declared itself independent of Russia and set about organizing forces under the capable General Carl Gustav Mannerheim even as the Reds were establishing militia centres in Finland. Helsingfors (now Helsinki) was already in Red hands, as were other urban centres, when the Reds launched a revolution against Finnish independence on 28 January 1918. Mannerheim responded rapidly: his initial move overwhelmed the Soviet garrison in Vaasa, where the Finnish military headquarters had been established, and secured a considerable arsenal for the use of the Finnish forces.

Mannerheim took Tammerfors (now Tampere) early in March, but was then checked by the Reds as his forces consolidated in preparation for an offensive into Karelia. The Germans now intervened, General Kolmar von der Goltz landing a force of 10,000 men at Hanko (now Hango) on 13 April. Von der Goltz moved rapidly and his force took

Helsingfors on 18 April to divide the Red-held area into two portions, Mannerheim's forces were also on the move once more, on 19 April driving through to Lake Ladoga and thus separating the Karelian isthmus from Russia. The remaining Russian forces in Finland attempted to break out to Russia, but were forced to surrender on 29 April. Desultory fighting continued along the front between the two countries, and the war was brought to an end on 14 October 1920 when the Treaty of Dorpat (now Tartu) recognized Finnish independence.

The situation was more complex to the south of the Gulf of Finland where the provinces of Estonia, Latvia, and Lithuania took advantage of the chaos attending the Soviet assumption of power to declare their independences. Estonia declared on 28 November 1917 and was immediately invaded by the Reds, who were then driven out by the Germans after the failure of the talks at Brest-Litovsk in February 1918. The German pulled out in November 1918 at the time of their armistice with the Allied

Evidence of Allied aid for the Whites: British and French guns captured by the Reds in Wrangel's final rout.

The exigencies of war created some strange 'weapons', including this paddle-wheel ferry used as a gunboat on the northern front by the British.

powers and the Reds wasted no time before invading once more, this time on 22 November.

Estonian resistance was determined and ably supported by the activities of a small British naval force in the Gulf of Finland, so in January 1919 the Reds were forced to pull back. The boot was now firmly on the other foot, and under the command of General Nikolai Yudenich a White force crossed the frontier near Narva on 6 October and struck towards Petrograd. The disorganized Red forces were able to offer only poor resistance to Yudenich's 20,000-man force, which reached the suburbs of Petrograd on 19 October. Sterling though panic-struck defensive measures organized by Trotsky then restored the Reds' equilibrium, and Yudenich pulled back into Estonia. A Treaty of Dorpat on 2 February 1920 recognized Estonia's independence.

On 18 November 1917 Latvia declared its independence and was promptly invaded by Red forces who took Riga on 4 January 1918 and re-established a Red government. In March a combined German and Latvian force drove the Soviets out of Latvia, but continued fighting became the order of the day as the Germans then sought to establish a German state in Latvia against Latvian resistance. An armistice came into force on 22 May but failed on 20 October as Latvians, Germans, and Soviets fought a small and extremely confused campaign for control of the country. Germany was forced to evacuate the country in November 1918. Sporadic fighting between the Latvians and Soviets followed, but by January 1920 the Latvians had finally succeeded in driving out the last Soviet troops, and the armistice of 1 February 1920 was formalized on 11 August by the Treaty of Riga, which recognized Latvian independence.

Lithuania was the last of the Baltic states to declare independence, this occurrence on 16 February 1918 prompting an immediate Soviet invasion and German counter-invasion. The Germans evacuated the country in November 1918, being replaced by yet another Soviet invasion which on 5 January 1919 took Vilnyus and prompted a Polish intervention from the south. This was one of the causes of the Russo–Polish War (see pages 16–20) but the independence of Lithuania was finally secured by the Treaty of Moscow signed on 12 July 1920. Poland was unhappy with the restoration of Vilnyus to Lithuania and seized the city and its environs on 9 October 1920; mediation efforts by the League of Nations were unsuccessful, and it was December 1927 before this Polish–Lithuanian squabble was finally ended.

The new Soviet state's problem to the east started with the Czech Legion, a force of some 100,000 Bohemian (later Czech) prisoners of war captured in Russia's war with Austria-Hungary. The Russian authorities had agreed to the repatriation of this force, which wished to see the establishment of an independent state of Czechoslovakia out of the Austro-Hungarian province of Bohemia. The plan was for the Czech Legion to come under French command for service on the Western Front against Germany, but when the Soviet regime began to interfere with its movement over the Trans-Siberian Railway towards Vladivostok, the Czech Legion seized control of this essential lifeline in June 1918.

Local Soviet forces were wholly incapable of handling this combat-experienced force, which soon captured sufficient arms to launch a westward move along the Trans-Siberian Railway towards Ekaterinburg (now Sverdlovsk), which was captured on 26 July 1918. The Czechs then opened negotiations with the Soviets and the anti-Soviet administration of the Omsk region. This latter was taken over on 18 November 1918 by the Whites under Admiral Aleksandr Kolchak, whose grandiose ambitions were signalled by his adoption of the title 'Supreme Ruler of Russia'. Kolchak offered the Czechs a 'deal they could not refuse' in order to secure their assistance, and in December the combined White and Czech army moved westward through the Urals to capture Ufa and Perm.

Trotsky rightly saw this thrust as the major threat to the fledgling Soviet state, and concentrated his major effort to halt Kolchak.

Under the able leadership of Tukhachevsky the Reds retook Ekaterinburg on 27 January 1919 and pushed east to capture Omsk

on 14 November. The Whites' eastern front now collapsed, and Kolchak was captured and executed. The Czechs remained a cohesive fighting force, however, and drove east towards Vladivostok and the Allied forces on the Siberian seaboard.

The last component of the threat to the Soviet regime was that of the Allies, which began with the Japanese occupation of Vladivostok on 30 December 1917. The size of the Japanese force, commanded by the respected General Otani, suggested to the other Allies that Japan had designs on the whole of the USSR's eastern seaboard, and prompted similar notions in France, the UK, and the USA.

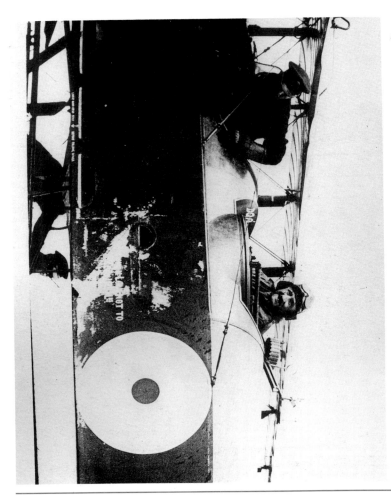

Top: Red prisoners of war captured by the British on the northern front and held in a camp at Troitsa.

Left: A British senior officer, General Walsh, prepares for a personal reconnaissance over the northern front in a Short 184 floatplane.

The first physical expression of this notion was the creation of an Anglo–American–French expeditionary force (under British command) that landed at Murmansk on 23 June 1918 before advancing on Archangel, which fell on 2 August within the context of a declared aim of regaining the supplies which the Allies had supplied to the Tsarist regime. The real objective, however, was a southward offensive to link up with the Czech Legion and (later) Kolchak's forces as part of the Allied effort to create a unified front against the Soviets.

Small-scale operations followed along the Vologda river but no major effort was undertaken and the Allied force began to disintegrate politically in August 1919 when the Americans pulled out. In September and October the French and British finally evacuated this northern lodgement.

The eastern lodgement enjoyed a longer life but ultimately no greater success. As the Japanese were consolidating their position in the region, the Americans in August 1918 landed a small force designed to ensure the extrication of the Czech Legion and to check Japanese ambitions, though the American commander was under explicit instructions to avoid combat if possible. The French and British tried to use this American detachment as the spearhead of a reinforcement effort for Kolchak and the Czech Legion, but the Americans adamantly refused to consider this, instead holding the Trans-Siberian Railway between Lake Baikal and Vladivostok until the Czech Legion arrived. The Americans and Czechs were then evacuated from Vladivostok in April 1920.

The Japanese retained Vladivostok and the area around it for a period, but then pulled out on 25 October 1922.

Top: *Allied troops in the dire winter conditions of the northern front.*

Right: *American prisoners are seen after their release by the Reds in August 1921.*

THE RUSSO-POLISH WAR (1920)

The course of World War I on the Eastern Front left all of Poland in the hands of the Central Powers, and on 5 November 1916 the independence of Poland was agreed by the Central Powers in an astute political move that brought a useful number of Poles to the ranks of the Central Powers. Yet full independence could not be organized in time of war, and a Regency Council was established to administer this semi-autonomous region. On Armistice Day (11 November 1918) the Regency Council took over from the Central Powers and named General Josef Pilsudski as commander-in-chief of the Polish armed forces.

Pilsudski's first two acts were to declare himself head of the Polish national government, and to

declare Poland an independent state. He was nothing if not ambitious for his country: with considerable approval from France, which saw a powerful and prosperous Poland as a potentially decisive French ally on the other side of Germany, Pilsudski set about restoring the boundaries of the new Poland to the lines they had occupied in 1772 – basically those of the Dvina and Dniepr rivers in eastern Russia. Pilsudski saw himself as the leader of an anti-Soviet confederation of states newly defected from Soviet Russia. In April 1919 the Poles invaded south-eastern Lithuania to take Lida and Vilnyus, and during May swept into eastern Galicia, part of the West Ukrainian Republic proclaimed by Petlyura in November 1918.

Such a situation clearly posed a severe threat to the Soviet state and its ambitions. In the short term Lenin and Trotsky offered to negotiate with the Poles, but though the offer of 22 December 1919 was accepted, no further progress towards negotiations, let alone a solution, followed. The Soviet leaders therefore fixed their determination on a rapid reabsorption of Poland into the Soviet state. The demands of the Civil War meant that the required Soviet build-up was slow, however, and was readily appreciated by the Poles. Pilsudski saw that Poland's best chance lay

The Ukrainian leader, Semyon Petlyura (left), with Marshal Pilsudski on a Polish train near the Front in April 1920.

with a pre-emptive campaign before the Soviets could muster their full strength.

To the north of the Pripet Marshes the Soviet forces were controlled by General Mikhail Tukhachevsky's Army of the West and comprised (from north to south) the 4th, 15th, 3rd, and 16th Red Armies supported by Gay Khan's III Cavalry Corps to exploit any breakthrough by the infantry armies.

The southern sector started at the southern side of the Pripet Marshes near Mozyr and ran westward to Rovno and Dubno before turning south along the line of the Zbrncz river and finally south-east along the line of the Dnieper river to Odessa. The Soviet forces here came under the command of General Yegorov's Army of the South-West and comprised (again from north to south) the 12th and 14th Red Armies supported by five divisions of cavalry commanded by General Semyon Budyenny.

The allied forces facing the Soviets were perhaps similar in overall strength, though an overall figure of 120,000 men is sometimes quoted (perhaps for the Poles alone). Facing Tukhachevsky in the north were the Polish 1st and 4th Armies under the overall command of General Wladislaw Sikorski, with a reserve (the Polish Reserve Army) in the process of forming to the north-west of Vilnyus. In the south were the Polish 3rd, 2nd, and 6th Armies under the overall command of Pilsudski. At the extreme south of the allied line was the Rumano-Ukrainian 7th Army under Petlyura.

Pilsudski was ready in April 1920 and on 25 April launched his forces in a drive east towards Zhitomir with the ultimate objective of Kiev before a left wheel up the Dniepr to take Tukhachevsky in his right flank. This was a plan of the most adventurous (or with hindsight foolhardy) strategic concept, demanding enormous performance from troops with only modest

horse transport capability. Yet all went well in the early phases of the offensive, and Kiev fell to the Poles on 7 May.

The balance of the front, with a strong Soviet right wing facing a weak Polish left wing and a weak Soviet left wing facing a strong Polish right wing, called for a rapid move by Tukhachevsky, and this was the move ordered by the Soviet overall commander, General Kamenev, as a means of

Units of the Polish 3rd Army enter the Ukrainian capital, Kiev, on 7 May 1920; however, the Poles' visit was to be short.

relieving the pressure of Yegorov. Tukhachevsky was only too eager to respond, and on 15 May launched his 15th Red Army against the strategic rail junction at Molodechno with the objective of driving the Polish 1st Army into the Pinsk swamps.

The Soviet forces made good initial progress against the weak Polish formations, but soon began to falter. Pilsudski saw this as the major threat to the complete front, and prepared to reinforce Sikorski's forces. But before he could do so he was undone by a move of the utmost operational boldness: on 18 May Budenny's cavalry force of the Army of the South-West (some 17,000 cossacks, 48 pieces of artillery, 5 armoured trains, 8 armoured cars and 12 aircraft) struck west through

Pilsudski's right wing from the region of Elizavetsgrad. Nearly capturing the right wing of Pilsudski's forces, Budyenny rampaged through the Polish rear areas after wheeling right: he disrupted the Polish forces south and south-west of Kiev, pressed on to take Berdichev and Zhitomir, and then advanced into Poland proper and the outskirts of Lwow. The Polish 3rd Army on Pilsudski's left flank would have been cut off had it not managed to break out to the west on 13 June.

To compound Pilsudski's problems, Tukhachevsky again started to move in July with a ponderous advance impossible for Sikorski's forces to check: Vilnyus

Top: The summer of 1920, and Poland's desperate position is exemplified by this unit of workmen about to depart for the front outside Warsaw.

Centre: The Poles throw up their defence lines as the Reds advance on Warsaw during the summer of 1920.

Above: *The face of Poland at war: Father Kosma-Lenkowski, a chaplain of the Polish army.*

Below: *The fledgling Polish tank corps was equipped with light vehicles such as these French Renault FT17 reconnaissance tanks.*

fell on 14 July and Grodno on 19 July, and Tukhachevsky loomed ominously closer to Warsaw which he expected to enter on 14 August. The position of the Poles was dire, with Pilsudski's armies centred on Lwow and Sikorski's on Warsaw. Into this situation stepped the French, dispatching General Maxime Weygand to offer strategic advice despite the fact that Pilsudski had asked for additional weapons and, perhaps more importantly in the short term, fresh supplies of ammunition for his existing weapons.

Pilsudski saw clearly that Tukhachevsky's momentum was fuelled by hunger rather than strategic necessity, and decided that Weygand's advice was wrong: the Polish blow would not be directed at the Soviet right wing, but rather at its centre with the object of breaking through the junction between Yegorov's and Tukhachevsky's forces before wheeling left to cut the latters' already overstretched lines of communication. And though the Soviets might at a pinch manage to live off the land for a short period,

they could not replenish their ammunition and other supplies in the same fashion. For this offensive the Polish dispositions were admirably suited, being based on the defence of Warsaw by 43 batteries of heavy artillery with the more mobile formations located largely to the north and west at Modlin and Plock, and to the south at Deblin. The defence was entrusted to General Haller, and Sikorski was entrusted with the urgent formation of the new Polish 5th Army. Pilsudski ordered a static defence of the Polish capital, and grouped the offensive forces for his plan around Warsaw and Lwow, linked by a weak centre.

Pilsudski marshalled his assault force at Deblin, some 50 miles (80 km) south of Warsaw. Speed was of the essence in case the Soviets should realize the weakness of their centre, and Pilsudski saw that as his 46th Army was already falling back towards the ideal start point for the offensive, it should become the focus of the planned offensive. Pilsudski finally committed the offensive on 16

August in the Battle of Warsaw. The Poles burst through the Mozyr Group in the Soviets' weakly held centre and drove straight towards Brest-Litovsk.

Caught between the Polish pincers, Tukhachevsky's armies fell apart: some 30,000 or more Soviets fled north into East Prussia, where they were interned, while the other shattered remnants of the Soviet armies sought to escape to the east. By a remarkable achievement of organization and personality, Tukhachevsky managed to stem the rout and restore order in his armies, so creating a defensive line between Grodno, Brest-Litovsk, and Włodawa on 25 August. Exhausted and virtually out of supplies, the Poles halted in front of this line. For the loss of some 50,000 of his own men, Piłsudski had inflicted a catastrophic defeat

on the Soviets who suffered about 150,000 casualties, which included 66,000 prisoners. The Poles also captured 230 guns, 1,000 machine guns, and 10,000 vehicles of various types.

An increasing stream of supplies enabled Piłsudski to build up his strength quite rapidly and on 12 September the Poles resumed the offensive with Piłsudski commanding the wing north of the Pripet Marshes and Sikorski the wing to the south of the Pripet Marshes.

In the south Sikorski made rapid progress, reaching Tarnopol to the south-west of Lwów by 18 September. But the greater level of success was enjoyed by Piłsudski, who stormed forward in a series of decisive engagements that kept the Soviets completely off balance. The Soviets were driven from their interim stop line

along the Niemen river in the Battle of the Niemen on 26 September, the 3rd Red Army being destroyed in the process and Grodno entered on the same day. On the following day Piłsudski offered the Soviets no respite, inflicting on them so decisive a defeat in the Battle of the Shchara (now Szczara) that Tukhachevsky's forces fell back as far as Minsk after losing 50,000 prisoners and 160 guns, as well as an unknown number of other casualties.

An armistice came in force during 12 October and the bone-weary troops of each side came to a halt. The war was finally brought to a close on 18 March 1921 by the Treaty of Riga.

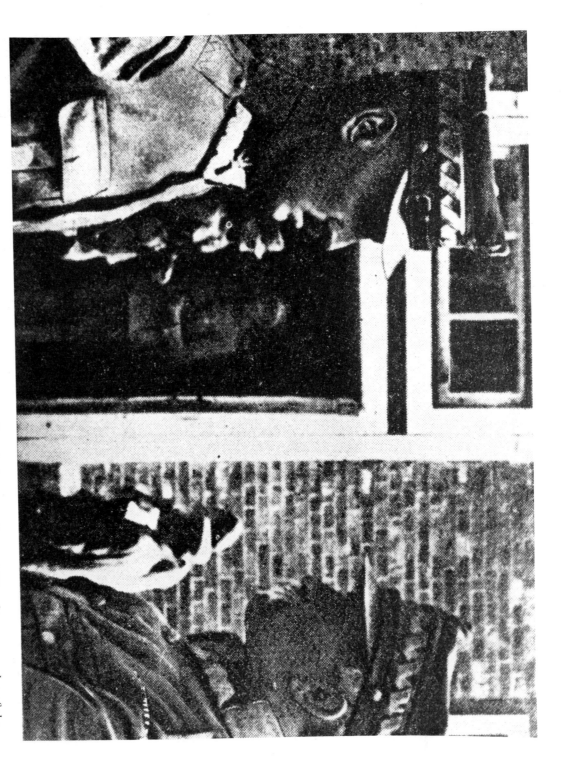

General Sikorski, commander of the Polish 5th Army, confers with the 17th Division's General A. Osinski in the dangerous days of August 1920.

THE GRECO-TURKISH WAR (1920-22)

After a series of campaigns in which the leadership of Turkish officers (frequently under overall German generalship) and the doggedness of Turkish infantry had caused the Allies a number of unpleasant shocks, in 1918 the dismal nature of Turkey's military infrastructure and logistical apparatus finally sapped the capabilities and morale of the country's field armies. The year was thus marked by a number of rapid British advances in Palestine and Mesopotamia and on 30 October 1918 the Ottoman Empire signed an armistice with the Allies. On 12 November an Allied fleet passed finally through the Dardanelles and dropped anchor off Constantinople (now Istanbul). The days of the Ottoman Empire were over and Turkey rapidly fell into virtual anarchy as the Allies started to squabble over the divisions of the spoils. Sultan Mohamed VI was ready to accede to all Allied demands, but this ready agreement to the dismemberment of Turkey (along the lines of a secret agreement between the powers in 1907 but finalized in the Treaty of Sèvres) further exacerbated the tensions already building in Turkey.

Signed on 20 August 1919 the treaty reduced Turkey to a geographical core comprising Anatolia in Asia Minor and the Chatalja peninsula in Europe, and pushed the nationalist party to action. Headed by Turkey's sole undefeated general of World War I, Mustafa Kemal, the nationalist party had come into existence during June 1919 and began to agitate against the Treaty of Sèvres the moment it was signed.

Before this time, however, the Greeks had begun to move into Turkey as the agents for the Allied powers: on 15 May 1919 a Greek force of 20,000 men began to come ashore at Smyrna (now Izmir) and develop a lodgement around this important port. The Allies

concurred with this move and the Italians also advanced from their local island toeholds (Rhodes and the Dodecanese, ceded to Italy by Turkey in the Treaty of Ouchy signed on 15 October 1912 to end the Italo-Turkish War of 1911–12), to occupy part of south-west Anatolia.

Kemal's nationalist party had lost patience by the beginning of 1920 and in April established a new national capital at Ankara as Constantinople was still occupied by the Allies. The Allies were highly disturbed by this resurgence of Turkish nationalism, much preferring the docile acquiescence of the sultanate, and when the Greek prime minister, Eleftherios

Venizelos, suggested that the Greeks should deal once and for all with the nationalist movement, the Allies were persuaded by the British prime minister, David Lloyd George, to agree without demur. In this simple decision the Allies indicated how little they really understood the temper of Turkey, where the nationalist cause was developing a momentum whose deep roots were unappreciated by the Allies with their feelers buried in the decadence of Constantinople.

Seen in 1922, these are Turkey's greatest political and military leaders of the Greco-Turkish War: Mustafa Kemal Pasha (left) and Ismet Pasha.

Greek operations were entrusted mainly to the force around Smyrna (grandiloquently titled the Allied Army in Anatolia under the command of General Paraskeropoulos), though on 22 July 1920 the European Turkish city of Adrianople (now Edirne) was taken by the Greeks after a cross-border operation from Thrace. The main effort was thus an eastward advance from Smyrna along the axis of the Gediz river. There was little that the Turks, outnumbered and outgunned, could do to oppose this initial Greek advance, and by 29 June the Smyrna force had advanced some 125 miles (200 km) to Ushaq (now Uşak), while a flanking movement by the Greek force from Thrace crossed the Bosporus to secure Panderma and Brusa (now Bandirma and Bursa) on the southern side of the Sea of Marmara by 9 July.

The continuance of the Greek effort was now delayed by the death of King Alexander on 25 October. Venizelos wished to instal Prince Paul as king (despite the fact that Alexander's morganatic wife Aspasia was pregnant) but the Greek people decided in an election to recall ex-King Constantine, the hero of the Balkan Wars, with Rhallis as his prime minister. Constantine had been pro-German in World War 1, and his resumption of power proved too much for the Allies, who withdrew their support for what was now a Greek adventure into central Anatolia. Constantine ordered that the advance be resumed, with Ankara as its objective as part of the overall Greek scheme to annex European Turkey and western Anatolia.

Now under the command of General Papoulas, the force still styled the Allied Army in Anatolia pushed farther to the east: moving on the main axis from Smyrna towards Afionkarahisar (now Afyon) was a force of seven infantry divisions and one cavalry brigade (30,000 men), and along the secondary axis 40 miles (65 km) to the north from Brusa towards Eskisehir was a force of four infantry divisions (18,000 men). Good progress was made initially, for Kemal was holding his forces around the two Greek target towns: 23,000 men to protect Eskisehir under the command of Ismet Pasha and 25,000 men to shield Afionkarahisar.

Numbers were about equal, and while the Greeks were superior in artillery and other *matériel*, the Turks had the advantage of fighting a defensive battle in prepared positions. It was the Greeks' northern thrust that made the first serious contact with the Turks as it pushed forward to Eskisehir: on 10 January 1921 it met the Turks at Inonu, some 20 miles (32 km) to the west of Eskisehir, resulting in the 1st Battle of Inonu. The Turks fought in their normal dogged fashion, halting the Greeks in conditions of melting snow on the first day and repulsing them on the second.

On 23 March 1921 the Greeks moved on to the offensive once more, Papoulas having built up his strength to a maximum of some 150,000, about 100,000 of which were disposed along the Greek line of communication with Smyrna. On 28 March the Greeks launched simultaneous attacks on Inonu, whose defence was still entrusted to Ismet Pasha, and on Afionkarahisar, whose defence was led by Refet Pasha. On the right flank the Greeks were successful, driving Refet Pasha's forces out of Afionkarahisar; on the left flank, however, Ismet Pasha again held firm against three determined Greek assaults in the 2nd Battle of Inonu. With Inonu and Eskisehir still in Turkish hands and threatening the left flank of any advance from Afionkarahisar, Papoulas was hamstrung and on 2 April again called off the offensive. Refet Pasha was summarily replaced by Ismet Pasha who became Ismet Inonu when the Turks adopted surnames.

Constantine now decided to assume personal control as the Supreme Commander of the Greek Forces in Asia. Strength was further boosted, this time to 200,000 men, but now the position of the Turks was improving on a daily basis.

Constantine's offensive was committed on 16 July 1921, and was skilfully executed. A feint towards the Turkish right flank at Eskisehir distracted Ismet Pasha just as the major assault fell on his left at Afionkarahisar. The Greeks then wheeled their axis to the north and swept towards Eskisehir, rolling up the Turkish defence in a series of frontal assaults combined with flanking movements. Eskisehir fell on 17 July despite a vigorous counter-attack by Ismet Pasha who was determined to fight to the finish. The saner counsels of Kemal prevailed, however, and Ismet disengaged with great losses to reach the comparative safety of the Sakkaria (now Sakarya) river, some 30 miles (48 km) to the north and only 50 miles (80 km) from Ankara. The Turks had lost about 11,000 men and the Greeks 8,000, but the Greek army was too tired to follow up this initial success with the required operational speed. Thus it was only on 10 August that Constantine was able to commit his regrouped forces to an assault against the much-strengthened Sakkaria Line. This is some of the most inhospitable terrain in all Turkey and the Greeks found themselves operating at the end of over-extended lines of communication in a virtual desert that killed horses, caused vehicles to break down, and prevented the movement of heavy artillery.

On 23 August battle was joined and, once a Greek enveloping movement against the Turkish left flank had failed, the Battle of the Sakkarya descended to a typical head-on confrontation of infantry, machine-guns and artillery. The Greeks launched their main effort in the centre, pushing forward some 10 miles (16 km) in 10 days. Astute as ever at the decisive moment, Kemal assumed personal

command and led a small counter-attack against the Greek left. The attack achieved limited success, but in fear that this presaged a major effort to outflank his forces as the severity of winter was approaching, Constantine broke off the Greek assault on 16 September and ordered a general retreat towards Eskisehir and Afionkarahisar.

In May 1922 Papoulas and his complete staff resigned, Papoulas being replaced by General Hajianestis who was mentally ill and who ran the campaign from his yacht moored in Smyrna harbour. In fact the only decisive move made by Hajianestis was the transfer of two divisions from Anatolia to eastern Thrace in an effort to blackmail the allies into giving up Constantinople. The Allies called the Greek bluff and discovered it to be just that.

On 26 August 1922 Kemal dispatched his army on a drive to the coast of the Aegean Sea. Afionkarahisar fell to the Turks on 30 August, followed by Brusa on 5 September. The Greeks could do nothing but retreat, and the retreat almost inevitably declined into a rout characterized by the most appalling Greek atrocities: rape, pillage, and arson became the order of the day and it is estimated that one million Turks were rendered homeless as the Turks pursued the shattered Greek army with an increasing ferocity that saw the massacre of many prisoners. No thought had been taken for evacuation and as the defeated Greek forces tumbled into Smyrna the city became a complete shambles. The Turks took Smyrna in a direct assault between 9 and 11 September and two days later the city went up in

Kemal Ataturk, the founding father of modern Turkey and victor in the Greco-Turkish War.

flames, to this day the Greeks blaming the Turks and the Turks counter-accusing the Greeks.

Kemal proclaimed a Turkish republic, and on 1 November the sultan fled his capital and his country on a British warship. The Greco-Turkish War was over, a fact formalized on 24 July 1923 by the signature of the Treaty of Lausanne, restoring to Turkey eastern Thrace as far west as the Maritza river. On 23 August the Allies quit Constantinople and on 29 October the Turkish republic came into formal being with Kemal, newly surnamed Ataturk (father of the Turks), as its first president.

THE SPANISH CIVIL WAR (1936-39)

On 18 July 1936 the military garrisons of 17 cities (12 on the Spanish mainland and 5 in Spanish Morocco) rose in rebellion against the communist government of Spain. The spark that triggered off the Spanish Civil War was the confrontation, in the Spanish Moroccan city of Melilla, between a unit of the Spanish Foreign Legion and a communist-led mob, but the real causes of any civil war must lie far deeper in the socio-political make-up of any country, and this was certainly the case with the Spanish Civil War.

It was the communists who predominated in the Spanish parliament after 16 February 1936 and who led the move that led to President Zamora's replacement by the Marxist president, Manuel Azana. The new administration promised to follow the guidelines of its predecessors, but was under great pressure from the CNT union and its extremist offshoot, the Federación Anarquista Iberica (FAI), for total revolution against the current political, social, and religious complexion of Spain. With the essence of Catholic Spain threatened in this manner, the army felt that it must act, but was poorly placed to do so as many of its ablest and most anti-communist/anarchist officers had been relegated to Spanish Morocco and the Canary Islands specifically to prevent their interference in domestic matters.

Throughout the spring and early summer of 1936 the generals laid their plans and finally came out into the open on 17/18 July with a

rising in Spanish Morocco, which was followed closely by risings in many of the major garrisons of the Spanish mainland. General Francisco Franco commanded in Spanish Morocco, after flying secretly from the Canaries in a chartered aeroplane, while the leader on the mainland was General Emilio Mola, commanding the garrison of Burgos. In general the Madrid region, the ports of the eastern coast, and the Basque and Catalan regions remained loyal to the republican government. By the end of July the initial division of the country had become clear: the republicans held the centre and east of the country with the exception of a nationalist enclave around Granada, a western tongue running from Ciudad Real to Badajoz and the Portuguese frontier, and the north coast with the exception of a nationalist enclave at Oviedo.

Centre: A heavily posed study of Moroccan colonial troops of the type so important to the Nationalist cause in the Spanish Civil War.

Right: Nationalist troops involved in a house-to-house search for republicans in Irun (northern Spain) during September 1936.

Right: *Troops advance towards the ruins of a Republican town under cover of a light tank being tested operationally by the Germans in Spain during 1938.*

Bottom: *Nationalist troops on the march, clearly in good spirits about the progress of their operations.*

The nationalist plan was to reinforce southern Spain as rapidly as possible with men and equipment from Spanish Morocco, and the sealift was augmented by an airlift by German transport machines in the ferry task to Algeciras and La Linea.

Thereafter Madrid was to be the target for the nationalists' two main forces: Franco was to strike north with his 30,000 Spanish and Moroccan troops while Mola was to strike south from Burgos with his 15,000 Spanish troops. On 15 August Franco's forces took Badajoz and Merida after an offensive into the republican corridor to the Portuguese frontier, followed by Caceres near the lower reaches of the Tagus river, and then swung north-west to move up this natural approach route to Madrid, in the process taking Talavera and on 28 September relieving Toledo after its 10-week seige.

The political overtones of the civil war inevitably resulted in international involvement and this became increasingly evident during September. The Soviets supported the republicans, supplies and equipment being brought in by sea to the ports of Barcelona, Valencia, Alicante, and Cartagena. The Germans and Italians supported the nationalists; and supplies, equipment, and complete military units were shipped into Huelva and Cadiz for the most part, together with a proportion through Portugal, which had sided with the nationalists in July 1936. International pressure forced Portugal to close its borders in April 1937, but by this time Franco's forces were able to secure deliveries through Spain's

north-western ports. The German contribution was centred on aircraft (transports, bombers, and fighters) and later a number of newer weapons which the Germans wished to subject to operational testing, while the Italians provided aircraft and tanks, plus a number of infantry and armoured units.

On 4 September the republican administration was re-formed as the Popular Front government under Francisco Largo Caballero. Basque and Catalan nationalist interests were incorporated into the government from its beginning, but the Anarcho-Syndicalists were adopted only in November, after the government had removed to safer quarters in Valencia as the nationalists laid siege to Madrid. In October Franco had been named head of the nationalist government and by 6 November Madrid was under siege by the combined forces of Franco and Mola, the latter commenting that in addition to the four columns he commanded outside the city he had a fifth column inside Madrid. The fighting for the city was bitter, and though the nationalists managed to take part of the northern and western suburbs, the defence under General Jose Miaja held firm in four months of virtually non-stop combat. The exhausted nationalists called off their offensive in February 1937 to rest and regroup before resuming the offensive in March.

As the siege of Madrid tailed off, the nationalists made two determined efforts to reduce the republicans' hold on south-eastern Spain. In the south a force commanded by General Gonzalo Queipo de Llano, with considerable Italian support,

captured Malaga on 8 February and extended the nationalist hold on the south almost as far east as Almeria. Less success attended the northern effort, however: here the nationalists attempted to push south from Teruel to cut Madrid's main supply line from Valencia, up which Soviet equipment and 'international brigade' volunteers were flowing in growing numbers to bolster the defence of Madrid. Another attempt to achieve the same operational purpose was mounted by the Italians in March. Striking south from Guadalajara, just the north-east of Madrid, two divisions supported by 50 tanks became stuck in thick mud and by 16 March had been destroyed as effective formations by repeated attacks by Soviet dive-bombers. Most of their equipment was lost, but most of the men finally regained the safety of the

nationalist lines. The republicans capitalized on this success by capturing the Italian base area around Brihuega on 18 March and making off with large quantities of invaluable stores.

Realizing that Madrid was for the time being out of his reach, Franco turned his strategic gaze on the north and the Basque capital of Bilbao, which was invested on 1 April. Soon after this, though, the nationalist cause suffered a severe public relations defeat when German aircraft attacked Guernica on 25 April, worldwide outrage at the civilian casualties being directed at the nationalists as a whole and not just at the Germans.

Men of the 15th International Brigade: the brigade included 26 nationalities, but these are men of the 600-strong 1st (British) Battalion.

On 18 June the 80-day siege of Bilbao ended when the nationalists under General Fidel Davila took the city and moved straight on to take Santander on 25 August. Despite the death of one of its abler generals, Mola, in an air accident on 3 June, the nationalist cause was faring well in northern Spain, and by the end of October 1937 the complete northern coast so valuable to the republicans was in the hands of Franco's forces.

Meanwhile the republicans were trying to lift the nationalist pressure from Madrid and on 6 June launched an offensive that initially gained useful ground. But the investing force, under General Jose Varela, brought the offensive to a halt by 25 June and this ended the dire warfare around Madrid for about two years. The republicans next switched their effort to Aragon, a major effort being made in August and September to enlarge the republican area west of Tarragona with an offensive up the Ebro river. Severe fighting resulted, the

Top: Rural operations in Spain: hugging the stone walls for protection against machine-gun fire, a small unit approaches a defended village.

Centre: From their commanding position on a hilltop, Republican troops await a Nationalist attack. The scene is probably Aragón, but is typical of Spanish operations.

nationalist garrisons at Huesca, Zaragoza, and Teruel all contributing to the halting of the offensive.

To even the most biased observer it was clear that the tide of the war was beginning to turn slowly but strongly in favour of the nationalists: in recent months there had been little movement in the front lines, but the nationalists had largely consolidated their previous gains, pinning the republicans in the eastern portion of the country where the nationalist naval blockade could slowly strangle them. On land the most serious threat posed by the nationalists in the short term was the salient centred on Teruel: should the nationalists succeed in driving forward from this position they could reach the eastern coast at Castellon and Valencia, so

cutting the republican area into northern and southern halves and effectively destroying the supply line to Madrid.

On 5 December, therefore, the republicans launched a major offensive to eliminate the Teruel salient. Extremely bitter and costly fighting eventually gave Teruel to the republicans, at the same time undoing the nationalist offensive to the north of the salient, but the campaign so exhausted the republicans that they could not sustain their effort when the nationalists launched their counter-offensive on 15 February 1938. In just five days the nationalists retook the area which the republicans had needed 40 days to capture and in the process pushed forward their left flank to the north of Teruel to straighten the nationalist line and so eliminate the salient.

Above: Brief interlude – Republican soldiers recover their energies and discuss the progress of operations with reporters, including Ernest Hemingway.

Left: Nationalist troops shelter at the bottom of a rock-covered hill whose summit is held by machine-guns unsilenced by an earlier artillery bombardment.

An experienced Nationalist commander explains the course of operations on the Ebro front to an eager reporter.

Then the republicans' worst fears were realized as the nationalists committed a major offensive to the east during February, reaching the coast at Vinaroz on 15 April: large portions of Aragon and the Levante were lost to the republicans, and Catalonia was cut off from the rest of republican Spain. Franco's forces pushed on towards Barcelona, but fanatical republican resistance on the Ebro river checked the advance by the end of July. Yet if the republican cause was to survive, the Catalan peoples and the industries around Barcelona must be reconnected with the anarchist-controlled agrarian areas of south-east Spain.

On 24 July a passionate offensive was launched by the republicans along the line of the lower Ebro with a view to breaking through the nationalist corridor to the sea. The battle ebbed and flowed up to 30 September in the area north-west of Tortosa, the

republicans making slow and appallingly costly progress over a total depth of about 10 miles (16 km). Ultimately, though, all that the republicans achieved was the elimination of the nationalist salient between Fayon and Cherta, and not the breakthrough to reunite Catalonia with the rest of republican Spain.

Franco had been able to husband his forces carefully during the Ebro battles, and on 23 December sent his troops forwards in a concerted effort against Catalonia, the main weight being directed north-east along the coast. By 17 January 1939 the area between Tarragona and Artesa had succumbed to the nationalists and the back of the republican effort had been broken: increasingly large numbers of republican troops fell back in growing disorder towards Barcelona and despite the appalling weather the nationalists pressed ahead with all possible vigour. On 26 January Barcelona

fell, and by 7 February the nationalists had compressed the last vestiges of republican defence into a narrow corridor between Andorra and Figueras with their backs to the French border.

Yet the republicans refused to capitulate, and decided to fight on from their strongholds in south-eastern Spain and Madrid, lying in the north-western corner of the republican area. Yet this determination was completely undermined by the disaffection between the various factions within the republican camp, and no effective resistance could be found against Franco's offensive against Madrid, launched on 26 March. Just two days later Madrid and Valencia surrendered, and the Spanish Civil War was finally over.

MIDDLE AND NEAR EASTERN WARS

THE 2nd ARAB-ISRAELI WAR AND THE SUEZ CAMPAIGN (1956)

The pace of the Israeli thrusts in November 1956 caught the Arabs completely flat-footed. This is Egyptian equipment abandoned in Sinai.

The creation of the Jewish state of Israel within a largely Moslem Palestine during 1948 caused a whole range of social, religious, political, and economic problems that are still with the world in the late 1980s and likely to continue into the foreseeable future. The initial reaction of the Palestinians and their Arab neighbours was an attempt to crush Israel at birth, but this 1st Arab-Israeli War (1948–9) served merely to secure Israel's tenure of the territory allocated to it in 1947 by the United Nations and to extend its area at the expense of the indigenous Palestinian population (most of modern Jerusalem and western Galilee, or West Bank). Palestinian refugees fled mostly to Egypt and Jordan.

By 1956 the three Arab states

directly in contact with Israel decided that a proper military solution was the only answer to the problem of Israel, and under the overall leadership of an Egyptian officer (General Abdal Hakim Amer), Egypt, Jordan, and Syria began to lay concerted plans for a three-pronged offensive to crush Israel. Israel's intelligence was fully up to the task of monitoring these Arab preparations, which became definitely threatening as Egyptian formations were pushed forward through Sinai on 25 October 1956. It was the moment against which Israel had been preparing.

The Israeli chief-of-staff in 1956 was General Moshe Dayan, and it was this officer who secured approval from Prime Minister David Ben Gurion and his cabinet

for a pre-emptive campaign against the Arabs, with emphasis on the Egyptians who were beginning to receive large shipments of Soviet weapons. Dayan conceived Operation 'Kadesh' in which mechanized columns, each with a penny packet of armour in support, would drive deep into Sinai on three main axes and, instead of directly engaging the 45,000 men (six brigades) of the two Egyptian infantry divisions which Amer was concentrating in a triangle bounded by Rafah, El Arish, and Abu Aweigila (supported by an Egyptian armoured division already on the eastern bank of the Suez Canal ready to move into Sinai and by a Palestinian division at Gaza), bypass the main centres of resistance and secure the chokepoints on Egypt's lines of communication. The Israeli offensive was committed on 29 October 1956 and secured total success: at the cost of 180 dead and 620 wounded, the Israelis completely routed the four Egyptian divisions massed behind the frontier and drove them in pellmell retreat towards the Suez Canal at the cost of 3,000 dead and 7,000 prisoners, plus an unrevealed number of wounded.

The operation began with the drop of just under 400 paratroops in the Mitla Pass, just 40 miles (65 km) east of Suez and dominating the most southerly of the three routes across Sinai. There was no opposition at Mitla and, as soon as the success of the drop had been confirmed, a mechanized column of the 202nd Parachute Brigade set out from southern Israel under Colonel Ariel Sharon to cross Sinai via El Kuntilla, Thamad, and Nakhl to reinforce the paratroops at Mitla. The relief column overran three Egyptian strongpoints as it advanced, and arrived at Mitla in just 28 hours after travelling 130

miles (210 km). Farther to the north the second Israeli mechanized column (the 7th Armoured Brigade and 4th Infantry Brigade) crossed the frontier and took El Quseima as part of an advance designed to place it in a position to reinforce Mitla should Sharon's column be delayed. But Sharon arrived in time to bolster the Israeli position at Mitla just before Egyptian reserve forces launched a strong counter-attack that was defeated in the evening of 30 October.

The Israeli armoured forces committed in Sinai were Brigadier Ben Ari's 7th Armoured Brigade equipped with American-supplied

M4 Sherman tanks, the 27th Armoured Brigade equipped with French-supplied AMX-13 light tanks, and the 37th Armoured Brigade equipped with a miscellany of types. As a result of local initiatives, the armour attacked 24 hours earlier than planned, and instead of supporting their associated infantry brigades (respectively the 4th, 1st, and 10th Infantry Brigades) played the primary role in the advances in the centre and north.

Israeli troops move through Gaza in their half-track, alert for the possibility of 'stay behind' parties of Palestinians.

Within the central advance, whose primary task was the seizure of Bir Gifgafa and an advance to Ismailiya in the middle of the Suez Canal, the Israeli offensive was launched in two parts. On the left, as mentioned above, the 7th Armoured Brigade (supported by the 4th Infantry Brigade) passed through El Quseima and Bir Hasana to envelope the Egyptian position around Abu Aweigla and the Dayka Pass. This opened the way for the 37th Armoured Brigade (supported by the 10th Infantry Brigade) to push through on the right towards Bir Gifgafa on the main route from Ismailiya. The armoured effort had not been planned as such, but this extemporized operation proved what the Israeli armour could achieve when imaginatively

handled, for it completely removed any chance the Egyptians may have had of reinforcing their forces in Sinai from the west.

The third Israeli advance was that launched in the north and its primary tasks were the capture of one of the main Palestinian refugee areas, and an advance eastward along the coast road to Port Said at the northern end of the Suez Canal. By the morning of 1 November the Israelis had pushed the 27th Armoured Brigade (supported by the 1st Infantry Brigade) through the south-western end of the Gaza Strip, suffering heavy casualties in the extensive minefields, and were driving east along the coast road towards El Arish.

On 30 October the Israelis were only 30 miles (48 km) from the

canal and halted only when the British and French issued an 'ultimatum' with a 12-hour time limit. The Israelis agreed but the Egyptians refused and scuttled some 27 cement-laden ships to block the Suez Canal when their refusal elicited an Anglo–French air attack. The Israelis finally called an end to the advance on 2 November, with their spearheads a mere 10 miles (16 km) from the Suez Canal. The main strategic objectives had been achieved and the two main tasks now left were the capture of the Gaza Strip in its entirety and the securing of Israeli maritime access through the Straits

Israel's effort in Gaza was rapid and ruthless: these are Palestinians rounded up in the advance and awaiting interrogation and possible release.

Soviet anti-aircraft artillery captured by the Israelis in the 2nd Arab–Israeli War.

of Tiran to the southern port of Eilat.

A specially trained force, the 12th Infantry Brigade, left in the wake of the 27th Armoured and 1st Infantry Brigades, secured the Gaza Strip, in the process discovering and capturing several 'stay behind' bands of Palestinian guerrillas. And in the south Brigadier General Avraham Yoffe's 9th Infantry Brigade, a reserve force, made incredible progress along the trackless eastern shore of the Gulf of Aqaba to debouch in the rear of the Egyptian garrison at Sharm el Sheikh, which fell without difficulty to give Israel control of the eastern side of the Strait of Tiran. Sinai had been taken in a lightning campaign completed in just 100 hours and yielding vast quantities of Egyptian *matériel*.

Despite their 'ultimatum' to the Israelis and Egyptians, the British and French were already deeply committed in secret against the Egyptians. Egypt had become independent of British control in June 1956, some five years later than planned because the occupiers had remained in place in a vain effort to quell the disorder that had toppled King Farouk in July 1952 to create an Egyptian republic and then attended the power struggle between General Mohamed Naguib and Colonel Gamal Abdal Nasser, resolved in favour of the latter during November 1954. Then, just over a month after the final British withdrawal, on 19 July 1956 Nasser announced the nationalization of the Anglo-French Suez Canal, thereafter refusing all attempts to turn the canal into an international waterway.

The British decided as early as 27 July that military intervention would be required and a royal proclamation was issued on 2 August to recall some 20,000 reservists. Two days earlier the French had decided to join the British, offering air and naval units in addition to the 7th Light Mechanized and 10th Colonial Parachute Divisions from the garrison of French Algeria. The Allied plan called for an invasion force of some 80,000 men and, as 50,000 of these were to be British, overall command was entrusted to General Sir Charles Keightley (commanding Middle Eastern Land Forces) with Vice Admiral Barjot (commanding the French fleet in the Mediterranean) as his deputy. This arrangement of a British commander and French deputy was retained for the individual land, sea, and air components of Operation 'Musketeer', which was designed to seize and hold the Suez Canal for the allies.

were to prove, were the airfields
that could otherwise have been
used by allied aircraft. The first air
drops encountered stiffer
opposition than expected, but all
went ahead without undue
difficulty and on the following day
the seaborne assault came ashore
without problems as allied forces
probed down the Suez Canal
towards Ismailiya, reaching a point
some 25 miles (40 km) south of
Port Said on schedule.

But as allied forces began to
enter Ismailiya, world disapproval
of such high-handed action began
to catch up with them, and the
reluctant British obeyed a United
Nations ceasefire demand on 7
November. The USA and USSR
were in agreement, and the British
felt compelled to halt operations,
the French following suit.
Between 19 November and 22
December the British and French
evacuated the canal zone, leaving
it in Egyptian hands once more.

'Musketeer' was now tied to the
Israeli timetable, and allowed the
Anglo-French partners to be seen
to intervene in the forthcoming
Israeli-Egyptian campaign,
demanding a ceasefire and a 10-
mile wide neutral zone on each
side of the canal: the object was
that the Israelis should accede to
the allied demand, leaving Nasser
in the difficult position of having
to accept a *de facto* loss of control
over the canal zone or of refusing
the allied demand and suffering
the military consequences of an
allied invasion which would pave
the way for a continued Israeli
thrust against Egypt.

At first all went to plan: the
Israeli 'Kadesh' operation
achieved all that was expected of
it, the ultimatum was issued, and
Nasser refused to consider it. Then
the next stage of the whole
ponderous allied plan was
committed: six days of air attack
were launched, initially scoring
few successes as the long-range
bombers from Malta could find
few aircraft to destroy, the
Egyptians having dispersed them
to the south at the time of the
ultimatum. The closer-range
attacks by carrier-based aircraft
proved more effective, and Egypt's
air force and air-defence system
were virtually destroyed: so too,
and most unfortunately as events

THE 3rd ARAB-ISRAELI WAR OR 'SIX-DAY WAR' (1967)

The pattern of events after the 1st Arab–Israeli War was repeated after the 1956 war. Increasingly under the moral leadership of Nasser and Egypt, the Arab nations moved closer to the USSR and in return received considerable military support as well as equipment at very beneficial terms: the Arab leaders realized that they could not yet hope to tackle Israel, which was receiving substantial assistance from France, the UK and – from 1962 – the USA, so while they re-equipped and retrained their enlarged forces, political and economic harassment of Israel became the pattern. The Palestinians also stepped up their terrorist activities, incurring the retaliatory responses from Israel that helped to keep Arab tempers on the boil. The most serious incidents of the period were attributable to the comparatively new Al Fatah, an umbrella organization for the disparate Palestinian terrorist groups led by Yasser Arafat.

Some ten years passed in uneasy peace of this type, and the advent of 1967 at first seemed to offer the prospect of continued inactive

The mood of the Six-Day War is well caught in this shot of UN troops relieved in Jerusalem by the Israelis.

hostility, for both sides were still in the throes of absorbing new equipment and refining new tactics: the Arab states had opted for the Soviet model of using mass rather than finesse, while Israel had now come to a beautiful appreciation of armoured warfare, in which mobile tank and mechanized infantry formations would avoid head-on confrontations if possible and search for the enemy's weak spots.

36

But the Soviets convinced the Egyptians that Israel was planning another offensive in Sinai and after demanding full mobilization on 14 May Nasser ordered an enormous increase in the Egyptian military presence in Sinai: perhaps 80,000 men and 1,000 tanks were moved into the region in well-publicized movements that raised nationalist fervour to fever pitch in Egypt.

Overall command in Sinai was entrusted to General Mortagy, with his headquarters in Ismailiya, while local command was entrusted to Lieutenant General Mohsen whose headquarters were in Bir Thamada. On 16 May Nasser demanded action that the

UN peacekeeping force be removed from Sinai, the evacuation being completed on 19 May, and then once again closed the Strait of Tiran to Israeli shipping on 22 May.

From the Israeli side of the frontier the Egyptian positions and strengths could mean only war and if Egypt was able to take the offensive then Jordan would possibly follow and Syria probably fall into line: indeed, by 25 May Israel's borders were faced by Egyptian, Iraqi, Jordanian, Palestinian, Saudi Arabian, and Syrian forces. Israel's military leaders and their highly efficient intelligence apparatus determined that the greatest threat was posed

by Egypt and it was decided that the optimum course of action was a pre-emptive war on three fronts, with Egypt selected as the primary foe to be eliminated first. By 2 June, when General Moshe Dayan was appointed chief-of-staff, mobilization and planning were well under way.

Egypt's dispositions in Sinai were typical of its army's operational thinking at the time: the forward line was based on infantry formations with powerful organic artillery and armour

Israeli commanders are firm believers in command from the front, and this is General Moshe Dayan seen with his daughter Yael.

support, while to the rear of this was a second line of infantry and armoured divisions with a heavier component of tanks and artillery for mobile counter-attack should the forward line be pierced. The disposition, it should be noted, was basically static and defensive.

Though still organized largely on the basis of specialized brigades, the Israeli army had recognized the tactical advantages of an all-arms divisional structure for detached semi-autonomous operations in regions such as Sinai, and the Israeli field force was therefore disposed in three

divisions (*ugdahs*) under the overall command of Major General Gavish's Southern Command. Major General Israel Tal commanded the northern *ugdah* in the Gaza Strip, with two armoured brigades and a paratroop force supported by a tank battalion: the northern *ugdah* was tasked with driving east along the coast road to Port Said.

The central *ugdah* under Major General Avraham Yoffe was tasked initially with a defensive role (as the Southern Command's reserve and protection against an offensive push by the Egyptian 4th

Armoured Division with support from Shazli Force); then it was given the offensive task of capturing the Mitla and Giddi Passes following a drive through central Sinai with two armoured brigades to defeat the Egyptian 3rd Infantry Division. This was after passing between the right flank of the Egyptian 4th Armoured Division and the left flank of the Egyptian 2nd Infantry Division.

Israeli 'tankers' prepare their Centurion tanks at a forward base in the Negev desert in anticipation of an Egyptian offensive.

The southern *ugdah* under Major General Ariel Sharon had one infantry and one armoured brigade, supported by two paratroop battalions, for the capture of the Umm Katef crossroads and the destruction of the Egyptian 3rd and 6th Infantry Divisions while bypassing Shazli Force. Covering the southern end of the Negev desert was an independent armoured brigade under Colonel Albert Mendler with 50 Sherman tanks. The initial Israeli objective in this preliminary part of the campaign, however, was the capture of key choke-points in Sinai (most notably El Arish, Jebel Libni, Bir Hasana, and Nakhl).

Israel decided to strike on 5 June, and on 3 June revised its overall scheme to include a pre-emptive air attack on the Arabs' main air bases, principally those in Egypt. With the aid of the USSR the Arab states now had some 800 advanced combat aircraft to Israel's 350 and the feeling was strong that this Arab numerical superiority in the air could tip the balance against the Israeli ground forces. By conventional standards the Israeli air force had neither the aircraft nor the capacity for the plan it developed in Operation 'Focus', but an extraordinary feat of maintenance and logistics opened the possibility of multiple attacks by the same aircraft if turn-round time and schedules were arranged with total accuracy.

The air attacks of 'Focus' ultimately decided the course of the war: the first wave of 185 Israeli aircraft attacked 11 Egyptian airfields in Sinai and Egypt proper, destroying 197 aircraft (189 on the ground and 8 in the air), and after a 7.5-minute turnround the aircraft were launched on a second attack, which tackled 14 more airfields and destroyed 107 aircraft. And in the second attack the Israelis also used 'dibber' bombs to crater the runways, so that surviving aircraft could not use them until they had been repaired. The blow was decisive: Egypt could not support

its forces in Sinai with air-cover and ground-attack missions, while the Israelis had a free hand to use both their modern and their obsolescent aircraft for a close support of their ground forces. And with the Egyptian air force effectively destroyed or rendered important, the Israelis switched their air effort to Jordan, Iraq, and Syria, whose air bases were attacked in the early afternoon for the destruction of 36 Jordanian, 10 Iraqi, and 53 Syrian aircraft. Israel's losses for the day were 19 aircraft (9 over Egypt and 10 over Syria) but only 14 pilots (10 dead and 4 taken prisoner).

The Southern Command's offensive was named Operation 'Red Sheet', and began at the time that Israel's first wave of air attacks was arriving over its targets. The whole campaign was a classic of mobile warfare characterized by individual initiative that did not exceed the limits of overall control, and without exception the Israelis out-thought and outfought the Egyptians. In the north Tal's *ugdah* pressed into the Gaza Strip with its 7th Armoured Brigade to the fore, took Khan Yunis and wheeled west along the coast road to break through the Egyptian position at Rafah and press on towards El Arish.

In the centre Yoffe's *ugdah* swept into terrain that the Egyptians had thought impassable, reaching Bir Lahfan and a position from which it successfully ambushed Egyptian forces moving up to

Above: The pace of operations was hectic, fast-moving light forces taking the war to the Arabs and pushing on regardless of casualties.

Opposite top: An Israeli Centurion main battle tank waits for the 'off' in the Sinai campaign, where Israeli tactics proved decisively better than those of Egypt.

Opposite bottom: Spoils of war: an Egyptian SA-2 'Guideline' surface-to-air missile abandoned by the Egyptians in their precipitate retreat from Sinai.

counter-attack Tal's *ugdah*. The Egyptian forces in the Gaza Strip were trapped when Tal's and Yoffe's *ugdahs* met at Bir Lahfan, and the Egyptian 4th Armoured Division's counter-attack was most severely handled.

In the south Sharon's *ugdah* had crossed the frontier early in the morning, but the commander was content to push a tank battalion across the Egyptians' only escape route during the day and launch his attack during the night. This was a set-piece assault typical of the tactics used by the Israelis to counter the Egyptians' use of entrenched positions with barbed-wire and minefield defences supported by artillery. The Egyptians generally selected positions with 'impassable' flanks, through which the Israelis passed light forces to engage the Egyptian artillery from the rear and flank before pushing into the main position.

On 6 June Tal's and Yoffe's *ugdahs* wheeled south to encircle the Egyptian airfield at Jebel Libni, but the defence of the airfield was not finally overcome until the next day after a large-scale attack. By now the Israelis were through the Egyptian forward defences in Sinai, and poised themselves to swoop

forward to take the three southerly routes to the Suez Canal, all of which could be blocked by determined Egyptian resistance: the road from Jebal Libni to Ismailiya via Bir Gifgafa (on Tal's axis), and the Giddi and Mitla Passes controlling the access to Suez (on Yoffe's axis and also planned for Sharon's *ugdah*). Terrain considerations meant that it was easier to fight through the retreating Egyptians than attempt large-scale movement through the desert, yet despite this fact the major Israeli problems were caused by mechanical failure more than enemy action.

By the early hours of 9 June the Israelis of Tal's and Yoffe's *ugdahs* had reached the eastern side of the Suez Canal in spots all along its length, and were mopping up in their rear areas. Sharon, meanwhile, had been co-ordinating the efforts of his own *ugdah* and Mendler's brigade in destroying the Egyptian 6th Infantry Division as an effective fighting formation. And on 7 June

Sharm el Sheikh had again fallen to the Israelis, this time in an airborne assault rapidly reinforced by sea to allow the Israelis the chance to sweep north up the eastern side of the Gulf of Suez as far as Abu Durba. The Sinai campaign was over.

Yet the campaign in Sinai was only one of the three simultaneous fronts being fought by Israel, for while the major effort was being made by Southern Command and the Israeli army's Central and Northern Commands were heavily engaged against the Jordanian and Syrian armies respectively. As noted above, the threat posed by Egypt had been judged paramount, so defensive operations were initially the order of the day against Jordan and Syria. Commanded by Major General Uzi Narkiss, the Central Command was faced by what was effectively

Cheerful Israeli troops examine an Arab MiG fighter knocked out by the Israeli air force's pre-emptive air attacks.

Above: A scene typical of the Israeli forces' lightning advance across Sinai in 1967: abandoned Egyptian equipment including tanks and AA guns.

Right: Israeli infantry advance after the objective has been 'softened up' by artillery fire and air attacks.

a west-facing Jordanian salient into Israel with its shoulders halfway up the Dead Sea and at Tirat Zvei in the central Jordan valley, and an east-facing Israeli re-entrant into Jerusalem.

The Israeli commitment to the area was inevitably centred on Jerusalem yet the geographical configuration of the battlefield meant that if the Jordanians could bring up armour and artillery from Jericho to a forward position at Ramallah, to the north of Jerusalem in the previous truce zone, the Israeli position would become impossible: the Jordanians could interdict the Israelis' sole line of communication into their western half of the city.

The Central Command had considerably smaller forces, and for obvious reasons the Israelis had therefore sought to persuade the Jordanians to remain neutral, but the failure of this effort became evident when Jordanian artillery opened fire against the positions of Colonel Eliezer

Amitai's Jerusalem Infantry Brigade and Jordanian army units were seen moving into forward positions in the erstwhile truce zone north and south of Jerusalem on Ramallah Ridge. Narkiss saw that he had to act and moreover to act quickly.

Already the Jerusalem Infantry Brigade had been in action, pushing through into eastern Jerusalem to relieve the United Nations headquarters caught in the crossfire: this was clearly an ideal opportunity to take the Old City and thus put the whole of Jerusalem in Israeli hands, and the

unit for the task was on hand in the form of Brigadier Mota Gur's 55th Airborne Brigade, which had been earmarked for the assault on El Arish rendered superfluous by the success of Tal's land offensive. During the evening of 5 June the brigade moved into its assault positions, knowing that it was faced with a hard task against the excellent troops of Iman Ali's reinforced 'King Talal' 3rd Infantry Brigade. The assault was committed early in the morning of 6 June and slowly made progress towards the capture of the complete city.

Meanwhile Colonel Uri Ben Ari's Harel Mechanized Brigade had moved from its reserve position which had been to the west of Jerusalem to an assault position on the left flank of the 55th Parachute Brigade and drove forward in heavy fighting to take Ramallah with the aid of an infantry brigade from Latrun, in the process destroying those remnants of the Jordanian 60th Armoured Brigade left by the Israeli air force. Further north still, an infantry brigade from Qalqilya moved east towards Nablus while Major General Elad Peled's *ugdah*, in reserve near Bet She'an lest the Syrians break into the Jordanian valley, was committed in a southward drive against the right flank of the Jordanian salient on the west bank of the Jordan. The Jordanians fought with determination and skill, the 40th Armoured Brigade managing to inflict severe losses on the tanks of Peled's *ugdah*, but when Jerusalem, Ramallah, and Nablus had fallen the Jordanian position on the west bank was no longer tenable and a wholesale retreat gave the whole area to the Israelis, who reached the line of the Jordan by 7 June. On the morning of 7 June, moreover, the

Israelis in Jerusalem had reached the Wailing Wall, their Holy of Holies, lost to them for 1,900 years. The southern half of the Jordanian west bank fell to the Jerusalem Infantry Brigade whose main prize after Jerusalem itself was Hebron.

The third foe faced by Israel in the 'Six-Day War' was Syria. Though largely responsible for persuading Nasser and Hussein to go to war, Syria itself took a back seat in the actual fighting in the first phase of the war. Syrian artillery did admittedly continue its heavy shelling of Israel's northern settlements and a number of small infantry attacks were launched but easily repelled. Yet, along the massively fortified front with Israel, Syria's army, under the local control of Lieutenant General Souedan, deployed some 40,000 men and 450 tanks in six infantry, one mechanized, and two armoured brigades.

Syria controlled the decisive Golan Heights where three infantry brigades were located, together with a useful number of obsolete tanks dug in as effective pillboxes, and additionally garrisoned the area around El Quneitra with one infantry, one

mechanized, and two armoured brigades. Major General David Elazar's Northern Command could initially muster forces that were considerably smaller than those of the enemy, and a careful defensive posture was adopted in the early days of the war.

Elazar decided the strike even as the reinforcements were arriving, to allow the Syrians minimum warning of impending operations given the rapid defeats of its allies farther to the south. Elazar's plan called for a four-axis advance, three directly east against the Golan Heights from the upper reaches of the Jordan to the north of the Sea of Galilee (Lake Tiberias) and the fourth on a north-easterly axis round the southern shore of the Sea of Galilee from Tel Kazir up the line of the Yarmuk river towards the left flank of the Golan Heights.

The full weight of the Israeli air force was available to support the Golan offensive, and this aerial firepower did much to destroy the Syrians' reserves and to interdict their lines of communication. This played an important part in aiding

Israeli infantry pause in an olive grove during operations on the Syrian front.

Above: *An Israeli jeep-mounted recoilless rifle in action against Syrian armour during the 1967 campaign.*

Below: *Israeli armour proved its overall superiority in the Six-Day War, even light types such as this AMX-13 being able to get the better of the inadequately-handled Arab tanks.*

the eventual success of the Israeli offensive, but could do little in the short term to support their monumentally difficult task in assaulting the Syrians' fully prepared defensive positions at the crest of steep slopes with artillery support from 265 guns. Elazar committed his offensive in the morning of 9 June, using the high-quality but untested Golani Infantry Brigade, Colonel Albert Mendler's 8th Armoured Brigade recently arrived from Sinai, and the reserve armoured brigade fresh from its successes in Samaria while supporting Lieutenant Colonel Moshe's mechanized brigade.

The fighting was bitter and intense, Elazar having to commit additional forces as these became available: the most important of these was the 55th Airborne Brigade, which was helicarried on the crests of the Golan Heights to oust fanatical Syrian resistance. The back of the Syrian defence was broken in the afternoon of 10 June and the disorganized Syrians

fell back towards Damascus, which was in full view of the victorious Israelis on the Golan Heights. Fearful that Israel was now about to take the war to them with a vengeance, the Syrians urged the Soviets to pressurize the Americans into imposing a ceasefire on the Israelis. This came into effect in the early evening of 10 June.

THE 4th ARAB-ISRAELI WAR OR 'YOM KIPPUR WAR' (1973)

With the Arab-Israeli conflict now firmly established as the primary world locus for the head-on confrontation of the superpowers through their proxies, the end of the 'Six-Day War' was the signal for a vast resupply effort in which the Egyptians received enormous quantities of Soviet *matériel*. Defeat in 1967 and 1973 had cost the Arabs dear, and the original concepts of crushing the small state of Israel through massive attacks by conscripted soldiery little able to get the best out of their weapons, let alone the tactics associated with them, were now abandoned. The Arabs, and in particular the Egyptians, appreciated that their numbers and brute strength still offered a useful advantage, but also realized that they now needed to acquire more skill.

At the heart of the Egyptian plan, at least in the short term, was artillery. Here the Egyptians followed Soviet military precepts, and on 8 September 1968 the Egyptians unleashed their first massive barrage against the Israeli positions on the eastern bank of the Suez Canal: Israel responded with a deep and destructive raid into Egypt, and there matters rested as the Egyptians swiftly recast their basic plans to bolster the defence of the canal's west bank against further Israeli incursions. The Egyptians felt themselves secure after March 1969, and resumed the barrage that was the primary feature of this so-called 'War of Attrition': Israel could not now commit ground forces across the canal and was unwilling to wear out its heavy artillery (in the process consuming vast quantities of

expensive ammunition) in a duel with the Egyptian guns, so turned to its air force for destructive attacks on the Egyptian gun batteries.

The Egyptians in turn committed their air force, but again found it no match for that of the Israelis. Another solution had to be found, and here the Soviets came up trumps: during 1970 these supplied Egypt with the latest version of the SA-2 'Guideline' surface-to-air missile, the new SA-3 'Goa' SAM and enormous quantities of radar-controlled anti-aircraft artillery. This allowed the Egyptians to establish a multi-layer air-defence umbrella over their artillery and this finally exacted a toll too great for the Israelis to bear. In August 1970 a ceasefire came into effect, and the Egyptians took advantage of this lull to move their air-defence umbrella right up to the west bank of the canal.

This was the first phase of Nasser's overall scheme for a revanchist war against Israel. After the successful completion of this phase, which embraced the wearing down of Israel's forces on the east bank of the canal, Nasser's scheme envisaged second

and third phases: the second phase was based on the infiltration of special forces into Sinai for reconnaissance and sabotage, in the process boosting Egyptian morale and sapping the confidence of the Israelis, and the third phase called for a full-scale assault crossing of the canal as the first step in a conventional military campaign to drive the Israelis out of Sinai.

To a high degree Nasser's plan proved far-sighted and successful. During the 'War of Attrition' the Israelis sought to protect themselves and their equipment against artillery fire. Thus there slowly developed the so-called Bar Lev Line: bomb- and shell-proof shelters were gradually extended into a string of huge sand-protected bunkers stretching the length of the Israeli line along the canal.

Nasser died in September 1970 and was succeeded by Anwar Sadat who continued with his predecessor's policy. In October 1972 Sadat decided that the time was nearly ripe for the Egypt's return to Sinai and plans were formulated with Syria for simultaneous attacks at both ends of Israel. The overall scheme

Israeli troops at prayer during a lull in the fighting.

envisaged an immediate war of attrition in Sinai and Golan to cripple Israel's dominant armour and air forces while causing manpower losses heavy enough to sap Israel's morale and determination, followed by simultaneous advances to make impossible Israel's favourite operational method of checking one foe while dealing with the other, and finally by a prolonged campaign designed to draw other Arab nations into a successful war and so cause the manpower and economic damage that would force Israel to the negotiating table.

The Egyptian assault was divided into two main sections: north of the Great Bitter Lake Major General Saad Mamoun's Egyptian 2nd Army was to push forward its 18th, 2nd, and 16th Infantry Divisions, while south of the Great Bitter Lake Major General Munim Wasil's Egyptian 3rd Army was to launch a more concentrated punch with its 7th and 19th Infantry Divisions. In the extreme north an infantry brigade was to cross the Suez Canal from Port Said to Port Fuad and advance along the strip of land beside the Mediterranean towards

Romani, a key junction through which reinforcements from Israel would have to pass.

In the case of the two major assaults the forward divisions were to push through the Israeli defences as rapidly as possible, leaving strongpoints to be neutralized by follow-up forces, and establish a dense bridgehead full of anti-tank and anti-aircraft defences on the west bank of the canal. This was to be the honeypot attracting the Israeli armour and air forces to their destruction. And with the Egyptian infantry formations firmly emplaced on the east bank, armoured forces were to be pushed across into the bridgehead for the exploitation phase of the offensive.

The day of renewed hostilities was fixed for 6 October, the Jewish Day of Atonement and thus the time at which the Israeli defences were likely to be manned at their lowest levels. This proved to be the case when the Egyptian and Syrian assaults were launched. In the short term the Syrian offensive was judged to pose the greater threat to Israel, and once the Egyptian advance into Sinai had been contained (or rather

The remains of a stone wall make a good ambush position for an Israeli recoilless rifle team operating on the Golan front against Syria.

contained itself), the Israelis opted to deal with Syria before turning their attentions to the Egyptians who were, after all, held further at bay from Israel proper by Sinai.

On the Golan Heights, a plateau area some 2,000–3,000 ft (610–915 m) higher than the rich lands of the upper Jordan valley, the Israelis had no buffer between themselves and Syria, and thus used the period after the Six-Day War to construct along the heights and on the vast massif of Mount Hermon which dominates the whole area from its peaks rising to a height of 9,220 ft (2810 m), a series of immensely strong fixed fortifications and a wide anti-tank ditch. Great reliance was placed on the 10-m (33-ft) wide water-filled ditch, and only two understrength brigades (the 7th Armoured and the Barak Armoured Brigades) were allocated as the garrison under Brigadier General Rafael Eitan. To break through this defence the Syrians allocated five divisions.

The Israelis had been able to watch the whole build-up of the Syrian assault, but for some inexplicable reason were taken by complete tactical surprise when the offensive was launched in the early afternoon of 6 October, simultaneously with the Egyptian assault crossing of the Suez Canal. The Israeli positions were heavily shelled, and were also subjected to massive air attack as the Syrian infantry assault gathered way, but as the observation post on Mount Hermon began to report this move it was captured by a heli-borne assault by the Syrian 82nd Commando Battalion.

Firing on pre-registered target areas, the Israeli tanks were able to knock out most of the Syrian bridgelayers attempting to bridge the anti-tank ditch, but the Syrians had anticipated this capability and

just kept feeding in more vehicles in the anticipation of over-whelming the Israelis by sheer numbers. Israeli attack aircraft were called in but these suffered devastating losses to missiles and anti-aircraft guns. The fighting raged all night, and though the Syrians made inroads into Israeli defences between Kudna and Rafid on the southern sector, the Israelis managed to stabilize the position despite a numerical inferiority of 1 to 15 in armour.

But on the morning of 7 October the Syrians continued their steamroller tactics and the Barak Armoured Brigade was driven back in the Kudha and Rafid sector by three armoured brigades, driving forward between the shielding flanks of the 9th and 5th Mechanized Divisions. The Barak Armoured Brigade was virtually

One of the keys to Israel's success – teams of mechanized infantry in half-tracks to support the armour used as the main offensive force.

wiped out, but its destruction gave the Israelis time to bring up the first of their reserve armour, which checked the Syrians just as they appeared on the crest of the rise leading up from the Israeli settlements in the valley below. A similar check was inflicted on the Syrian 43rd and 51st Armoured Brigades just as they reached the Israeli headquarters at Nafakh, where Eitan and his staff were preparing to sell their lives as dearly as possible: at the crucial moments the first tanks of the Israeli 79th Armoured Brigade arrived and their fresh crews and plentiful ammunition cut up the exhausted Syrian armour.

The Syrians had fared less well in the north, where the experienced 7th Armoured Brigade excelled its own gunnery records in picking off vast numbers of the tanks launched against its position over three days by the 3rd Mechanized and 7th Armoured Divisions supported by the elite Assad Force. So worried by the continued resistance of the Israelis did the Syrians become that they resorted to a dangerous expedient. A commando force with 'Sagger' missiles was helicoptered into the Israeli rear: it was spotted in time and wiped out.

Yet again, though, the efforts of the regular force had bought just enough time for the reserves to mobilize and reach the front: just as the 7th Armoured Brigade expended its last few rounds of ammunition the first reserves arrived and poured a withering fire into the massed Syrian armour.

Additional reinforcement was already on its way to the Israelis on the Golan Heights: Brigadier General Moshe Peled's division was pushing forward from En Gev and Major General Dan Laner's division from Yahudia. Command in the northern sector was now being exercised by Major General Yitzhak Hofi and he concentrated a pincer attack against the Hushnia crossroads where the

Syrians had concentrated two armoured brigades of their 1st Armoured Division. Caught in an enveloping movement, the Syrians fought with great determination but were decisively beaten despite a relief attempt by the 3rd Armoured Division.

Now was the moment for a counterstroke, and the Israelis determined to drive the Syrians back towards Damascus before reinforcements from Iraq and Jordan could arrive. First the Israelis had to cripple the Syrians'

Above: Israeli armour rumbles past a dump of crates and containers used for the mass transport of artillery shells and their propellant cases.

Below: By 1983 most of Israel's first-line mechanized forces were mounted in the capable M113 tracked armoured personnel-carrier, adapted with additional firepower.

Soviet-designed air-defence network, and into the bargain retaliate against Syrian missile attacks against civilian targets in the Jordan valley.

Hofi's plan called for the major effort to be made by the forces in the northern half of the Golan sector, commanded by Eitan and containing the reinforced 7th Armoured Brigade but increased to divisional size for the assault on the front held by the Syrian 7th Mechanized Division. At the same time Laner's division, with support from Peled's division, was to advance in the southern sector with the task of taking positions above the Awag river from which an assault on Damascus could be launched. The Israelis failed to dislodge the Syrian commandos from their eyrie on Mount Hermon, and the Syrians were thus kept informed of Israeli movements leading to the attack in the late morning of 11 October.

Massed tank firepower can achieve impressive results, as did these Israelis on the Syrian front, but can also suffer heavy losses to artillery.

PART I EUROPEAN WARS

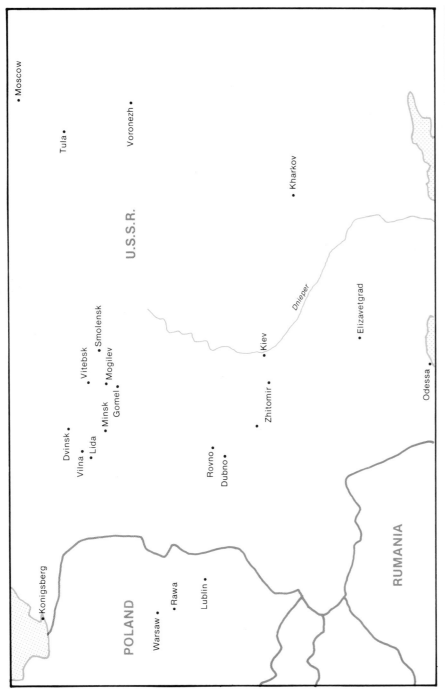

POLAND

Konigsberg

Warsaw
Rawa
Lublin

RUMANIA

U.S.S.R.

Moscow

Tula

Voronezh

Kharkov

Dvinsk
Vilna
Lida
Minsk
Vitebsk
Smolensk
Mogilev
Gomel

Rovno
Dubno

Zhitomir

Kiev

Dnieper

Elizavetgrad

Odessa

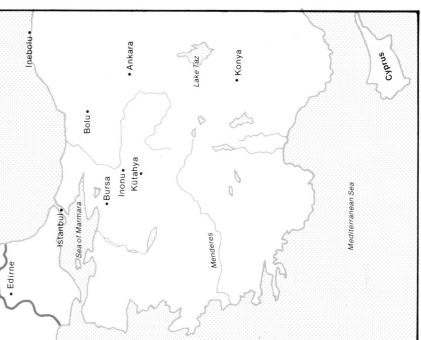

Inebolu

Ankara

Bolu

Lake Taz

Konya

Bursa
Inonu
Kütahya

Istanbul
Sea of Marmara

Edirne

Menderes

Mediterranean Sea

Cyprus

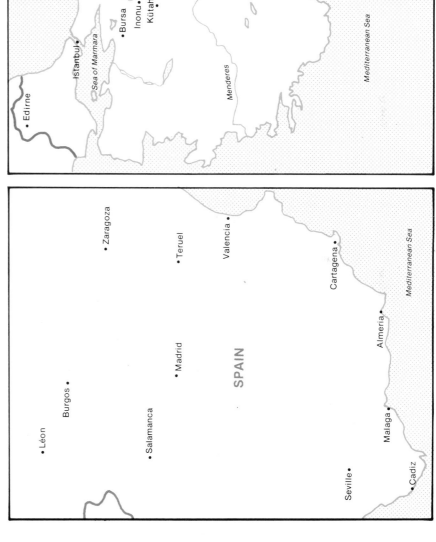

Zaragoza

Teruel

Valencia

Cartagena

Léon

Burgos

Madrid

SPAIN

Salamanca

Almeria

Mediterranean Sea

Seville

Malaga

Cadiz

Right: Both sides in the Gulf War have received substantial arms supplies from the Soviets; this is a ZU-23 anti-aircraft mounting with twin 23-mm cannon effective against low-level air attack.

Below: The guided-missile frigate USS Stark lies dead in the water after being hit by an Iraqi-launched Exocet anti-ship missile in a May 1987 attack that heightened yet further the tensions of this multi-faceted war.

Desperate fighting followed on both sectors and eventually the Israelis began to see cracks in the Syrian defence. But just as Laner was about to push through the broken Syrians to his front, on his right flank fresh forces arrived: these were the vanguards of the Iraqi 6th Armoured Division and Jordanian 40th Armoured Brigade. Laner drew them into a trap and decimated them, but lost much time and impetus to this flank assault. Farther to the north Eitan made better progress and from 15 October the Syrians lost ground more rapidly as their nerve and ammunition failed. The campaign petered out on 22 October, the Israelis taking Mount Hermon as the finale to this remarkable defensive/offensive effort.

The Egyptian assault across the Suez Canal was launched during the afternoon of 6 October with complete tactical surprise: the Israeli defences were pinned down with a heavy artillery barrage and air attacks as assault pioneers

crossed the canal to push through the defences into the interior of Sinai. Pontoon bridges rapidly created the means of vehicles to cross the canal and, to the total surprise of the Israelis, the sand defences of the Bar Lev Line were washed away with high-pressures hoses to create the gaps through which vehicles quickly passed.

By the early evening the Egyptians had pushed ten bridges across the canal, and during the night the five infantry divisions were pushed across, together with the first elements of the Egyptian armoured force. It was only on the morning of 7 October that the Israelis began to understand the gravity of the situation as reconnaissance aircraft and probes by Israeli reserve forces in the west side of Sinai started to reveal the Egyptians' success.

Under the command of Major General Albert Mendler the Israeli Sinai Command was starved of information and could only push forward its 300 tanks

towards the probable Egyptian main axes: Colonel Gaby's armoured brigade was ordered forward from Bir Gifgafa towards Tasa and El Kantara in the north, Colonel Amnon's armoured brigade towards the Bitter Lakes in the centre, and Colonel Dan's armoured brigade towards the area south of the Bitter Lakes. The Egyptians were waiting for this inevitable move and their new anti-tank tactics proved excellent: as they had learned to do in the 'Six-Day War' the overconfident Israelis committed their armour without the infantry support which could have dealt with the 'Sagger' teams and soon a mere 100 Israeli tanks were all that stood between the Egyptians and the strategic passes into central Sinai, and the Egyptians already had 500 tanks across the canal.

Here, however, the Egyptians had already sowed the seeds of their own defeat, for instead of creating a deep bridgehead to allow the concentration of a layered defence, they had evolved a long but very shallow bridgehead along the full length of the canal, so that the air-defence umbrella on the west bank of the canal protected it.

Unfortunately for the Israelis they attempted too much too soon: during 7 October the leading elements of two armoured divisions, under the command of Major Generals Avraham Adan and Ariel Sharon, arrived in the northern and central sectors of the front, and an ambitious plan was created to roll up the Egyptians with a north-to-south counter-offensive on 8 October. The Israeli effort was a total failure as yet again no infantry was used to support the armour, which had suffered heavy losses by the time the counter-offensive was called off in the middle of the day. The Israeli command now appreciated that considerably stronger forces would be needed to counter the Egyptians and were thankful only that the enemy were being so slow to develop their lodgement, which was only some 6 miles (10 km) deep by 13 October.

Left: Egyptian soldiers examine part of the wreckage of an Israeli F-4 Phantom II fighter knocked down by their comprehensive air-defence 'umbrella'.

Bottom: A wounded Israeli soldier is about to be ferried to hospital in a 'Huey' helicopter.

Israeli tanks move warily through Suez after General Sharon's immensely daring push across the Suez Canal.

Forward reconnaissance on this day revealed to the Israelis the fact that major movements were afoot in the Egyptian camp. These movements were in fact the arrival of the 21st and 4th Armoured Divisions, in the 2nd and 3rd Armies' sectors respectively, presaging the long-anticipated Egyptian breakout effort. Anticipating this, the Israelis (not without dissension amongst their senior commanders) had ordered their numerically inferior armoured forces into strong defensive positions with a view to breaking up the Egyptian tank offensive. But then, instead of going straight over to a concentrated counter-offensive

while the Egyptians were still reeling from the first blow, which would have been a predictable Israeli response, the Israelis husbanded their strength for the tactical surprise of a delayed counter-offensive. The Egyptian offensive was committed on 14 October and was completely destroyed.

The tide had turned and the Israelis now launched their decisive counterstroke. Under the command of Sharon a force of one airborne and two armoured brigades – supported by the armoured divisions commanded by Adan and, further to the south to pin the 3rd Army, Major General Meron – attacked at the thinly

held junction of the Egyptian 2nd and 3rd Armies just north of the Great Bitter Lake. Desperate fighting followed before the Israelis secured a firm foothold over the Suez Canal in an area known as the Chinese Farm (in fact an experimental agricultural station built by the Japanese). Sharon was effectively cut off by the furious Egyptian counter-attacks, but instead of adopting the conventional answer of consolidating and awaiting relief, he fanned out into the Egyptian rear areas and caused havoc.

It was 36 hours before the Egyptians fully appreciated the danger posed to their rear by Sharon, who was about to be reinforced by Adan's division, and when they did their first response was to urge the USSR to call for a ceasefire. The Israelis were now rampaging through the Egyptian rear areas, Sharon and Adan being reinforced by Major General Magen, who had taken command of Mendler's division when the latter was killed in action on 14 October. Against stiffening resistance the Israelis advanced south along the western shore of the Bitter Lakes to reach Suez and so cut off the entire 3rd Army. At

A comparatively informal triumph for Israel's returning tank crews at the end of the Yom Kippur War.

the same time units had probed west and by the time of the ceasefire that came into effect on 24 October these forces were a mere 60 miles (95 km) from Cairo.

THE AFGHAN WAR (1979-)

From the 1830s to the early-1940s the main arbiter of Afghan matters was the UK, but with the death of King Amanullah in 1953 Afghanistan emerged into a more independent country under Mohammed Daoud Khan, who solicited and received aid from both the USA and USSR. In the early 1960s the USA terminated its aid programme and in 1963 Daoud resigned in protest at the increasing reliance placed by Afghanistan of Soviet aid. Daoud returned in 1973 but was assassinated in 1978 during a coup that finally brought Nur Mohammed Taraki to power as president. Committed to a policy of dragging Afghanistan into the 20th century, Taraki acted so autocratically against traditional Afghan and Moslem *mores* that

the whole country, with the possible exception of the region around Kabul, was soon in a state of undeclared revolt against the central government by April 1979.

In January 1979 the Moslem fundamentalist revolution headed by the Ayatollah Khomeini had succeeded in toppling the modernizing regime of the Pahlavi dynasty in neighbouring Iran, Shah Reza Pahlavi and his family fleeing into exile, and the USSR was becoming increasingly worried that the fundamentalist Moslem feelings thus displayed in Afghanistan and Iran might spill over the frontier into the Moslem republics in the southern USSR. Moscow urged the Taraki regime to slow the pace of its modernization but, when this plea failed to secure results against the

hard communist line of the regime, decided to intervene militarily. On the pretext that the government had asked for support against increasing rebellion in the provinces, in December 1979 the USSR committed large numbers of troops to an invasion, whose reality was emphasized by the death of the Afghan prime minister, Hafizullah Amin, in the fighting for Kabul. The Afghan army put up only token resistance, and it has been estimated that perhaps half of its 80,000-man strength deserted almost immediately after the Soviet invasion.

A Soviet BTR-series armoured personnel carrier on guard at Kabul airport, a link with the USSR the guerrillas would have liked to cripple.

The war between the *mujihadeen* on the one hand, and the Afghans and Soviets on the other lacked the shape to make a detailed description of any use. Indeed, it was probable that the *mujihadeen* had no overall strategy: these freedom fighters had little in the way of heavy equipment, and generally operated in small bands against Afghan army or Soviet convoys, patrols, and bases. Thus the *mujihadeen* effort was one of hit-and-run tactics, designed to keep the Soviets and their Afghan puppets under constant pressure with small-scale attacks designed to inflict casualties and *matériel* losses to an extent that they became a running sore in the USSR's determination to continue the occupation. The *mujihadeen* generally enjoyed free run of the country outside the major towns, using this freedom to strike where and when they pleased, usually with rockets (designed to be fired from the tubes of multiple launchers but generally used straight from the ground on an improvised launcher of earth or stones) against military garrison areas and Soviet air bases. When the Soviets responded with a counter-attack the *mujihadeen* had the option of fighting from pre-prepared ambush positions, or of melting away to fight another day. The terrain constantly favoured the lightly equipped *mujihadeen*.

During the war's early years, the Soviets came to distrust the

Afghan guerrillas with a captured ZPU-4 quadruple mounting for 14.5-mm heavy machine-guns, ideal for engaging low-level helicopters.

Afghan guerrillas distributing weapons in a border town before moving into their operational areas. Most of the weapons are of Chinese origin.

unreliable Afghan army, so while it was often used for tasks in which the Soviets felt they might suffer inordinate casualties, it was relegated largely to the defence of important installations while the Soviets used their own forces for offensive operations against the *mujihadeen*. Yet the mobile *mujihadeen* continued to control most of the country outside the major towns and, having no need for bases other than their home areas from which they could draw food and young men, were difficult for the Soviets to pin down. So the Soviets ran through the gamut of counter-guerrilla tactics, apparently without success, and up to May 1988 continued their effort to halt the *mujihadeen* by eliminating their local support and bases: the young were shipped off to the major cities or even to the USSR for indoctrination, crops were burned, livestock killed, water supplies cut, and villages razed. One of the most unpleasant, but perhaps most effective, weapons in the Soviet arsenal was the anti-personnel mine, small enough for widespread

The 500-mile road from the Soviet frontier to Kabul, the umbilical for the USSR's effort in Afghanistan.

scattering over *mujihadeen*-infested areas – these nasty little mines cause a constant trickle of casualties amongst the *mujihadeen* but also exact a high penalty from the local populations. This all reduced local support for the *mujihadeen* to a certain extent but, given the widespread exodus of refugees to Pakistan, could never eliminate this support. The Soviets undertook a constant regime of search and destroy operations, but it was rare for a sizeable body of the *mujihadeen* to be trapped and eliminated by con-

Where isolated garrisons could not be air-supplied, the Afghans and Soviets had to run the road convoys that were among the guerrillas' favourite targets.

ventional means. Until May 1988 the Soviets had to escort supply convoys, and the scale of the occupation meant the *mujihadeen* could pick and choose which of these convoys to ambush at any time. Thus the Soviets had to provide a heavy escort for all convoys and this was a further drain on their resources.

Such military supplies as the *mujihadeen* needed were generally received via Pakistan from the West and from Moslem countries which felt the need to oppose Soviet expansion, and it was only here that the Soviets could effectively strike at the *mujihadeen*. The main supply route ran from Peshawar in northern Pakistan over the Khyber Pass towards Jalalabad, but the lightly equipped *mujihadeen* could then fan out over mountain tracks virtually impossible for the more heavily equipped Soviet troops to use. Occasionally the Soviets managed to pin down such bands and inflict moderately severe casualties through the use of Mil

Mi-24 'Hind' helicopter gunships escorting helicoptered ground forces. But the *mujihadeen* in recent years received British Shorts Blowpipe and American General Dynamics FIM-92 Stinger shoulder-launched surface-to-air missiles, and these effective weapons severely curtailed the Soviets' use of low-level tactical air power.

The Soviets finally saw that they could not win such a war. The *mujihadeen* had shown that they could make the war too costly for the Soviets, whom they could not defeat in any conventional military sense. Faced with continued opprobrium at the international level, and by increasing Soviet

Soviet prisoners shown off by the Afghan guerrillas.

dissatisfaction with the cost of the war in men and resources, Secretary Gorbachev decided that it was time to cut the USSR's losses in line with his new policies of cost-effective government. An agreement guaranteed by the two super-powers was signed by Afghanistan and Pakistan in April 1988 for the evacuation of foreign troops by mid-May, and non-intervention by outside parties. Afghanistan can now try to put its house in order so that Afghan refugees can return home to a country offered the possibility of peace and reconstruction.

THE GULF WAR (1980-   )

The Gulf War that has raged between Iraq and Iran since 1980 is on everyone's lips yet remains distinctly misunderstood, principally because the combatants have been remarkably tight-lipped, indeed secretive, about the course of events in all but their most obvious forms.

In 1979 Saddam Hussain became president of Iraq. Like neighbouring Iran, Iraq is staunchly Moslem but, whereas in Iran the population is mainly of the Shi'a Moslem persuasion, in Iraq the Shi'a Moslem majority is controlled by a Sunni Moslem minority. Iraq is also troubled by a potent Kurdish separatist movement in the north of the country; however, the problem of Kurdish separatism also spreads into Iran and Turkey.

In 1937 the Hashemite monarchy of Iraq had become party to the Treaty of Saadabad, a non-aggression treaty between Afghanistan, Iran, Iraq, and Turkey. Within this treaty were various measures to reduce the causes of local friction, and one of these allocated the Shatt-al-Arab waterway to Iraq, with the frontier between Iran and Iraq fixed as the eastern bank of this waterway. Connecting the joined Tigris and Euphrates rivers, plus the Karun river in Iran, with the northern end of the Arabian (or Persian) Gulf, this waterway is of seminal importance to both Iran and Iraq. Iran's mainland oil terminal at Abadan lies on the eastern side of the Shatt-al-Arab, while Iraq's second city and major port of Basra lies just to the north-west, about halfway between the sea and the confluence of the Tigris and Euphrates. Iran was always unhappy with the allocation of the Shatt-al-Arab to Iraq and in 1969 Shah Reza Pahlavi of Iran refused to be bound any longer by the decision of the Treaty of Saadabad.

The Shah was firmly assured by his military leaders that Iraq lacked the military muscle to intervene against this unilateral decision by what was clearly the predominant military power of the Middle East, but there immediately flared a number of border incidents, and diplomatic

relations between the two countries were severed. Iran exacerbated an already tense situation in 1971 by annexing the islands of Musa, Greater Tunb, and Lesser Tunb on the western side of the Strait of Hormuz at the mouth of the Gulf. Iran was clearly bent on securing strategic control of the Gulf, much to the worry of Iraq which relies on this maritime route for most of its important and export trade. In 1975 matters were apparently cleared up by the Treaty of Algiers, which fixed the boundary between Iran and Iraq as the deep-water channel in the Shatt-al-Arab, but Iraq was clearly still troubled by the slight to its sovereignty and the threat to its trade.

Then in 1979 the Pahlavid dynasty was overthrown by the fundamentalist Moslem revolution led by the Ayatollah Khomeini, and Iraq began to fear that the problems it had endured with the Pahlavids would be small by comparison with those likely to emerge from a republican Iran that was both fundamentalist in its own constitution and self-appointed standard bearer for a Shi'a Moslem renaissance. Hussain felt that Iraq could wait no longer, and in September 1980 Iraq issued Iran with a four-point ultimatum: the evacuation of its annexed islands in the mouth of the Gulf, the renegotiation of the Treaty of Algiers, the granting of autonomy to the Arabs of the Khuzestan province (south-western Iran, centred around Ahwaz), and the cessation of Iranian interference in the internal affair of the Arab states. Iran rejected the ultimatum out of hand, and on 12 September 1980 the Iraqi forces launched their offensive against Iran, initially with an attack into

Kordestan, the Iranian province in about the mid-point of the Iraqi-Iranian border, just to the north-east of Baghdad.

The gamble of the Iraqis was enormous, for the deposed shah had been fully justified in his belief in the Iranian armed forces' strength in comparison with those of considerably smaller and less affluent Iraq. The reasoning of Hussain and his politico-military advisers was that the revolution had affected the fighting capabilities of the Iranian forces to a very severe degree: supplies from the USA and other Western nations had been cut off, greatly reducing the serviceability of the Iranian's main weapons, while the political and religious culling of the armed forces' officers corps had ruined Iranian military leadership. Coupled with the fact that the Iraqis believed the

majority in Iran to be opposed to the regime of the ayatollahs, this persuaded Hussain that a sharp offensive would gain great areas and also cause Iran to crumble. To its dismay Iraq found that exactly the opposite happened: though bereft of high-quality leadership, the Iranian forces responded with exceptional tenacity and generally prevented the Iraqis from effecting deep penetrations, and the threat of the Iraqi war brought the majority firmly into line behind the country's politico-religious leadership.

The war had continued in fits and starts since that time, with neither side able to break the deadlock of static warfare in the

Iraq's defensive posture against numerically superior Iran is based on fixed positions of great strength and depth plus powerful artillery support.

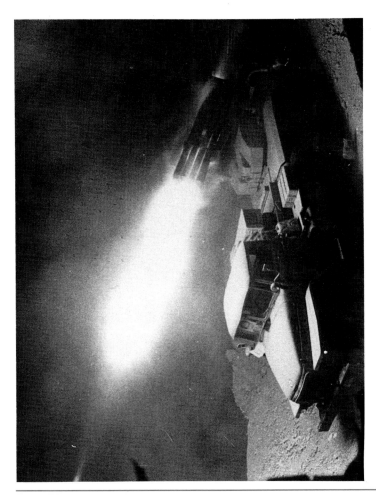

Right: A favourite Iranian weapon is the multiple rocket-launcher, which is comparatively inaccurate but can saturate a large area with heavy fire.

Bottom: Iran's strategy is based on heavyweight land offensives in which lack of matériel is balanced by masses of men with light equipment.

three main operational areas: Kurdistan in the extreme north, Kordestan in the centre, and Khuzestan in the south. Iran has been unable to match the weaponry of the Iraqis, and its major offensives (numbering seven so far) have therefore been conducted on the 'human wave' principle using masses of poorly trained and poorly equipped infantry to break through the Iraqis' defences, which are based on natural features supplemented by minefields and barbed wire, all backed by devastating long-range artillery. Estimates of the casualties to date differ wildly, but a figure of 700,000 to 1 million

seems a reasonable estimate. Iraq's initial gains were eradicated and the Iranians have now pushed forward in the main operational theatre, in the south, to points

within artillery range of Basra, in the process securing a useful bridgehead on the western bank of the Shatt-al-Arab on the Fao peninsula.

Serviceability of heavy weapons is a major problem for the Iranians, who must therefore husband their armour.

Iranian training and tactics have matured with considerable speed, and the land war is now nicely balanced between Iranian training and numbers of the one hand and Iraqi doggedness and *matériel* on the other. There have been (and continue to be) various efforts at mediation, but while Iraq is prepared to entertain the possibility of ending the war, Iran steadfastly refuses even to consider the matter unless Iraq agrees to pull back its forces and is internationally recognized as the aggressor. The land war seems set to continue, therefore, with the Iranians gradually having assumed the dominant position in terms of strategic initiative from the end of 1981 as the Iraqis lost their gains in Iran and thereafter seemed content to remain on the defensive. This has helped to reduce the enormous capital cost of the war for Iraq and has also helped to husband the country's more limited manpower reserves.

Given the stalemate on land, both countries looked to alternative methods of striking at the enemy. The air offers possibilities, but Iran's air force is too small and lacking in spares to allow a sustained offensive. Iraq, on the other hand, continues to make attacks on Iran's oil installations and, when provoked, on Iranian cities. This campaign began early in the war with mutual attacks on each other's oil installations, but has now settled down to a regime of occasional Iraqi attacks, sometimes on Iranian cities but more generally against offshore oil installations

Both Iran and Iraq depend on oil for their economic lives, and the oil assets of both countries (and of their allies) have thus become priority targets.

and 'large naval targets' (the Iraqi euphemism for the tankers plying down the Gulf with Iranian oil exports). Iran's counter-attacks are limited by the country's lack of an effective air force, and are generally undertaken with missiles such as the Soviet-supplied 'Scud' against area targets such as cities. In 1987 Iran began to receive useful supplies of Chinese 'Silkworm' surface-launched anti-ship missiles, and these have so far been used against the oil installations of Iraq's Arab neighbours to the south, most

notably Kuwait and Saudi Arabia.

Neither side has a navy sufficiently large or powerful to make possible the conduct of any formal naval warfare, but a number of hit-and-run attacks have been made, especially by the Iranians whose Revolutionary Guard Corps seems to enjoy a virtual autonomy from the rest of the armed forces and operates from forward bases in the Gulf ports and islands with speedboats to attack tankers with rockets and small arms. These attacks are very difficult to counter, and have

resulted in substantial losses and damage to the world's tanker fleets. The Revolutionary Guard Corps has also attempted a number of small minelaying offensives, and combined with the speedboat attacks this has at last in 1987 prompted international effort, spearheaded by the US Navy, to protect the tanker trade in the Gulf.

Being heavily outnumbered by Iran, Iraq relies on matériel superiority as well as the high quality of specialist troops such as these commandos.

There have been several clashes between US Navy forces and the Iranians, but the particular bent of mind that makes the Iranian form of Moslem fundamentalism so dangerous a foe also makes it impervious to the logical conclusion that an armed confrontation between US and Iranian forces must inevitably see victory going to the former. The US Navy is now convoying US-flagged tankers as far north as Kuwait, while an international but

disunited force of British, French, Italian, Belgian, and Dutch warships operates only into the southern reaches of the Gulf, largely for mineclearing operations.

There is no end in sight for this ghastly war and, while international attention remains fixed on the Gulf proper, there is no doubt that the greatest losses are incurred in the deadlocked land campaign, which must ultimately decide the outcome of

An increasingly large part of Iran's infantry burden is borne by youth units, in whom political and religious fervour is thought to outweigh any lack of pure military skills.

the war. Iran seems content at the moment to rely on the religious fervour of its young volunteers to make the massed attacks that clear Iraqi minefields and allow the conventional forces to advance and sometimes secure positions in the face of Iraqi counter-attacks.

ASIAN WARS

THE RUSSO-JAPANESE WAR (1904-05)

The key to Japanese military ambitions in the first half of the 20th century lies in the nation's industrialization from the 1870s. This extraordinarily rapid progress demanded the raw materials and the markets which densely populated Japan did not have and inevitably drew ambitious economic and political eyes to the Asian mainland, where the dominant nations were a decadent China and an expanding Russia. In the short term Japan coveted Korea, a semi-independent vassal of the Chinese empire, and parts of Manchuria.

In 1894 the Japanese fomented riots in Korea to destabilize the situation and both China and Japan rushed troops into the area to quell the disorder. The trouble was quickly crushed but neither side would withdraw its forces until the other did and this ultimately provoked the Sino–Japanese War (1894–5) desired by Japan. China was comprehensively defeated, and in the Treaty of Shimonoseki, signed on April 1895, recognized the independence of Korea, agreed to pay Japan a vast indemnity, and ceded to Japan the Pescadores, Formosa, and the Liaotung peninsula together with its important Port Arthur.

Worried by this considerable expansion of Japanese power onto the Asian mainland, the Western nations demanded comparable concessions from China, and finally edged Japan from the Liaotung peninsula, which was then leased by Russia in 1898 as the southern end of a major spur of the Trans-Siberian Railway,

Tsar Nikolas II holds up an icon before kneeling troops about to set off for the defence of Port Arthur in the Russo–Japanese War.

Russia having already occupied much of Manchuria. This persuaded Japan that Russia was the main threat to its growing hegemony in northern Asia, and between 1900 and 1903 large-scale preparations for war were made. The key to Japan's position on the Asian mainland was clearly Korea, where substantial forces were garrisoned, but this key was wholly dependent on superiority at sea. Japan rightly reasoned, therefore, that a cornerstone of the impending war with Russia was the destruction of the Russians' Far East Fleet based at Port Arthur.

Though the Russian forces totalled about 4.5 million men in all, those in eastern Asia amounted only to some 50,000 garrison troops and a field army of 83,000 men supported by 196 guns. Against this the Japanese could deploy, after securing command of the sea, its total regular army of 283,000 men and 870 guns, backed by about 400,000 highly trained reserves available very rapidly after mobilization. In the Far East the Russian navy could call on 7 battleships (all elderly), 9 armoured cruisers, 25 destroyers, and about 30 smaller craft: this force was concentrated at Port Arthur, the only dispersion being 2 cruisers at Chemulpo (now being Inchon) and another 4 at Vladivostok. Against this the Japanese could deploy 7 battleships (6 modern and 1 old), 8 armoured cruisers, 25 light

cruisers, 19 destroyers, 85 torpedo boats, and 16 smaller craft. Just as important as numbers in any war are, of course, doctrine, leadership, morale, and training, and in all these departments the Japanese had a decisive edge over the Russians.

Surprise was clearly important and for this reason the Japanese did not wait for a formal declaration of war before launching a surprise torpedo boat attack on the Russian naval units at Port Arthur on 8 February 1904. Considerable damage was caused and the Japanese commander, Vice Admiral Heihachiro Togo, then engaged the shore batteries and surviving ships with long-range fire from his main force cruising just offshore. Togo then initiated a close blockade of Port Arthur. Under the command of Vice Admiral

Hikonojo Kamimura, a Japanese cruiser force was already escorting the first troop convoys to the mainland at Chemulpo, and on the following day this cruiser force attacked the two Russian ships in the harbour, sinking one with gunfire and damaging the other so severely that the crew scuttled her. On the following day Japan declared war on Russia.

One week later General Tamesada Kuroki's Japanese 1st Army began to come ashore at Chemulpo, and immediately advanced north through Korea to the line of the Yalu river as the covering force for the operations planned against Port Arthur. As

The 1st Brigade of the Russians' 41st Mounted Division on the move in Manchuria. Poor communications placed great emphasis on such mounted formations.

PART I   MIDDLE AND NEAR EASTERN WARS

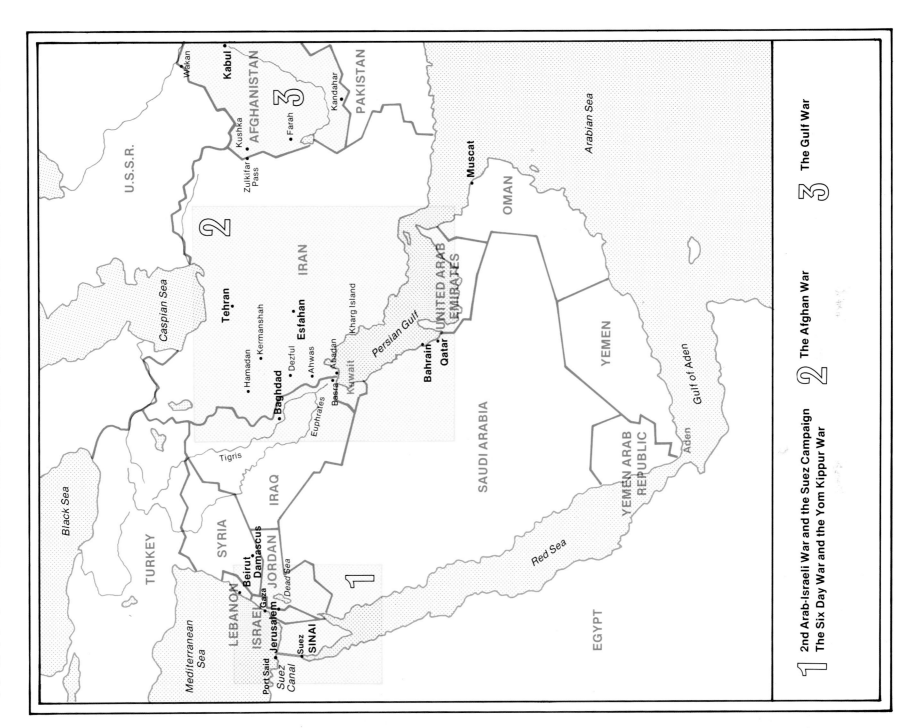

Black Sea

TURKEY

Mediterranean Sea

LEBANON
Beirut
SYRIA
Damascus
ISRAEL
Jerusalem
JORDAN
Gaza
Dead Sea
Port Said
Suez Canal
Suez
SINAI

EGYPT

U.S.S.R.

Caspian Sea

IRAN
Tehran
Kermanshah
Hamadan
Dezful
Esfahan
Ahwas
Abadan
Baghdad
Basra
Kuwait
Kharg Island
IRAQ
Tigris
Euphrates

Wakan
Kabul
AFGHANISTAN
Kushka
Zulkifar Pass
Farah
Kandahar
PAKISTAN

SAUDI ARABIA

Bahrain
Qatar
UNITED ARAB EMIRATES
Persian Gulf

Muscat
OMAN

Arabian Sea

YEMEN

Red Sea

YEMEN ARAB REPUBLIC

Aden
Gulf of Aden

1 2nd Arab-Israeli War and the Suez Campaign
The Six Day War and the Yom Kippur War

2 The Afghan War

3 The Gulf War

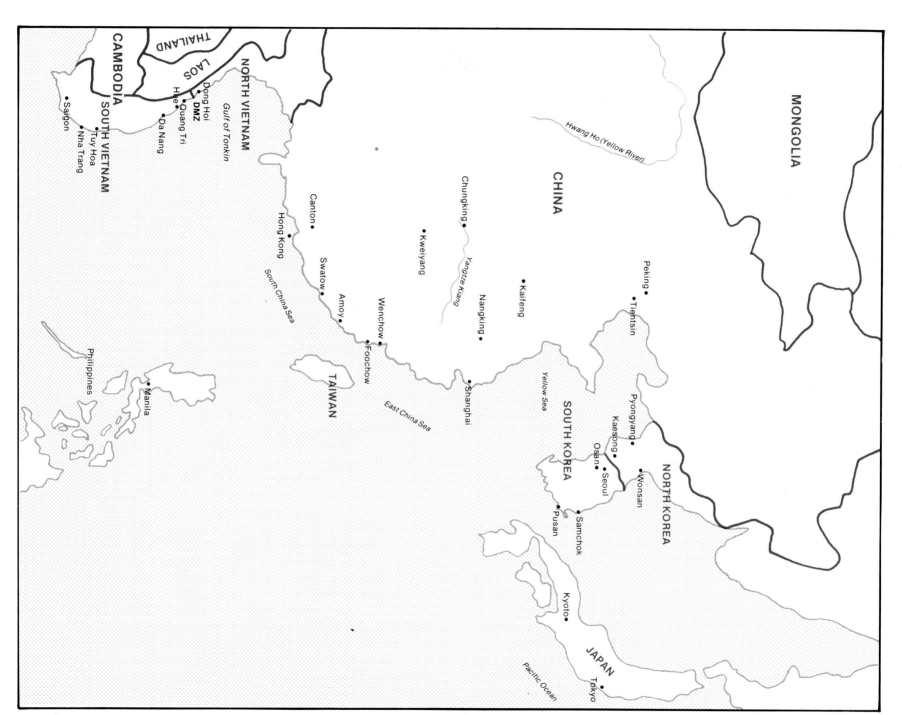

PART I ASIAN WARS

MONGOLIA

CHINA

Hwang Ho (Yellow River)

Chungking

Kweiyang

Yangtze Kiang

Nangking

Kaifeng

Peking

Tientsin

Canton

Hong Kong

Swatow

Amoy

Wenchow

Foochow

South China Sea

TAIWAN

East China Sea

Shanghai

Yellow Sea

SOUTH KOREA

Pyongyang

Kaesong

Osan

Seoul

Wonsan

NORTH KOREA

Pusan

Samchok

Kyoto

JAPAN

Tokyo

Pacific Ocean

Philippines

Manila

THAILAND

LAOS

CAMBODIA

SOUTH VIETNAM

Saigon

Tuy Hoa

Nha Trang

Da Nang

Quang Tri

Hue

Dong Hoi

DMZ

NORTH VIETNAM

Gulf of Tonkin

this Japanese advance was moving north, the Russians sent Admiral Stepan Makarov to assume command in Port Arthur. Arriving on 8 March, the able Makarov immediately set about measures to break the Japanese naval blockade: realizing that he could not match Togo's main force, he used his ships for harassing raids on the Japanese cruisers forming the close blockade. However, on 13 April Makarov's flagship *Petropavlovsk* struck a mine and was lost with all hands. Thereafter the Russians remained in port and judged the loss of Makarov must be the most decisive blow yet suffered by the Russians.

During April and May the Russian commander in the Far East, General Aleksei Kuropatkin, was working towards denying the Japanese the short-term victory they clearly wanted. Kuropatkin appreciated that his forces were in poor condition for sustained operations and thus concentrated his available strength in three groupings: immediately to the north of Port Arthur, in the area of Hai-cheng and Kai-ping, was General Stakelberg's force of 35,000 men; guarding the passes to the west of the Yalu was General Count Keller's force of 30,000 men, with an advanced guard of 7,000 men under General Zasulich watching the Yalu crossings; and at Liao-yang was the main reserve of 40,000 men under Kuropatkin himself.

Port Arthur itself was garrisoned by almost 40,000 men under General Anatoli Stesel. Kuropatkin's strategic plan was based on a rational assessment of his forces' limited capability to check the Japanese: he therefore planned to allow the Japanese to invest Port Arthur, whose basic strength, garrison, and supplies should be sufficient to withstand a lengthy siege, while his mobile forces allowed themselves to be pushed slowly back towards Harbin, checking any headlong Japanese advance into Manchuria and so buying the time needed for additional forces to arrive from

western Russia. Kuropatkin estimated the capacity of the Trans-Siberian Railway at 40,000 men per month, so that by the end of the summer the Russians would have sufficient manpower for the relief of Port Arthur and the expulsion of the Japanese from Manchuria.

Kuropatkin's plan was a model of sensible planning but was thrown away by Admiral Evgeni Alekseyev, an incompetent political appointee to the post of viceroy of the Far East. Alekseyev demanded that Kuropatkin undertake an immediate offensive. The folly of such a course was made immediately apparent when Zasulich's force lost 2,500 of its 7,000 men in attempting to halt the Japanese 1st Army's crossing of the Yalu on 30 April and 1 May: Kuroki lost only 1,100 of his 40,000 men and was not delayed in his advance into Manchuria. Further Japanese moves were also afoot, General Yasutaka Oku's Japanese 2nd Army landing

between 5 and 19 May at Pitzuwu on the Liaotung peninsula, a mere 40 miles (65 km) north-east of Port Arthur. Oku advanced on Port Arthur without delay, but was checked at Nanshan Hill, where the Russians had constructed their main defensive line across the narrowest portion of the peninsula. Further Japanese forces were coming into the field, however, with the disembarkation of General Michitsura's Nodzu's Japanese 4th Army at Takushan to the west of the Yalu. With Port Arthur clearly about to come under close siege Alekseyev decamped to join Kuropatkin in Liao-yang.

On 25 May the siege of Port Arthur began with the Battle of Nanshan: this set the scene for the campaign that was to follow. Oku's force attacked the 3,000

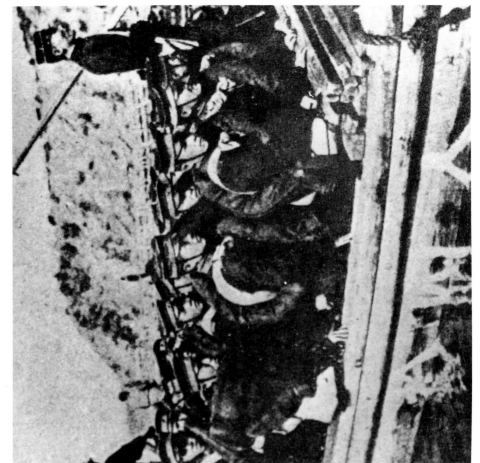

Well-equipped and ably led, the Japanese had all the advantages of shorter lines of communication and, in many cases, combat experience.

Russian artillerymen rest by their piece of field ordnance on a hill overlooking the Japanese line of advance.

defenders of Nanshan Hill frontally, was decisively repulsed, and then found its way round the Russians' left flank by wading through the sea to force the Russians to fall back: the Russians lost half their men, and Oku 4,500 of his 30,000-strong force. The loss of Nanshan Hill uncovered Dalny (now Dairen), which was seized by the Japanese as their main base and supply port in the area. Port Arthur was now completely cut off by land and sea, and at Dalny another Japanese formation, General Maresuke Nogi's Japanese 3rd Army, began to arrive. It was Nogi who had taken Port Arthur from the Chinese in 1894, and this same leader was again entrusted with the prosecution of the current siege while the Japanese 2nd Army headed north to deal with the offensive being unwillingly

undertaken by Kuropatkin, using Stakelberg's force, on the ill-advised instructions of Alekseyev.

Port Arthur was the primary prize of the Japanese war and it is convenient to deal with the course of the complete siege before turning to other operations. Between 1 and 26 June 1904 the Japanese were content to build up their forces under Nogi, the process being disturbed on the latter date by a sortie undertaken by the dithering Stessel. The sortie was quickly pushed back and during July the Japanese 3rd Army launched two probing attacks of its own (on 3 and 4 July, and on 27 and 28 July) to assess the capabilities of the defence. By the end of July Nogi had 80,000 men and 474 guns, facing a garrison of 40,000 men and 506 guns.

The defences comprised three main lines: from inner to outer

these were an entrenchment around the old town; 4,000 yards (3660 m) farther out the so-called Chinese Wall made up of concrete forts tied together by strongpoints and additional entrenchments; and outside that an outer lines based on a series of fortified hills, some of which were incomplete. The Russian garrison still had its warship strength, and on 23 June Admiral Vilgelm Vitgeft sortied against Togo, whose strength had been reduced by the loss of two battleships to Russian mines on 15 June. When it came down to action, though, Vitgeft decided that discretion was the better part of valour and retired to port, much to the relief of Togo.

By August Nogi decided that he had sufficient strength to assault Port Arthur, and on 7 and 8 August the Japanese 3rd Army launched its first major effort against the city, taking the hill defences at the eastern end of the Russian defences after severe fighting. This made it clear that the position of Port Arthur was genuinely threatened and, on the express instructions of Tsar Nikolas II, Vitgeft broke out of Port Arthur to link up with the cruiser force from Vladivostok, which had evaded the search of Kamimura's armoured cruiser force. Vitgeft set sail with a force of 6 battleships, 5 cruisers and 8 destroyers, and on 10 August met Togo in the Battle of the Yellow Sea. Japanese gunnery carried the day, and once Vitgeft had been

killed on the bridge of his flagship the Russian squadron lost cohesion and fled towards safety: most of the ships regained Port Arthur, but one cruiser was sunk and others were interned in neutral ports. Four days later Kamimura finally caught up with Admiral Jessen's cruiser force from Vladivostok, and in the Battle of Ulsan sank one of the three Russian ships.

Between 19 and 24 August Nogi launched his second major attack on Port Arthur. Some gains were made by Japanese, but casualties to Russian machine-guns were extremely heavy: for the loss of 3,000 of their own men the Russians inflicted more than 15,000 losses on the Japanese. Nogi now decided to call a halt to such frontal attacks and demanded

a train of siege artillery from Japan. In preparation for its arrival the Japanese started to develop a comprehensive system of saps and mines, and between 15 and 30 September Nogi launched his third major assault, in this instance against the northern and north-western sectors of the Russian position. The Japanese took their northern objectives on 19 September, but failed to secure the pivotal 203-Metre Hill. Yet again the Japanese losses were enormous, the vast majority of the casualties being inflicted by well-sited Russian machine-guns firing onto massed frontal assaults.

The machine-gun, on both ground and 'artillery' mountings, played a decisive part in the Russo–Japanese War.

Above: A Russian prisoner is brought into the Japanese lines.

Below right: General Kiten Maresuke Nogi, commander of the Japanese 3rd Army.

On 1 October the Japanese siege artillery began to arrive and with the aid of 19 280-mm (11-in) howitzers the Japanese began to batter the Russian defences, particularly those on 203-Metre Hill, which was also approached by the Japanese sapping and mining effort. While this artillery and engineer effort was underway, Nogi carefully prepared an assault against the eastern side of the Russian defences. On 30 October and 1 November Nogi launched his fourth general assault, this time against the northern and eastern sides of the defences. Once more the Russians decimated the attackers, whose massed ranks were an ideal target for machine-gun, artillery, and grenade attack. On 26 November Nogi tried again, launching the Japanese fifth general assault to the same

siege artillery began to arrive and with the aid of 19 280-mm (11-in) howitzers the Japanese began to batter the Russian defences, particularly those on 203-Metre Hill, which was also approached by the Japanese sapping and mining effort. While this artillery and engineer effort was underway, Nogi carefully prepared an assault against the eastern side of the Russian defences. On 30 October and 1 November Nogi launched his fourth general assault, this time against the northern and eastern sides of the defences. Once more the Russians decimated the attackers, whose massed ranks were an ideal target for machine-gun, artillery, and grenade attack. On 26 November Nogi tried again, launching the Japanese fifth general assault to the same

inevitable toll without tangible result. It was abundantly clear that the key to Port Arthur was 203-Metre Hill and here Nogi at last concentrated all his efforts.

The position was truly formidable, being based on a large redoubt flanked by subsidiary fortified positions, liberally protected by barbed wire as well as weapons manned by the 2,200-man garrison under Colonel Tretyakov. Nogi launched his forces once more on 27 November after 203-Metre Hill had been subjected to an intense artillery bombardment.

The Japanese assault reached the barbed wire in the dusk of the first day and in the face of all Russian efforts managed to hold on through the next day. Wave after wave Japanese attacked every day, and despite two successful Russian counter-attacks the Japanese finally took the fort from its last few defenders. The Japanese had lost some 11,000 dead in the attacks on 203-Metre Hill, but once in possession were able to bring up the artillery that began to shell the Russian ships in the harbour.

There was still much for the Japanese to achieve, and fort after fort had to be subdued in desperate hand-to-hand fighting. The last Russian defence fell on 1 January 1905 and Stesel surrendered Port Arthur and its starving garrison, now reduced to about 10,000 able-bodied men, on 2 January.

In the first part of June 1904 Alekseyev had demanded that

Kuropatkin take the offensive against Oku's Japanese 2nd Army, advancing up the rail line from Port Arthur towards Harbin. Kuropatkin entrusted Stakelberg, commanding a force of some 25,000 men, with this ill-conceived task. Moving south Stakelberg met Oku at Telissu and, realizing his difficulty against a numerically superior foe, dug in.

There followed the Battle of Telissu on 14 and 15 June, and after losing some 3,600 men Stakelberg pulled back to prevent the Japanese from outflanking him. The Japanese lost a mere 1,000 of their 35,000 men and moved in pursuit, only to be checked on 24 June at Tashichia with 1,200 casualties by General Zarubayev's small covering force. Farther to the east Keller's force was attempting to prevent Kuroki's Japanese 1st Army from linking up with the Japanese 2nd Army, but was severely handled in the Battle of the Moteinlung River between 17 and 31 July. Yet Kuroki was little able to press on with vigour as Keller's force was able to check it effectively.

Kuropatkin now decided to concentrate his forces in the area of Liao-yang and pulled his separate groupings back towards this important rail junction between 1 and 25 August. This was also the point at which the converging forces of Kuroki, Oku, and Nodzu were to meet, setting the scene for a decisive encounter.

The combined Japanese force was now placed under the direct command of Field Marshal Iwao Oyama, who carefully organized the approach of the three Japanese armies to the entrenched positions prepared by Kuropatkin's forces around Liao-yang. Kuropatkin had at last been reinforced from European Russia, and could deploy a total of 158,000 men to Oyama's 125,000 men. Working on the principle that attack is the best defence, Kuropatkin moved south on 25 August, but was checked before advancing past his own forward positions.

Switching the main effort against the Japanese 1st Army on his right, Kuropatkin renewed the offensive, but was again halted by the offensive tactics used so aggressively by the Japanese. The Battle of Liao-yang ended inconclusively on 3 September, the Russians having lost 19,000 men and the Japanese 23,000 men, but Kuropatkin decided that he had been worsted and opted to pull back to the north.

As he fell back, Kuropatkin was further reinforced and at Sha-Ho decided to halt and fight again. With a strength of 200,000 men to the Japanese 170,000, Kuropatkin went over to the offensive on 5 October, launching his main effort again at the Japanese 1st Army, this time on the right of the Japanese advance. Kuroki's army hastily dug in and checked the Russian effort, which had the effect of weakening Kuropatkin's centre just as Oyama threw his main weight against it. The Russian commander called off his own drive against the Japanese right to re-establish his centre, and by the time the Battle of Sha-Ho petered out on 17 October, both sides were exhausted.

With the fall of Port Arthur in the very beginning of 1905 Kuropatkin realized that he would soon be faced by additional Japanese forces in the form of Nogi's Japanese 3rd Army and decided to strike before the Japanese had thus been bolstered. With a strength of 300,000 men in three armies (commanded by Generals Grippenberg, Kaulbars, and Linievich) Kuropatkin launched the Battle of Sandepu (now Hai Kou-tai) on 26 January against the 220,000 men under Oyama. The attack was committed under cover of a snow storm and came very close to success. But Kuropatkin lost heart at the crucial moment and instead of pressing his attack allowed himself to be checked by Oyama's counter-attacks. The stalemate was resumed on 27 January and each side recovered its strength for the decisive encounter.

Men of the 1st Royal Regiment in an ambush position. As the war progressed the Russians gave an increasingly better performance on a man-to-man basis.

This was the Battle of Mukden which opened on 21 February. The two groups faced each other on a 40-mile front, each mustering about 310,000 men. The failure of frontal assault was clear to both sides and Oyama tried to turn Kuropatkin's right flank with the Japanese 3rd Army. Steady pressure pushed back the Russian right and by the end of the day Nogi's army had wheeled Kaulbars' army through 90° so that it faced west rather than south. This was clearly the cardinal point of the battle and Kuropatkin kept feeding additional troops into this sector to prevent its dissolution.

The Japanese managed to push into Mukden in a fortnight's heavy fighting, but failed to break the Russian right wing. Oyama further reinforced Nogi's army and between 6 and 8 March this left wing of the Japanese force pushed back the Russian right so far that Kuropatkin worried that his lines of communication would be severed. Breaking off with great skill, Kuropatkin pulled his surviving forces back to Tieling and Harbin, while the shattered Japanese were left victors of the battlefield and its masses of matériel; the Russians had lost

about 100,000 men and the Japanese 70,000 men. This marked the effective end of the land campaign, both sides being still in the process of recovery when political events overtook them.

These political events resulted from the Russian realization after the Battle of Tsushima that they could not win. This was the decisive encounter of the war, and one of history's great turning points. After the dismal showings of his admirals in the Battles of the Yellow Sea and Ulsan during August 1904, the Tsar had ordered naval reinforcements to the Far East. Unfortunately the selected force, the Baltic Fleet, was commanded yet again by an incompetent, in the form of Admiral Zinovy Rozhdestvensky. Rozhdestvensky sailed from his final port of call in Indo-China on 14 May with 8 battleships, 8 cruisers, 9 destroyers, and a number of smaller craft. The Japanese intelligence apparatus had kept careful watch on the Russians' progress and in December Togo's fleet had left the water around Port Arthur for a thorough refit.

Thus the Japanese fleet of 4 battleships, 8 cruisers, 21

destroyers, and 60 torpedo boats was in excellent physical shape and at the height of its morale when Togo prepared to meet the advancing Russians in the Strait of Tsushima on 27 May. The result was almost inevitable and was sealed by Togo's superior leadership and the better gunnery of his crews. For the loss of 3 torpedo boats and 1,000 men, Togo completely destroyed the Russian fleet and inflicted 10,000 casualties: with the exception of 1 cruiser and 2 destroyers that reached Vladivostok, and 3 destroyers that reached the Philippines and internment, the Baltic Fleet was sunk or captured.

Both sides were exhausted and ready to accede to the mediation of President Theodore Roosevelt of the USA. The Treaty of Portsmouth was signed on 6 September 1905: Russia ceded Port Arthur and the southern half of Sakhalin Island to the Japanese, evacuated Manchuria and recognized Korea as falling into the Japanese sphere of influence.

The Japanese battleship Asashi (preceded by the Fuji, Shikishima and Mikasa) opens fire on the Russian Baltic Fleet in the Battle of Tsushima.

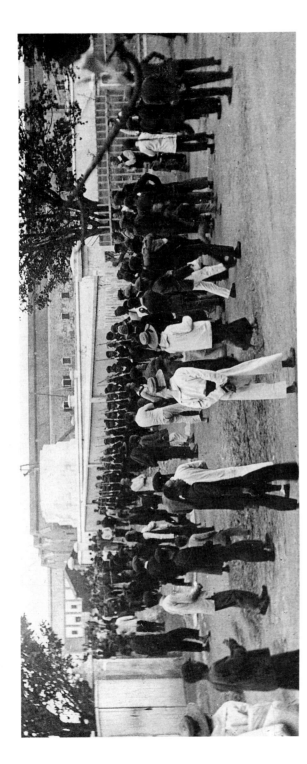

The last years of the 19th century and the first years of the 20th century were a disaster for China: defeat in the Sino-Japanese War was followed almost without respite by territorial losses to the European powers, the acceptance of inequitable trading conditions, the terrible Boxer Rebellion, and the fighting of the Russo-Japanese War largely on Chinese territory. Internally the Chinese could take this out only on the Manchu dynasty and, following a period of intense nationalist revival between 1905 and 1911, a mutiny by the garrison of Wuchang in October 1911 led rapidly to the revolt of the complete army under Marshal Yuan Shi-kai. The Manchu dynasty was overthrown (the ruling emperor being Pu Yi, then aged three) and China was declared a republic in February 1912 with Yuan as its first president. Tibet took the opportunity to drive out the Chinese and become independent, the British preventing the Chinese from any attempt at reoccupation of the country.

Yet even in the vast body of China proper unrest seemed endemic: in 1913 the so-called 'Summer Revolution' broke out in the valley of the Yangtze river but was crushed, while Yuan's announcement of the restoration of the monarchy with himself as emperor led to a larger uprising in December 1915. This had been put down by March 1916, but unrest continued even after Yuan announced a change of plans. Yuan died in June 1916 and was succeeded as president by Li Yuan-hung, who was then faced by military revolt against parliamentary democracy.

The northern military governors established their rival capital at Tientsin during May 1917, and in July 1917 one of the governors, Chang Hsun, pretended to a wish for agreement but then overthrew the Peking government and for 12 days restored the Manchu dynasty. But Chang was repudiated by his fellow military governors who attacked Peking, forced Chang and the restored Manchus to quit, and installed Feng Kuo-chang as president.

Top: The scene after the taking of the Manchu courts at Chao Foo in 1912, with curious civilians watching the troops.

Left: China was liberally endowed with European concessions. These are the 1st Somerset Light Infantry, the garrison of one such British enclave.

By 1920 central authority had disappeared from China and the military governors became in effect independent in the period between 1920 and 1926, known to history as the time of the war lords. The war lords fought almost constantly between themselves, China's one ray of hope being the congress of the Kuomintang (national people's party) in Canton during January 1924. Under the leadership of Sun Yat-sen, the Kuomintang began to prepare for the reunification of China under a central authority with the help of its own army, eventually led by General Chiang Kai-shek, head of the Whampoa Military Academy at which German and Soviet advisers helped to create a new officer corps for the Chinese.

So began the Chinese Civil War which saw Chiang move north from Canton in July 1926 to begin the programme of defeating the war lords and bringing their territories under central control of the Kuomintang. First on the list was Wu Pei-fu who controlled the region round Hankow and Wuch'ang, which were taken in September and October 1926. This allowed the capital to be moved from Canton to Hankow. Again advised by the Soviet General Vasili Blucher (known to the Chinese as B. K. Galin), Chiang next turned against Sun Ch'uan-fang, whose capital of Nanking in the lower reaches of the Yangtze valley was captured in March 1927.

Left: Recruits learn the intricacies of loading a bolt-action magazine rifle in 1923, a period of considerable growth in the Chinese army.

Bottom: Cantonese soldiers supplied for the defence of Hankow provide evidence of the Soviet involvement in this episode, all being well provided with Soviet weapons.

Above: Japanese troops cut the rail line at San-tai-tzu, to the north of Mukden, so hindering the arrival of Russian reinforcements in the Russo-Japanese War of 1904–05.

Right: A stylized impression of the Japanese battle line in the Battle of Tsushima on 27 May 1905, the engagement that decided the outcome of the Russo-Japanese War.

Overleaf: A Russian troop train being shelled by Japanese artillery during the Russian retreat from Mukden to Tieh-ling-hsien.

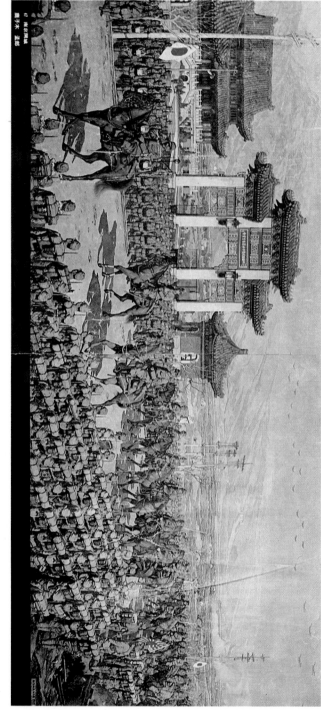

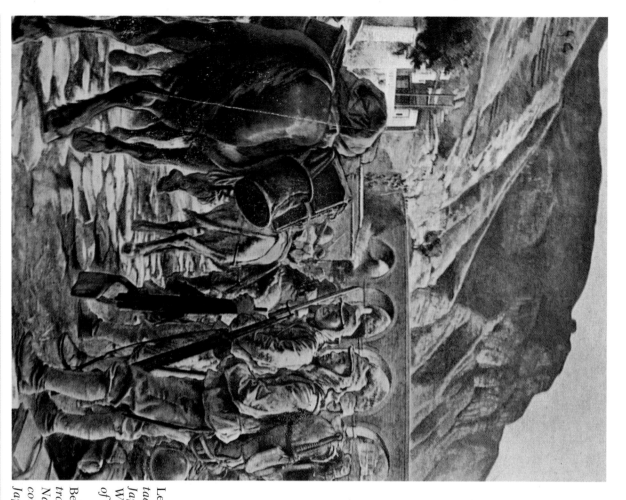

Left: Transport at all levels from tactical to strategic was vital to Japan's success in the Russo-Japanese War: here troops watch the passage of a mule train.

Below: Watched by his victorious troops, General Matsui enters Nanking in December 1937 in the comparatively early stages of the Sino-Japanese War.

Part of the British defences for the protection of its interests in Shanghai during this turbulent period of Chinese history.

The problem of reunification was now greatly hampered by the emergence of the Chinese communist party as an active force. In March 1927 the communists seized control of the Chinese portion of Shanghai and, suspicious of possible collusion between the communists and left-wingers of the Kuomintang, Chiang took Chinese Shanghai on 12 April, some 5,000 communists, trade unionists, and left-wingers being killed. This action caused a split in the Kuomintang: the communist-leaning left wing, centred on the Kuomintang capital of Hankow, condemned Chiang's action in Shanghai, so Chiang formed a new nationalist government under his own leadership with its capital at Nanking.

The two nationalist governments now launched independent campaigns against the northern war lords in April and may 1927. The Hankow regime concentrated its efforts on Wu Pei-fu and Chang

Hsueh-liang of Manchuria and north-east China, failing to win any conclusive result in a campaign fought mainly in northern Hupeh and southern Honan. Chiang fought a more conclusive campaign against Sun Ch'uan-fang, pushing through Anhwei towards Hsuchow. At this point the 'Christian War Lord', Feng Yu-hsiang of Shensi, joined forces with Chiang against the

other northern war lords, but the combined offensive of Chiang and Feng was blocked by the Japanese occupation of Shantung, a temporary measure in May and June 1927.

January 1927, and a 'bomber' of General Chang Chung-chang's air force receives its main payload before a mission against the Cantonese 'Reds'.

Meanwhile the influence of the communists on the Hankow branch of the Kuomintang had been growing steadily and, fearful lest the communists seize control, the leadership of the Hankow party broke off relations with the USSR in July 1927 and sent home all Soviet political and military advisers. At the same time left-wing members of the party were purged, and this cleansing of the stables provoked communist elements in the garrison of Nanchang to mutiny in the hope of sparking off a national communist uprising. The uprising was led by dissident Generals Yeh T'ing, Ho Lung, and Chu Teh, but was rapidly crushed by loyal troops. The generals fled, and despite a co-ordinated effort by both branches of the Kuomintang, the rebels for the most part managed to escape. The most important escape was that of Chu Teh with

a small but capable group of supporters to the mountainous region of western Kiangsi, which marks the real beginning of the civil war between the Kuomintang and the communists, eventually settled by the success of the latter in 1949 after an often-broken truce period between 1937 and 1945, when the Japanese were officially deemed to pose the greater problem.

As the military revolt was failing, a peasant revolution was organized in Hunan by Mao Tse-tung during August and September 1927. The revolution failed, and Mao fled south towards Kiangsi, where he and Chu eventually joined forces.

In spite of the temporary rapprochement with the Hankow faction during the search for Chu, Chiang remained strongly opposed to any remarriage of the two factions of the Kuomintang and on 27 August 1927 resigned in protest at the efforts of the two factions to merge. With Chiang absent in Japan after his resignation, the two wings of the party united, the Hankow faction moving to the new combined party capital of Nanking. The political and military upheavals attendant on these travails in the affairs of the Kuomintang were just what was wanted by the northern war lords, and under the overall command of Sun the 70,000 men raised by the war lords moved south towards the Yangtze valley, crossing the river to the west of Nanking.

The Kuomintang rallied their forces under General Li Tsung-jen, and in the Battle of Lungtan used their field forces with river gunboat support to defeat Sun's forces, which lost 20,000 dead and 30,000 prisoners. The remnants of the war lords' army fell back and by the end of October the offensive had been called off. Further south the problems of the

Torture was endemic to all parties in the Chinese Civil War, most civilians being thought to be spies for any of the other factions.

Kuomintang were exploited by the communists in Canton, who declared the city a communist commune on 11 December 1927. The Kuomintang moved swiftly and by 15 December had ruthlessly crushed the rising. The party realized that it lacked true leadership of a high-quality kind and on 6 January 1928 Chiang returned as commander-in-chief and chairman of the party's central executive committee. Chiang rapidly restored order and set about the preparation of

another northern offensive within his long-term plan of unifying the country. The offensive was launched on 7 April and was a truly large-scale effort by some 700,000 men under the command of Generals Li, Feng, P'ai Ch'eng-hsi, and Ho Ying-ch'in, together with those of Yen Hsi-shan, war lord of Shansi.

The three northern war lords put about 500,000 men into the field under Chang Tso-lin but were defeated and could not oppose the Kuomintang's advance

across the Yellow (Huang) river. The Japanese intervened between 3 and 11 May at Tsinan and pushed the Kuomintang out of Shantung, in which the Japanese claimed a special interest, but the nationalist forces drove forward to take Peking (then renamed Peiping) on 4 June. On the same day Chang Tso-lin was killed

Troops of the northern warlords begin their evacuation of Shantung province in the face of a powerful advance by the armies of Chiang Kai-shek.

when his train was blown up by the Japanese as the war lord withdrew towards Manchuria with the rest of his forces. Manchuria now became the province of Chang Hsueh-liang who acknowledged the overall authority of the Kuomintang.

Then in July 1930 the communist problem reared its head in a major fashion. Li Li-san, the communist party chairman, believed the time ripe for an uprising to overthrow the Kuomintang and ordered a rebellion in Kiangso and Fukien as part of a communist drive to seize the central area of China. Li believed that the revolution must stem from the country's urban masses and overruled the objections of Mao, the major proponent of the belief

in the superiority of a rural revolution by the peasants. Under the command of General P'eng Teh-huai, the communist forces seized Ch'angsha on 28 July 1930 but then withdrew. Li ordered the city captured once again, but the delay allowed Chiang to reinforce the garrison of the city, which defeated all efforts by reinforced communist forces led by P'eng, Mao, Chu and Ho. The campaign was called off by the communists, and when Li was recalled to Moscow the star of Mao moved into the ascendant.

Chiang now decided that the time was ripe to eliminate the communist threat, and between late 1930 and 1934 the nationalist leader launched a number of so-called 'extermination' or 'bandit-

Arrest of a communist agitator flushed from a haystack by Kuomintang troops equipped with long lances for just this purpose.

suppression' campaigns. The first and second (between December 1930 and January 1931, and between April and May 1931) were largely unsuccessful, being defeated by an incessant communist guerrilla effort that prevented the nationalists from pinning down their opponents, so Chiang decided to lead the third campaign himself. Launched in July 1931, the campaign was moving nicely toward the communist capital of Juichin when news of the Mukden Incident persuaded Chiang to call it off in September: in their policy of absorbing Manchuria the Japanese pretended that the Chinese were plotting to destroy the railway between Mukden and Port Arthur, using this fable to justify the seizure of the arsenals of Mukden and other Manchurian towns by their Kwantung Army; the Chinese were forced to withdraw and by February 1932 Manchuria was firmly in Japanese hands despite the crippling blockade of Japanese goods by the Chinese.

Chiang was able to launch a small-scale campaign in the summer of 1932, eliminating the Oyuwan Soviet in Anhwei, Hunan, and Hupeh. The fourth main campaign was thus the one launched in April 1933, again disrupted by communist guerrilla tactics and finally abandoned in June when the Japanese again began to stir themselves against China. The fifth campaign was undertaken from December 1933 after careful preparation under the control of a German adviser, General Hans von Seeckt.

Moving slowly and thoroughly, with their progress marked by the construction of a series of block-houses, the nationalists closed in on the communists and caused heavy losses eventually coming to a halt in September 1934 as Mao persuaded the communists to fall back and avoid further losses.

The nationalists took the field against the communists once again in the summer of 1936, in response to a communist effort into Shansi. Chiang put some 150,000 men under the command of Marshal Chang, with his headquarters in Sian. However, towards the end of the year little had been achieved by Chang, and when Chiang flew to Sian on 7 December 1937 to urge greater effort, he was greeted with the information that the troops would rather fight the Japanese than their fellow Chinese. Chiang refused to consider any such alteration of basic effort and was arrested. There followed a series of still-unexplained negotiations including all relevant parties (the communists being represented by Chou En-lai), resulting in the agreement of 25 December 1936: Chang was arrested and the freed Chiang agreed to end the campaigns against the communists by the nationalists. In July 1937 war broke out between China and Japan, and Chiang was forced to abide by the Sian agreement and devote his major efforts to the Japanese threat.

Government troops prepare to search a village for 'bandits' during 1923.

THE SINO-JAPANESE WAR (1937–41)

For sound strategic reasons Japan concentrated her efforts of the early 1920s on consolidation of its position in northern China, gradually easing the area from any semblance of American, British or Soviet influence. The Chinese Civil War played right into Japanese hands, this internecine struggle allowing the imperial empire to increase its hold on China's northern territories to the extent that the Japanese could use military force to expel Chinese armies, as in the Tsinan incident of May 1928 during Chiang Kai-shek's drive towards Peking.

By 1930 Japan's economic position in China proper was sufficiently secure for the imperialists to cast increasingly covetous eyes on Manchuria, already firmly within the Japanese sphere of influence but wanted as part of the Japanese empire for its markets and raw materials. On 19 September 1931 the Japanese sprang the 'Mudken Incident' on the Chinese; claiming that the Chinese had attempted to blow up portions of the rail line between Mukden and Port Arthur, the Japanese seized the arsenals of Mukden and other Manchurian cities and forced the Chinese to pull out their troops. Within a few

months Manchuria was under effective Japanese control, and the only weapon available to the Chinese was a boycott of Japanese goods. This proved remarkably effective, and the Japanese responded with an attack on Shanghai using forces sea-lifted from Japan. The 1st Battle of Shanghai was fought between 28 January and 4 March 1932: a total of 70,000 Japanese troops was used and had to wage a surprisingly protracted campaign within the city against the Chinese

Above: A Japanese reconnaissance biplane swoops down to impart information during the Japanese seizure of Manchuria in 1932.

Below: Chinese troops in action against the Japanese during March 1932.

19th Route Army, which pinned the Japanese into the waterfront area for about a month. The Japanese eventually overcame the Chinese resistance and China

Chinese 'Big Sword' troops, numbered among the defenders of Jehol in March 1933.

reluctantly agreed to lift its boycott of Japanese goods. To emphasize their defeat of China at this time, the Japanese on 18 February declared Manchuria to be the independent kingdom of Manchukuo under Pu Yi, the former Chinese emperor. This was, of course, a puppet state over which Japan immediately threw a protectorate.

In January 1933 Japan moved to increase its holdings in Asia, advancing from Manchukuo into Inner Mongolia (Jehol) on the pretext that this was in fact part of Manchukuo. There was little that the Chinese could do and with

Peiping threatened they had to agree to the armistice of Tangku on 31 May, which forced them to cede Jehol, evacuate Tientsin, and create a demilitarized zone in eastern Hopeh. Between 1934 and 1937 the Japanese moved further into China, advancing westward through Inner Mongolia to take Chahar and the northern part of Hopei. Chiang was firmly distracted by his 'extermination' campaigns against the communists, and the Japanese now thought the time ripe for a major effort against China.

The *casus belli* was another Japanese-fabricated occasion, the

'China Incident' of 7 July 1937: claiming that their troops on night manoeuvres near the Marco Polo Bridge in Lukouchiao, near Peiping, had been fired upon, the Japanese clashed with the Chinese and so initiated a full-scale war. Though little considered in the West, this war blended into Japan's operational scheme in World War II and may thus be considered the start of that huge conflict.

the Japanese took Tsinan, the capital of Shantung, and were thus left in control of the area north of the Yellow river.

To pave the way for further advance in 1938 the Japanese had decided to open a second front around Shanghai and on 8 August 1937 an amphibious invasion was launched. Yet again the Japanese encountered resistance far more determined than they had anticipated and the 2nd Battle of Shanghai was for a time in the balance until the Japanese rushed in reinforcements. For two months the Japanese were able to hold on to their beach-heads only with the aid of intense naval gunfire

Below: Japanese occupation forces in Shanghai, China's major link with the rest of the world.

Above: Japanese troops cross an extemporized footbridge to the captured walled city of Nanking on the Yangtze.

The first phase of Japan's war was concentrated north of the Yellow river, where the forces of Japan's North China Area Army captured Peiping and Tientsin on 28 and 29 July respectively. The seizure of these vital cities paved the way for Japan's two-axis advance: to the west the Japanese army moved through Chahar and part of Suiyuan to reach the upper reaches of the Yellow river at Paotow, while to the south a larger effort saw the Japanese army advance along the rail lines to Hankow, Nanking, and Sian. The Japanese progress was initially fast, but as the Chinese forces gained in combat experience they began to slow the pace of the Japanese advance, which was further limited by the need to divert troops back to the rear areas, where the Chinese civil population became an increasing thorn in Japan's side. Then logistical difficulties, compounded by poor winter weather, took a hand and the Japanese offensive was halted in December. Just before operations were called off,

The Japanese attack served to unite many parts of a disunited China in resistance. These are female guerrillas armed only with spears.

support and a series of devastating air attacks on Shanghai city. Additional reinforcements arrived in October, allowing the Japanese to undertake landings north and south of the main assault area. Outflanked by these new beach-heads, the Chinese were forced to pull back and the Japanese secured their hold on Shanghai on 8 November. With Shanghai secured the Japanese were able to push west along the line of the Yangtze river against wholly ineffective Chinese resistance.

To the surprise of nearly all, including the Japanese, the reverses at the start of the Japanese invasion failed to destroy either the cohesion or the will of the Chinese, who fought on with increasing skill in small-scale operations designed to restrict rather than defeat the Japanese.

Thus when the Japanese 1st Army resumed its southerly advance towards Nanking and Hankow during January 1938, it made steady progress along the main rail lines but failed to extend its control laterally from these main lines of communication. By April the Japanese had reached Taierchwang and here a force of some 60,000 Japanese was surrounded by upwards of 200,000 Chinese regular and guerrilla troops under General Li Tsing-jen. The Japanese eventually managed to fight their way north out of the encirclement at the cost of 20,000 dead and most of their equipment, and though this success did much to boost Chinese morale it played no decisive part in the overall scheme of things.

In May and June the Japanese recovered their strength and

nerve, and relaunched their offensive with converging attacks from north and south. The Japanese made steady progress along the rail line and by the end of June the whole length of the rail line between Peiping and Nanking was in Japanese hands and the eastern corridor of China from Shanghai to the north was under Japanese occupation. Chiang had meanwhile agreed to support another communist field force and the New 4th Army was created under the command of Ye T'ing with the objective of fighting a guerrilla campaign behind the Japanese lines south of the middle Yangtze.

With the main north/south lines of communication safe, and their forces firmly lodged (even though under constant pressure) in the north-eastern part of mainland China, the Japanese sought to extend their territory to the west. In June 1938, therefore, the China Expeditionary Army launched an offensive west from Kaifeng up the Yellow river with the task of taking the rail junction at Chengchow. This prize was desired as it would seriously affect the mobility and supplies for the Chinese forces and also open the way for a southward advance towards Hankow.

The position of the Chinese was potentially desperate, and therefore desperate counter-measures were required: the Chinese broke the banks of the Yellow river,

flooding vast areas and diverting the river into its original course to debouch many hundreds of miles from its recent descent to the sea in the Gulf of Chihli. The man-made disaster secured its objective, the Japanese offensive having to be cancelled during July in a sea of shallow water and mud that completely halted movement. Yet the Japanese were determined on the seizure of Hankow and shifted their effort further to the south, advancing up the line of the Yangtze during July.

The nationalists were equally determined that the Japanese should not capture their capital and the result was some of the severest fighting of the whole Sino-Japanese War. Yet with the aid of their unopposed air force the Japanese were able to make

slow and steady progress, capturing Hankow on 25 October. Chiang had already realized the inevitable loss of his capital and moved west to Chungking in the heart of mountainous (and thus less vulnerable) Szechwan province. Japan's effort for the year was completed by the capture of Canton on 21 October, amphibious forces for the assault having been landed near Hong Kong on 12 October. This gave the Japanese China's second largest port and as they already had Shanghai this further turned the screw on Chiang's acute supply problems.

Japanese troops man a commandeered junk on the Yangtze river for the movement of supplies.

The winter of 1938 gave the Japanese time for a radical reappraisal of their task in China. A quick victory was clearly out of the question, Chinese determination and the sheer distances to be covered having proved too sapping for the completion of major offensives. The Japanese therefore decided on a war of attrition to wear down the Chinese.

Over the next few years the forces of the China Expeditionary Army thus confined themselves to local offensives designed to draw out the Chinese on terms favourable to the Japanese, who could then destroy sizeable field forces with minimum effort. And as part of the attritional effort

Japan took China's last sea ports in an effort to starve Chiang's armies of weapons and logistical supplies from the West: in 1939 the Japanese took Hainan island, plus the ports of Wenchow, Foochow, Amoy, and Swatow. Shortly after this the communists began to shoulder at least part of the burden in their so-called 'Hundred Regiments Offensive'. This was a large campaign of small guerrilla attacks against Japanese communications and outpost, planned by Mao Tse-tung and launched on 20 August throughout Shansi, Chahar, Hopeh, and Honan provinces: before its end on 30 November the campaign proved highly successful in

disrupting the Japanese rear areas and causing an unpleasant flow of morale-sapping casualties.

The 'Hundred Regiments Offensive' had hit Japanese pride as well as Japanese capabilities, and in response the China Expeditionary Army launched a number of hard-hitting offensives against communist-controlled areas between 1941 and 1943. These cost the 8th Route Army perhaps 100,000 casualties and kept it permanently off balance. As a

The juxtaposition of old and new was commonplace in China, as revealed by this home guard unit with spears and the occasional rifle.

result there was heightened animosity between the already mutually suspicious nationalists and communists, whose relations had worsened drastically because of the 'Anhwei Incident' of January 1941. In December 1940 Chiang had ordered the New 4th Army, whose operational area lay in Anhwei province to the south of the Yangtze, to move across the river and tackle the Japanese occupation forces on the left bank. Yeh refused to consider such a move, undoubtedly with the support of Mao, and this prompted Chiang to repeat the order and shift nationalist troops into Anhwei.

Late in December the New 4th Army yielded to this threat and began slowly to cross the Yangtze. Then the nationalists launched an attack on the New 4th Army's rearguard when just this force was left south of the river: all 10,000 men were killed or captured, the latter category including Yeh, who was wounded.

When properly led and adequately equipped (as these men are), the Chinese at times put up a capable defence.

swinging out of China for the war planned against the British and Dutch in South-East Asia and the Americans in the Pacific. The rest of 1941 was thus relatively quiet for the Chinese, their bitter struggle against the Japanese about to be absorbed within the altogether greater compass of World War II.

Japan's attention was by now

THE CHINESE CIVIL WAR (1945-49)

With the collapse of Japan in August 1945 after the devastation, both physical and psychological, by the American atomic bombs dropped on Hiroshima and Nagasaki, the civil war in China flared up again. On 14 August the nationalists signed a treaty of friendship and alliance with the USSR: Dairen and the Manchurian Railway were to be held in joint ownership for 30 years, Port Arthur was to become a joint Soviet/Chinese naval base, and China was to recognize the independence of Outer Mongolia, which had freed itself from Chinese suzerainty in 1911 but failed to secure any Chinese admission of this fact. But even as Chiang was negotiating, the communists had swept in to seize as much as possible of Japanese-occupied China. Chiang ordered them to halt, but Mao's forces took not the slightest notice.

The Americans feared the immediate outbreak of renewed hostilities, and from 30 September had been landing American forces, spearheaded by the 1st Marine Division and eventually totalling 53,000 men to hold Hopeh and Shantung provinces, together with the cities of Peiping and Tientsin. But it was altogether too late to prevent the outbreak of hostilities and on 15 October the communists destroyed a force of five nationalist divisions in the region of Tunliu and Hsiangyuan in eastern Shansi. Just six days later Mao announced the withdrawal of all communist forces to areas north of the Yangtze river, but ten days later a major battle in northern Honan resulted in the total destruction of two nationalist armies.

Chiang decided that his forces must deal first of all with the communists in Manchuria and, denied permission by the occupying Soviets to move his troops by sea into the Liaotung peninsula, used sea lift to move a substantial force to Chinwangtao on the northern side of the Gulf of Chihli. The landings were effected on 15 November and by 26 November the nationalist forces had advanced north-east (but outside the Soviet-occupied area) to take Chinchow. But on 30 November as the nationalists moved into Manchuria the communist New 4th Army under Chen Yi advanced to occupy those parts of Shantung province not held by the US forces. The nationalists were not to be deterred and by 13 December were in possession of Mukden after a large-scale air lift.

The USA was becoming increasingly worried by the spread of renascent civil war and President Harry S Truman appointed General George C. Marshall, the recently retired US Army chief-of-staff, as his personal mediator in the dispute. Marshall arrived on 14 December and within a month had secured both parties' agreement to a truce, which failed to stick in Manchuria but elsewhere held, with frequent violations, for about six months as Marshall attempted to find a solution agreeable to both sides.

The failure of the February 1946 accord signalled a general outbreak of hostilities by the two parties in the Chinese Civil War, the main theatres being in Manchuria and in northern and central China. The catalyst for the resumption of hostilities in Manchuria was the Soviet evacuation of that former puppet state of Japan, beginning on 1 March 1946. To fill the vacuum (increased by the Soviets' removal of industrial plant then valued at US$858 million) the nationalists advanced on a basically north-eastern axis up the roads and rail lines from the Gulf of Chihli through Mukden (now Shenyang) towards Harbin, while the

Under Mao Tse-tung, the Chinese communists shifted from an urban to a rural base, and concentrated their efforts on the rise to power rather than the defeat of the Japanese.

communists concentrated their previously scattered groups of forces into the main cities and towns, where the Soviets had left sufficient Japanese *matériel* to equip the whole of the communist forces at a level that lifted them almost immediately from lightly armed guerrilla bands to comparatively modern formations with heavy weapons. On 9 March the Soviets evacuated Mukden and on the following day a six-day battle for control of the city erupted between the nationalists and communists, the former emerging victorious and driving on towards Harbin.

Two days later, however, the communists launched a major counter-attack and halted the nationalists in the 1st Battle of Szeping (now Szepingkai), an important rail junction that was rapidly fortified by the communists. Chiang attempted to circumvent this block by airlifting a special force of 4,000 troops to Ch'angch'un, about one-third of the way north from Szeping

towards Harbin, but this bold move was rapidly defeated by numerically superior communist forces in the 1st Battle of Ch'angch'un. Chiang now decided to concentrate his effort on a piecemeal 2nd Battle of Szeping in which General Sun Li-jen's New 1st Army, 70,000 veterans of the nationalist Chinese effort in Burma during World War II, pushed 110,000 communist troops out of the city between 16 April and 20 May 1946.

The nationalists immediately surged forward, though the communists had already strengthened their overall grasp on northern Manchuria by seizure of Harbin and Tsitsihar on 25 and 28 April respectively. On 3 May the Soviets completed their evacuation of Manchuria, and the two warring Chinese factions were left to settle their differences with little hindrance from outside forces. The communists decided in the short term to consolidate in northern Manchuria, and on 22 May pulled back from their

Immediately after Japan's surrender the communists move to assume the reins of power and defeat the Kuomintang.

advanced position at Ch'angch'un, leaving the nationalists to push north-east towards Harbin.

On 1 June the nationalists crossed the Sungari river, just short of Harbin, but on 7 June a temporary halt to operations followed an armistice arranged by Marshall, with the nationalists at Shuangcheng just 25 miles (40 km) from Harbin. The armistice failed on 30 June but the communists had used the breathing space to strengthen their defences and there followed a stalemate right through to the end of the year.

In January 1947 the communists fully appreciated that Chiang had ordered a strategic defensive in Manchuria to allow the continuance of offensive operations elsewhere, and also felt their strength and training were adequate for a sustained offensive. Under General Lin Piao the communists got the ball rolling with a series of probing attacks across the Sungari to the south-west of the main nationalist positions during the first three months of 1947: all three attempts were repulsed. But in May Lin struck south with three offensives aimed at Ch'angch'un, Kirin, and Szeping; and with a force of 270,000 men cut off all three cities, which the nationalists had to supply by air, after the Sungari bridgehead had been hastily abandoned, as a relief force of two armies was pushed forward from the Liaotung peninsula.

By 16 June the communists had reached Szeping but were ejected in the 3rd Battle of Szeping before both sides collapsed into temporary exhaustion during July and August. The communists got under way again on 20 September, launching an offensive designed to cut the Liaosi corridor, and with it the nationalists' overland communications with Mukden. General Cheng Tung-kuo, the nationalist commander in

Manchuria, responded with vigour, and by 10 October the corridor had been secured for the nationalists. In January 1948 the communists renewed their offensive against the Liaosi corridor and so desperate did the situation become that Chiang flew in to assume personal command of the defence effort. The corridor was again secured by February, allowing Chiang to fly south to his capital at Nanking.

The decisive moment in the Manchurian campaign arrived on 12 September when a rapidly developing communist offensive seized the Liaosi corridor. Furious nationalist counter-attacks were defeated and, arriving in Peiping to assess the situation, Chiang saw that the nationalist position was untenable. He ordered his Manchurian garrisons to fall back, the first step being the evacuation of Ch'angch'un on 21 October. Under the command of General Liao Yueh-hsiang, another competent nationalist leader who had won his spurs in Burma during World War II, the three nationalist armies fought their way south, but were overwhelmed by a communist counter-offensive that completely destroyed them in the Battle of Mukden-Chinchow between 27 and 30 October. On 1 November Mukden fell and by the end of the year the communists were in firm control of Manchuria, the nationalists having lost at least 300,000 of their best troops.

Further to the south on 1 May 1946 Chiang switched his capital from the wartime expedient of Chungking back to Nanking near the mouth of the Yangtze river above Shanghai and settled to the routine of prosecuting the war against the communists in north and central China. Despite the truce arranged in January 1946, the region was racked by a series of small but troublesome communist uprisings, the most nasty of which was that occurring in Hankow (now Wuhan) on 5 May. The communists hoped to keep the nationalists off balance with this programme of pinprick problems in their heartlands, but by July 1946 Chiang was ready for his first major offensive in northern China, claiming the series of communist attacks as the reason for the drive.

The real motive for this offensive, which was undertaken between July and November and proved highly successful, was to prevent the communists from consolidating their position in the area. The nationalists retook most of Kiangsu province to the north of Nanking, reopened the rail line between Tsingtao and Tsinan in Shantung province, and made deep inroads into Jehol and Hopeh.

Chiang now ordered his forces to assume a defensive posture in all areas but Shensi, where a successful offensive was continued for a limited time, taking the communist capital of Yenan (now Fushih) on 19 March before petering to a halt by the end of the month. Mao was forced to abandon the city, but it was only a minor setback for the rapidly improving communist effort: this is signalled by the fact that Mao steadfastly refused to allow the recall of communist troops from more important theatres to stem the nationalist effort in Shensi.

In retrospect it is possible to see that the unilateral ceasefire and the decision to fight a defensive campaign were disastrous mistakes by Chiang, and the communists gratefully seized the mantle of offensive initiative so offered by the nationalists. The whole of 1947 was marked by a gradual consolidation of communist power in the country, leaving the nationalists virtually isolated in the cities and along the main rail lines. By October, however, the communists felt themselves secure enough to mount an offensive carefully co-ordinated with the slightly earlier Liaosi corridor offensive in Manchuria to split the nationalists' defence capability.

Chinese 'landlords' escape death at the hands of the communists by witnessing the executions of other opponents of the emergent regime.

The operations in north and central China were entrusted to General Liu Po-ch'eng's Central Plains Army and General Chen Yi's East China Field Army: striking far and wide in Shansi, Honan and Shantung provinces, the communists made great efforts between the Yangtze river and the Lunghai railway, one of the most important successes being the cutting of the Pinghang Railway north of Chengchow on the junction of the east/west Lunghai Railway and north/south Pinghang Railway. This effectively cut off the nationalist armies in north

China from the main body of nationalist strength.

The winter of 1947–8 passed relatively uneventfully but in March the communists went over to the offensive in Shensi and at the end of April forces under the command of General P'eng Teh-huai recaptured Yenan. By May the offensive had spread to involve the armies of Liu and Chen, which made important gains in the Yellow river valley, gradually eliminating the nationalist garrisons north of the river in Shantung and Hopeh provinces before moving to the

decisive Battle of Tsinan (14–24 September 1948), when some 80,000 nationalists were killed or captured in the struggle for this important Yellow river city, which is also the primary junction of the Kaotsi Railway from Tsingtao and the Tsingpu Railway from Nanking.

Yet these moves were on a small scale compared with the campaign that began in November 1948. This is generally known as the

Execution of an 'enemy of the people' (a landlord) at the hands of a communist soldier.

Inhabitants of the Tachen islands are seen as they prepare to leave almost all their possessions in an evacuation to Formosa (Taiwan).

Battle of the Hwai Hai, and lasted into January 1949. Under the overall leadership of Chen the communist Central Plains and East China Field Armies engaged the nationalist 2nd and 7th Army Groups deployed along the line of the Lunghai Railway. Each side deployed about 500,000 men. The East China Field Army pinned the 7th Army Group between Hsuchow and the East China Sea, allowing the Central Plains Field Army to crash through the right flank of the 2nd Army Group west of Hsuchow, making for the Hwai

river and positions in which it could prevent any attempt by the 2nd and 7th Army Groups to fall back south into the nationalist heartlands. Some elements of the 2nd Army Group managed to break through to the south, but the 7th Army Group was cut off and destroyed. Nationalist losses are estimated at 250,000 men and vast quantities of *matériel*.

On 21 January Chiang resigned as president of nationalist China, being replaced by Li Tsung-jen, previously the vice president. Then just one day later Peiping

fell when General Fu Tso-yi surrendered his nationalist garrison after a long siege. Mao immediately shifted his capital from Yenan to Peiping. The nationalist cause was clearly in desperate straits and was further disheartened by the evacuation of the US Marine garrison of Tientsin during February 1949. On 1 April Li sent a telegram to Peiping to

The evacuation to Formosa was undertaken by Chinese Nationalist landing craft with escort from the US 7th Fleet.

ask for communist agreement to divide China (along the line of the Yangtze) into communist northern and nationalist southern halves. The proposal was refused adamantly by the communists who demanded nothing short of total surrender by the nationalists.

And in pursuit of his objective of total power the communists were soon on the offensive once more: on 20 April Liu's and Chen's forces, redesignated the 2nd and 3rd Field Armies respectively, swept south over the Yantze on a wide front between Nanking and Hankow. The nationalists had started to move their capital from Nanking to Canton (now Kuang-chou) during January and the process was now implemented with greater energy

as the communists closed on Nanking, which fell on 22 April. Further communist success followed rapidly: by the end of May other major nationalist centres that had succumbed to the communists included (in order of loss) Taiyuan, Hsuchow, Hankow, Sian Nanchang, and Shanghai. The rot of the nationalist cause swiftly gathered momentum, many commanders and their troops defecting as the communists continued to squeeze the nationalists into an ever-smaller pocket in south-east China around Canton.

On 15 October Canton fell to the communists without a fight, the nationalists having already switched their capital to Chungking, where Chiang again

took the reins. On 30 November Chungking fell and the nationalists moved their capital to Chengtu. There was no chance for the nationalists on the mainland and Chiang decided that the only viable option was a withdrawal to China's offshore islands, inaccessible to the communists for lack of a navy. On 7 December the surviving nationalist forces completed their withdrawal to Formosa, retaining toeholds close to the mainland in the form of the small island groups of Quemoy (off Amoy), Matsu (off Foochow) and Matsu (off Wenchow).

THE KOREAN WAR (1950-53)

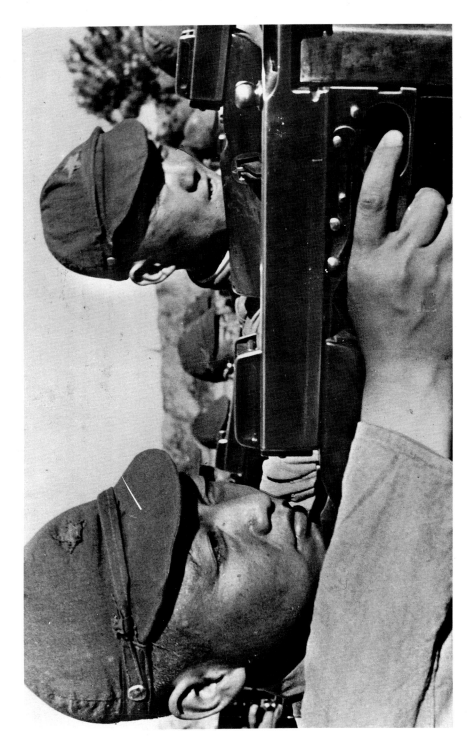

Unhappy Korea was the scene for the next major war to afflict eastern Asia, a mere six months after the final defeat of the nationalist cause in mainland China. Annexed by Japan in 1910 after the Russo–Japanese War (1904–5), Korea was promised independence by the Allied conference at Cairo (December 1943) and this promise was confirmed at the Potsdam conference (July 1945). When Japan surrendered at the end of World War II Soviet forces were already sweeping south from Manchuria and an extemporized dividing line was fixed along the 38th parallel: north of this line the Japanese would surrender to the Soviets, south of it to the Americans. The Soviets then decided that the 38th parallel was a convenient political boundary for the communist regime it envisaged and two years of US demands refused to budge the communists.

In 1947 the USA referred the problem to the United Nations, which undertook to create a unified and independent Korea after the implementation of nationwide elections. The USSR refused to co-operate in the organization of such elections and the Republic of Korea was formally established on 15 August 1947 with its capital in Seoul. The communists responded with the establishment of the Democratic People's Republic of Korea with its capital in Pyongyang.

The Soviets completed their evacuation of North Korea in December 1948, though leaving vast quantities of *matériel* and advisers for the creation of a large North Korean army, while the Americans pulled out of South Korea in June 1949, leaving only small quantities of *matériel* and a small adviser group for the nascent South Korean army.

This allowed the North Korean

China foresaw little difficulty in expelling democracy from Korea, but underestimated the effect of capably used Western weapons and air power.

army to complete its preparations for the planned military solution to the unification problem. Against South Korea's 100,000 men in eight divisions without armour or artillery, North Korea massed 130,000 men in ten divisions with modest armour (one brigade of T-34 tanks) and excellent artillery. On 25 June 1950 North Korean forces poured south over the 38th parallel in two main groups. Under the command of Marshal Choe Yong Gun seven infantry divisions and the armoured brigade moved south with the intention of taking Seoul on the right before advancing south along the west coast and of taking Pusan after a southward advance by smaller forces along the east coast.

North Korean tactical surprise was complete and rapid gains were achieved as the western advance smashed through the screen of four South Korean light divisions. The border town of Kaesong fell to the communists on the first day of the war and on 28 June Seoul was captured as part of the North Koreans' determined effort to win the war before the non-communist world could intervene: it was fully appreciated in the north that a *fait accompli*, with all of Korea in communist hands, was the optimum manner to secure success.

An emergency session of the United Nations Security Council had been convened on 25 June, but the Soviet boycott of the council removed the USSR's chance to use its veto and by 30 June positive action had been agreed and set in train. The council called for an immediate ceasefire preparatory to a North Korean withdrawal and asked for physical as well as political support from the member nations of the UN. Already the USA was moving to intervene, President Harry S Truman on 27 June having ordered General Douglas MacArthur to use the forces at his disposal as commander of the US forces in the Far East to cover the South Koreans' defence with air and naval power. MacArthur visited the front even as the US Navy instituted a blockade of North Korea and the US Air Force

struck at the North Koreans' lines of communication. MacArthur reported that the severely handled and poorly equipped South Korean army was incapable of halting the North Koreans, and on 30 June Truman gave permission for the deployment of US combat forces into Korea, starting with the 24th Division.

Between 6 and 21 July the 24th Division fought a succession of rearguard actions as it was pushed south down the Korean peninsula. On 16 July the North Koreans were able to pin the remnants of the 24th Division and attack from three sides, but the American defence bought another five days

of invaluable time. Major General Dean remained with the rearguard as the rest of his division escaped at the end of the Battle of Taejon, and though Dean's force was captured on 20 June the rest of the 24th Division was relieved by the 1st Cavalry Division on 22 July, just as the 25th Division began to come into the line on its right.

Above: Amphibious capability was very important to the UN forces, giving them an unequalled tactical flexibility in offence and defence.

Below: When supplied with US heavy weapons, the South Korean divisions were well able to handle their North Korean counterparts.

Throughout the rest of the month the North Koreans pushed increasingly slowly to the south and by the beginning of August the allied position was looking increasingly desperate. Clearly a major port was essential to continued defensive capability on mainland Korea and the logical choice was Pusan at the very south-eastern tip of the peninsula. This was the ultimate objective of the North Korean drive and here the US 8th Army was established under Major General Walton Walker to assume command of the US and South Korean forces flowing into the area. By 5 August Walker had created a thin but comparatively secure perimeter around the Pusan beach-head, running from a point on the coast west of Pusan some 90 miles (145 km) north up the Nakong river to Taegu before bending east for the 60 miles (95 km) to the coast of Korea at Pohang.

The main weight of the North Koreans' continued offensive fell on the Americans, but it was discernible from the middle of the month that the scale and intensity of the attacks were dwindling as

A dozer-fitted tank works to clear a stockpile area on Wolmi Island as part of the massive logistic effort to support the US Marine Corps landing at Inchon.

the 7th Fleet's aircraft, complemented by those of the Far East Air Forces and one group of the Royal Australian Air Force, began to interdict the North Korean lines of communication. The allied aircraft were also able to furnish much needed close air support and, in concert with Walker's use of a mobile reserve that could be moved rapidly over the allies' interior lines of communication, this allowed the North Koreans' attacks to be beaten off.

MacArthur by now had some 180,000 men available to him, while the North Koreans had been

US armour (in the form of three M26 heavy tanks) could be moved rapidly and in substantial quantities by the use of tank landing ships.

whittled down to some 92,000 men. The Pusan perimeter was still under pressure but was deemed sufficiently secure by MacArthur for the planning of a major counter-offensive to begin. Most of his contemporaries disapproved of the plan, which must go down in history as one of the most ambitious strategic strokes ever envisaged when it was launched on 15 September.

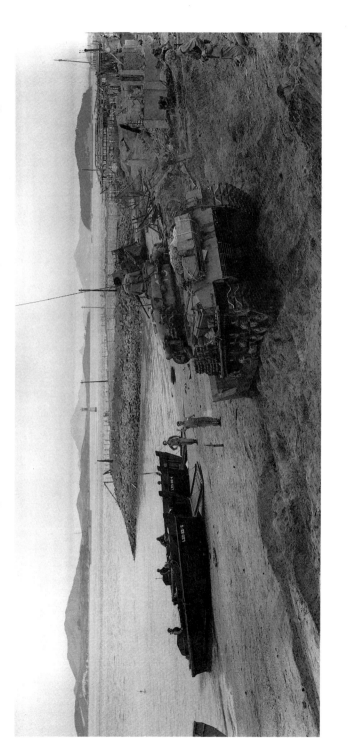

The counter-offensive was divided into two major portions. The more obviously logical of these was a break-out from the Pusan perimeter by the 8th Army, spearheaded by the 1st Cavalry Division with the immediate objective of enlarging the perimeter to both the north and west, but with the longer-term objective of driving a narrow corridor to the north, thereby cutting the North Koreans' lines of communication and destroying the investing force around Pusan. The more dangerous, and potentially decisive, portion of the two-part counter-offensive was a large amphibious assault on Inchon, the port of Seoul and now 200 miles (320 km) behind the North Korean front.

Distance was only one of the problem's faced by MacArthur's planning staff, who had also to contend with the difficulty of throwing ashore an amphibious force in an area where tides of 40 ft (12.2 m) are common. The formation selected for this formidable task the US X Corps under Major General Edward Almond, comprising the US 1st Marine and 7th Divisions.

The two portions were launched simultaneously, and secured complete strategic surprise. Despite a two-day naval bombardment that appears not to have alerted more than the local defence forces, the Inchon landing went ahead smoothly and the 1st Marine Division moved rapidly inland to secure Kimpo airport outside Seoul on 17 September while the 7th Division moved further to the right, cutting the rail and road lines feeding the North Korean forces in the south, and investing Seoul. In the south the already strained communist forces disintegrated as the 8th Army swept forward and as the North Koreans learned that their lines of communication had been severed. The 1st Cavalry and 7th Divisions met at Suwan, just south of Seoul, on 25 September and Seoul fell to the allies one day later.

Top: US Marines inspect equipment captured from the communists.

Left: Part of the US invasion force makes rendezvous off Wolmi Island before the Inchon landing of 15 September 1950.

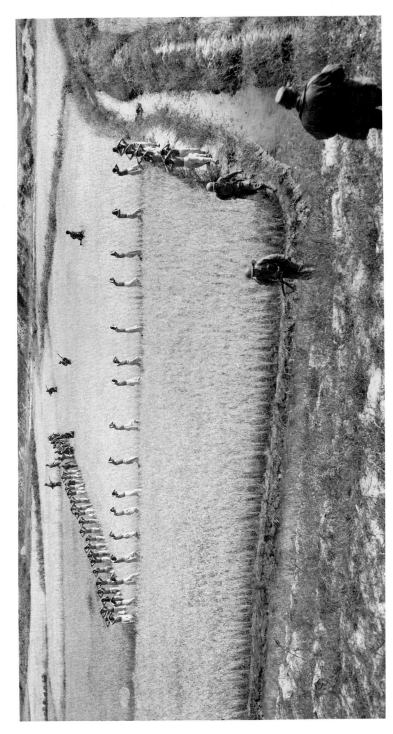

On 1 October MacArthur launched his forces in a general offensive north across the 38th parallel towards the Yalu river. The South Koreans led the offensive, the Americans following on 9 October after detaching two divisions to secure the allied lines of communication and to continue the mopping-up operation in the south. Under the overall command of the 8th Army the allied forces moved north on a broad front, taking Pyongyang on 20 October (with a small but effective combined operation by ground forces and the airborne 187th Regimental Combat Team) and forcing the North Koreans to move their capital to Sinuiju on the lower reaches of the Yalu. The defence was so fragmented that some allied formations forged far ahead, the most telling of these deep penetrations being that of the South Korean 6th Division which reached the Yalu at Chosan on 26 October.

This period was also notable for the influx of allied forces (in addition to the British brigade already present), generally of a comparatively small size and thus better integrated into the existing US structure rather than combined into new formations: Turkey supplied a brigade, and battalions arrived from Australia, Canada, the Netherlands, the Philippines, and Thailand. Meanwhile it was becoming clear that the 8th Army had its hands full with its northward advance to the Yalu and could not divert sufficient troops to advance into the north-eastern corridor of North Korea running from the Chosin Reservoir to the upper reaches of the Yalu north-east of the port of Chongjin. Thus X Corps re-embarked at Inchon on 16 October and disembarked in the captured port of Wonsan on 26 October, a seven-day delay in the programme being attributable to the need to sweep Wonsan of Soviet mines. X Corps then moved north-east between the Chosin Reservoir and the sea before striking towards Hyesanjin.

Top: *US Marines bring in a column of North Korean prisoners of the war taken in an engagement in the hills.*

Left: *US Marines call on a party of North Koreans to give themselves up before an assault is put in against their position in an isolated farm.*

China had been threatening military intervention should the allied forces advance over the 38th parallel but, as the chance of aerial reconnaissance was denied him, MacArthur was operating in the dark to a certain extent. The Chinese were in fact massing forces north of the Yalu and, unknown to the allies, already passing sizeable detachments across the river to support the North Koreans. In a sudden spate of tactical reverses the allies became conscious of this new dimension as South Korean and American spearheads were pushed back in several spots. Not knowing or being able to find out what was faced by his forces, Walker made the sensible decision to call a temporary halt to his offensive and to consolidate an intermediate position along the line of the Chongchon river, halfway between Pyongyang and the Yalu.

MacArthur had different ideas, based largely on his belief that the Chinese were bluffing about a large-scale intervention, and therefore planned a massive offensive designed to eliminate the North Korean army. This plan was based on a vast enveloping movement in which the US X Corps (1st Marine and 3rd and 7th Divisions) and the South Korean I Corps (3rd and Capital Divisions), which had already reached the Yalu at Hyesanjin (7th Division), and Chingjin (Capital Division) would sweep west to drive the North Korean forces on to the main weight of the advancing nine divisions of the 8th Army's US I, US IX, and South Korean II Corps.

The 8th Army started its cautious northward movement on 24 October and just one day later was struck by the hammerblow of a communist counter-offensive, directed chiefly against the right flank of the allied army: 18 Chinese divisions, with some 180,000 combat troops, punched through the South Korean II Corps and began to pivot west on the US 2nd Division, the right-hand

formation of the US IX Corps. The Chinese appeared to have every likelihood of enveloping the entire 8th Army, especially after the 2nd Division fell into a major ambush while trying to refuse its right flank, the resultant Battle of Kuni-ri costing the American division 4,000 men and most of its heavy weapons. Walker threw in his reserve, the British 27th and the Turkish brigades, to stabilize the position as the 8th Army pulled back. The Turks took heavy casualties, but the two brigades bought the time for Walker to disengage in good order by 5 December. The Chinese had spent their energy in the hammerblow and were not capable of pursuing as the cautious Walker retreated some 130 miles (210 km) to the better defensive position available along this line of the 38th parallel.

Much of the fighting in Korea was undertaken in poor terrain and at very close quarters.

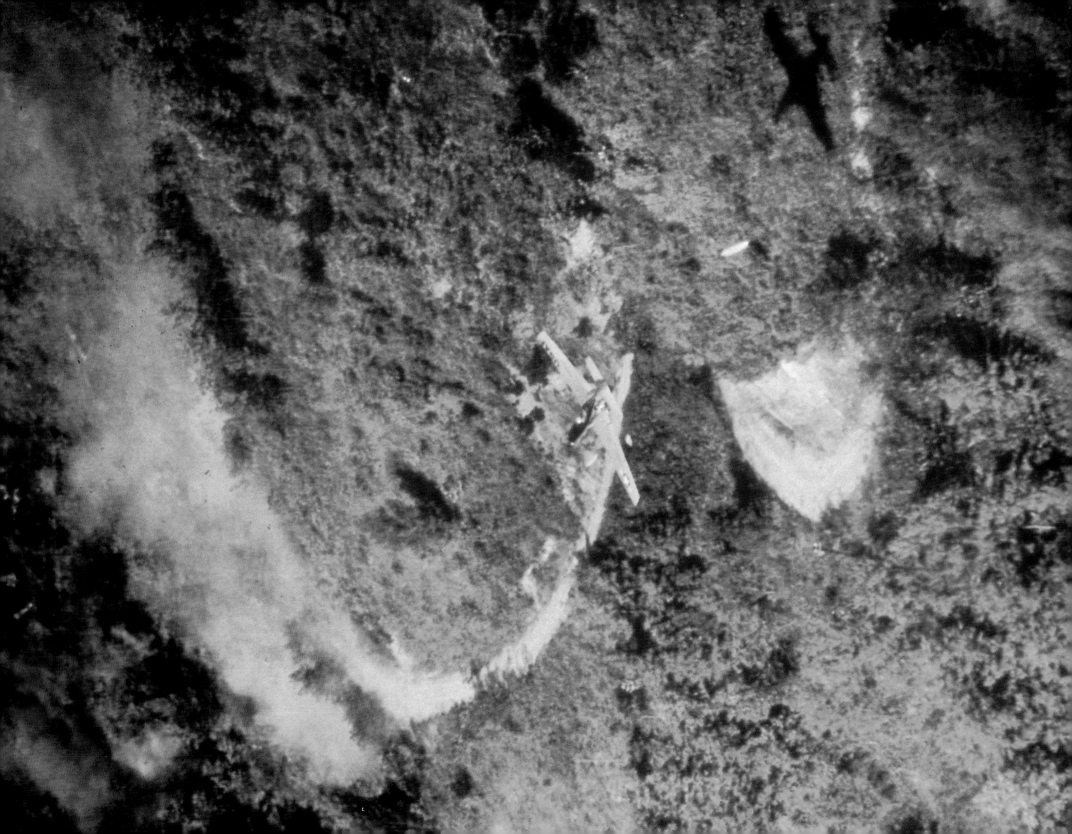

Preceding page: Air power was all-important to the UN effort in Korea: here a North American F-51 Mustang fighter drops napalm on communist troops during the fighting of late 1951.

Right: Obsolescent aircraft are often used for tasks that are technologically less demanding: this is a Lockheed F-80C Shooting Star fighter practising for the 'tank-busting' role.

Below: M4 Sherman tanks of the US 2nd Division give covering fire to men of the 187th Regimental Combat Team during an assault north of Pambol-ni on 7 February 1951.

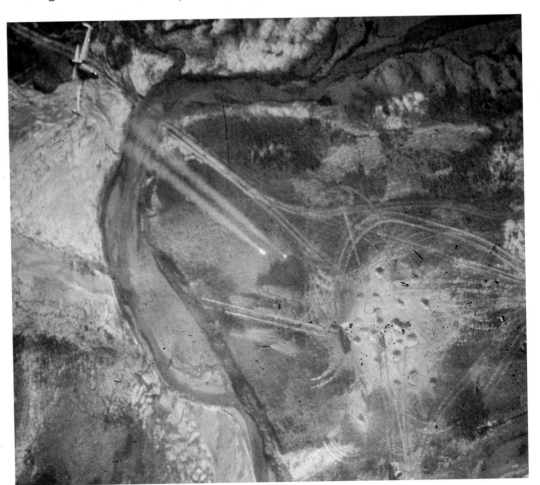

At the other end of the allied front the position was no less precarious for the US X and South Korean I Corps. About 120,000 Chinese troops pushed round both sides of the Chosin Reservoir on 27 November, cutting off the 1st Marine Division and pushing back the 3rd and 7th Divisions. Realizing that I Corps might be cut off in the far north-east of North Korea, Almond ordered it to fall back towards Wonsan and this sensible retreat was managed without any severe interference from the Chinese. MacArthur now saw that his eastern forces could perhaps be destroyed piecemeal by the Chinese offensive towards Hungnam and Wonsan, and he ordered a general withdrawal to these two ports, where the 3rd and 7th Divisions established defensive perimeters pending the arrival of the ships for an evacuation. Cut off and invested by eight Chinese divisions just to the south of the Chosin Reservoir,

Major General Oliver Smith's 1st Marine Division slowly fought its way south towards Hungnam with massive air support.

On 23 December Walker was killed in a vehicle accident, being replaced on 26 December by Lieutenant General Matthew Ridgway. MacArthur entrusted the command of all ground operations in Korea to Ridgway. Ridgway had little time to settle into his new command for on 1 January 1951 the communists launched a huge offensive over the 38th parallel: 400,000 Chinese and 100,000 North Korean troops fell on the 200,000 men of the 8th Army, forcing Ridgway's command to give ground towards Seoul. The main weight of the communist offensive fell on the allied left until 3 January, when the main thrust was switched further to the east with a thrust line into the Chungpyong Reservoir area.

The US 2nd Division was exposed by the collapse of the

South Korean divisions on its flanks and the situation was remedied only when Ridgway committed his reserves, the 3rd and 7th Divisions. Seoul was evacuated on 4 January but by 15 January the allies had halted the communist offensive some 50 miles (80 km) south of the South Korean capital along a line running from Samchok on the east coast to Pyongtaek on the west coast. Ridgway wasted no time in planning his riposte, though when launched on 25 January this took the forms of a number of limited-objective assaults rather than a general offensive, preventing the communists from consolidating their new-won territory and by the end of February forcing them back towards Seoul at the western end of the line and past Kangnung at the eastern end.

In defence as well as offence, a tank makes a handy way of avoiding movement on foot.

Men of the US 25th Division take cover behind rocks as mortar bombs explode immediately to their front somewhere in central Korea.

Between 7 and 31 March Ridgway undertook Operation 'Ripper', a limited offensive designed to inflict casualties rather than make ground, though the opportunity was taken for I Corps to retake Seoul on 14 March against negligible opposition, the Chinese having withdrawn, and capture the communist rear area supply concentration just north of Chunchon. After the fall of Seoul communist resistance stiffened and it was only with the aid of an airborne operation by the 187th Regimental Combat Team at Munsan, some 25 miles (40 km) north of Seoul, that the communist right flank was opened, allowing the allies to push north to the general line of the 38th parallel by the end of March.

MacArthur and Ridgway now planned a major effort against the 'Iron Triangle', the main

communist communication, supply and assembly area bounded by Chorwan, Kumhwa, and Pyongyang. Relations between MacArthur and Truman had been strained since the two men disagreed on the overall conduct of the war at the Wake Island conference of 15 October 1950, and on 11 April MacArthur was relieved. His position was assumed by Ridgway and Lieutenant General James Van Fleet took over the 8th Army.

On the 22 April the communists launched the first phase of their spring offensive, breaking through the allied front to the west of the Chungpyong Reservoir in the area. The two flanking formations were the US 24th and 1st Marine Divisions and, though these refused their flanks to the commu-

nists, Van Fleet felt that his advanced positions were no longer tenable and ordered a retreat by his left wing (I and IX Corps) to the prepared defensive line. The Chinese maintained their pressure against I Corps to the direct north of Seoul. The South Korean 1st Division fell back too rapidly, exposing the flank of the British 29th Infantry Brigade, and the position was retrieved only by the magnificent stand of the Gloucestershire Regiment on the Imjin river. By the end of the month the communist offensive had petered out, the front-line forces fell back out of range of the allied forces' superior artillery to recoup their losses, estimated at 70,000 to the allies' 7,000.

On 14 May the second phase of the offensive got under way, the communists having switched their main weight from the west to the east. Based on Chinese divisions flanked by North Korean divisions, some 20 communist divisions fell on X Corps to the east of Seoul, the main blow falling on the South Korean 5th and 7th Divisions on the corps' right flank. The two South Korean formations, together with the South Korean III Corps on their right, fell back in some disorder, the situation being stabilized as the US 2nd Division (on the left of the 5th Division) and the South Korean I Corps (on the right of III Corps) channelled the communist advance into a narrowing corridor.

Van Fleet had anticipated the point of the communists' second-phase offensive and located his reserve in the appropriate position. The drive was already being blunted by counter-attacks from the 2nd and 1st Marine Divisions on the western flank, and when the army reserve (the US 3rd Division and the 187th Regimental Combat Team) went into action the communists called off their offensive on 20 May.

The boot was now on the other foot and on 22 May the allies unleashed a general offensive along the entire length of the front. A preliminary effort secured the allied left along the Imjin and the offensive proper made steady progress, especially at the extreme eastern end of the front where the South Korean 2nd and Capital Divisions encountered virtually no resistance as they outpaced companion formations to reach Kansong after a 35-miles (55-km) advance. Elsewhere progress was initially slower but by the end of

May was beginning to quicken against clear evidence that the communists were in poor shape. Van Fleet was prepared to push harder against an opposition on the verge of collapse but on 31 May was ordered to halt by a US government increasingly worried by Soviet threats of interference. Van Fleet therefore used the first half of June 1951 to consolidate his current position and to improve the overall allied line with local offensives at the southern edges of the 'Iron Triangle' and 'Punchbowl' areas.

On 23 June the Soviets proposed

a ceasefire, and in July and August 1951 delegations from both sides met at Kaesong, in the communist area at the western end of the front. Negotiations were all but impossible, the communists using the forum to abuse the allies and generally to buy time as their mauled forces were rehabilitated. The front was a scene of constant small actions throughout the period as each side sought to gain the tactical upper hand, but in general the allies came out on top and at the end of August the communists broke off the negotiations.

Centre: *An infantryman of the US 2nd Division receives medical attention while his wounded South Korean comrade is helped to safety.*

Right: *Artillery of the 936th Field Artillery Battalion, US 8th Army, fires on communist Chinese positions near Choriwon in Korea.*

Right: *T66 rocket launchers of 2nd Field Artillery Battery, US 40th Division, in action against communist positions.*

Centre: *The impressive but somewhat revealing signature of a mobile 4.5-in rocket-launcher of the US Marine Corps in action against the communists.*

Van Fleet was cleared to resume limited offensives and seized the opportunity during the period from September to November to clear the 'Iron Triangle' and 'Punchbowl' areas, at the same time ejecting the Chinese from the regions north of the Hwachon Reservoir and along the rail line connecting Chorwan and Seoul. These allied successes persuaded the communists that further procrastination might pay handsome dividends and on 12 November a further round of negotiations started at Panmunjon, a village in no man's land just south-east of Kaesong.

The rest of the war was now characterized by small-scale operations, sometimes of an extremely intense nature, along an essentially static front as each side sought to secure the morale and tactical advantage while the negotiations continued apparently interminably at Panmunjon. In May Ridgway was posted to a NATO command and replaced by General Mark Clark, who maintained the policy of an actively fought defence. The communists continued their force build-up and by the end of 1952 are thought to have reached a strength of 600,000 Chinese and 200,000 North Koreans, supported by vast quantities of Soviet *matériel* including the latest artillery and radar-controlled anti-aircraft guns. This failed to impede allied control of the air, and much of the bitter but small-scale fighting was confined to nocturnal operations that cost a steady trickle of casualties on both sides without altering the tactical situation to any marked degree. In October the communists again

broke off the negotiations, and in the presidential elections of that year General Dwight D. Eisenhower was elected on a platform that included the promise to bring the war to a speedy but honourable close.

Little was achieved in the first months of 1953, but on 28 March the communists' local leaders, Kim Il Sung of North Korea and

General Peng Teh-huai of the Chinese People's Volunteer Army, made the first real move towards peace, going back on their 1952 refusal to offer an exchange of wounded and sick prisoners of war. Decisive negotiations resumed on 20 July and just seven days later an armistice was signed to end the fighting along the current front line.

THE VIETNAM WAR (1956-75)

The Geneva Agreement signed on 21 July 1954 formally ended the existence of France's empire in Indo-China: Cambodia and Laos, which had declared their independence of France on 9 November 1953 and 19 July 1949 respectively, were recognized as fully independent nations, while Tonkin, Annam and Cochin-China were recognized as an independent Vietnam, temporarily divided by the Demilitarized Zone on the 17th parallel into a communist North Vietnam and democratic South Vietnam. The agreement stipulated that in July 1956 there should be free elections to establish 'the national will of the Vietnamese people' with regard to unification of the two components of the country. The South Vietnamese prime minister was Ngo Dinh Diem and on 26 October 1955 he overthrew Emperor Bao Dai and declared a South Vietnamese republic with himself as president.

On 16 July 1956 Diem called off the proposed election, pleading that the North Vietnamese would not be allowed to vote freely by the regime of Ho Chi Minh. This date in 1956 may be taken as the start of the undeclared Vietnam War, which immediately came into being as a campaign of insurrection, terrorism, and assassination inside South Vietnam.

The Viet Cong relied in this initial stage of their campaign on eliminating the educated middle classes, especially in rural area where the insurrection could be expected to flourish most readily, and there followed a widespread assassination campaign aimed at teachers, doctors, civil servants, and village leaders, who refused to support the Viet Cong. In the rural areas the Viet Cong were soon supreme, reprisals by urban-based soldiers serving to widen the growing rift between rural and urban populations.

This communist campaign grew in scope and pace during the late 1950s while the USA, apparently mesmerized by President Dwight D. Eisenhower's October 1954 commitment to supply direct aid 'for maintaining a strong, viable state capable of resisting attempted subversion or aggression through military

A large part of the allied effort in South Vietnam was devoted to starving the Viet Cong of support by removing villagers to protected villages.

means', responded with increased levels of assistance to the South Vietnamese forces.

The terrorism campaign in South Vietnam was now escalating to the point at which the Viet Cong could engage the South Vietnamese army in small-scale conventional operations, one step up from the purely guerrilla stage of an insurrectionist war. This capability was signalled in part by the formation of the National Front for the liberation of South Vietnam, a North Vietnamese-sponsored front organization designed to attract the growing number of South Vietnamese affronted by the combined autocracy and venality of Diem's administration. But on 11 October 1961 President John F. Kennedy pledged further support for the South Vietnamese government's fight against communist guerrillas and General Maxwell Taylor was despatched to South Vietnam to

The first US military presence in Vietnam was a unit with Piasecki H-21 helicopters to give the South Vietnamese army tactical mobility.

The 'strategic hamlets' programme involved immense physical effort to create impenetrable defences – which were often 'opened' by the presence of Viet Cong among the villagers.

assess how best the USA could support Diem's government.

Taylor's initial conclusion was that the South Vietnamese forces lacked the mobility and speed of reaction to counter the Viet Cong, and the USA responded by despatching a small helicopter force to aid the South Vietnamese army, though there was a specific injunction against the US soldiers becoming involved in combat. The US army appreciated that the South Vietnamese lacked the technical expertise to operate a helicopter force, but could benefit

from the level of air-mobility that could be supplied by an American-manned transport force. The two US Army helicopter companies arrived in Saigon on an American aircraft-carrier during 11 December 1961 and this occasion marks the beginning of the USA's direct involvement in the rapidly growing Vietnam War.

By this time the South Vietnamese had some 400,000 men under arms (comprising a substantial regular establishment and large paramilitary support forces), and the Americans concurred with South Vietnamese expectations of being able to meet the Viet Cong on more than equal terms, and thus to bring the long war to a satisfactory conclusion.

On 8 February 1962 a US Military Assistance Command Vietnam was established in Saigon under General Harkins, its specific role being the technical and operational support of the South Vietnamese forces with American expertise. One of the MACV's first suggestions led to the 'Strategic Hamlets' programme, an American development of the 'Briggs Plan' used successfully in Malaya by the British: the object was to resettle the inhabitants or scattered hamlets in larger villages that could be protected against the depradations of the Viet Cong, thereby reducing the amount of support (both voluntary and forced) for the communists and easing the task of the central government in raising the living standards and security of the villagers, an essential component in the plan to wean them from their hatred of the government.

In parallel with the 'Strategic Hamlets' policy went the 'Open Zone' concept: this designated any area into which the government forces had not penetrated a zone open to artillery and air attack. From the zones emerged a constant stream of refugees and, while the government claimed that these were fleeing the Viet Cong, in reality they were just escaping from zones into which the government forces dumped indiscriminate fire. These homeless refugees were an administrative thorn in the side of the government and a fertile source of Viet Cong recruitment as the 'Strategic Hamlets' concept collapsed.

The fortunes of the government inevitably continued to decline throughout 1963, exacerbated by the evident corruption of Diem and his adherents. The period between May and August was marked by a series of widespread Buddhist demonstrations, whose

main target was the authoritarian yet inefficient civil administration, and the armed forces had finally had enough: on 1 November 1963 they undertook a coup against Diem, who was killed together with his brother. A provisional government under Nguyen Ngoc Tho was recognized by the USA, though this was a legal fiction to conceal the real government, a junta headed by Major General Duong Van Minh. Even this failed to survive and on 30 January 1964 another coup brought Major General Nguyen Khanh to power. Corrupt as he had been, Diem had at least generated a certain political stability in South Vietnam, and his overthrow and death merely added uncertainty to a continuing state of inefficiency as regime supplanted regime in a series of short administrations.

Throughout 1964 the war progressed as it had in earlier years, with the Viet Cong slowly gathering strength as the government failed to grasp the nettle of how best to tackle an insurrection that was beginning to show potent signs of developing from guerrilla to conventional warfare. During 1964 the Viet Cong grew to a strength of some 35,000 men in military units, supported by 100,000 in the political infrastructure that supported the field forces. Already sizeable bodies of South Vietnamese troops had been destroyed in Viet Cong ambushes and other conventional military operations, undertaken in regimental and even divisional strength from the autumn of 1964, the government forces proving themselves incapable of pinning their elusive enemy.

Top: *South Vietnamese troops were sometimes of high quality, but were often conscripts of doubtful loyalty and indifferent performance.*

Right: *A Bell UH-1B utility helicopter about to be offloaded from a Douglas C-133 transport after arrival from the USA to support the South Vietnamese army.*

The South Vietnamese government also found it impossible to stem the flow of weapons and other supplies to the Viet Cong over the Ho Chi Minh Trail, a series of tracks running south just inside Vietnam's frontiers with Cambodia and Laos before branching east into Vietnam at any desired point. The trail allowed labourers and soldiers to move south, generally under cover of the thick tree canopy, from its sources at the Ne Pa and Mupla Passes from North Vietnam into Laos, skirting round the western end of the Demilitarized Zone before crossing into Cambodia and then feeding into South Vietnam via a myriad untraceable tracks.

The preferred method of transport along the trail was a modified bicycle, which was easy to maintain, required no fuel, and could carry a sizeable load when manhandled by a single person. And from 1967 the Ho Chi Minh Trail was supplemented by the shorter Sihanouk Trail through southern Cambodia. This allowed Soviet ships to unload their cargoes in the port of Sihanoukville for onward movement over the southern trail into the Fish Hook and Parrot's Beak areas of South Vietnam, the

areas flanking the Iron Triangle salient jutting into Cambodia between Phnom Penh and Kampong Cham.

On 20 June General William Westmoreland assumed command of MACV and the pace of US assistance was stepped up. But in 1964 there also occurred the first of the incidents that finally drew the USA into an active involvement in the Vietnam War: on 2 August three North Vietnamese fast-attack craft engaged an American destroyer in the Gulf of Tonkin. All three were sunk or damaged by fire from the destroyer, supplemented by an air attack, but two days later the North Vietnamese tried the same ploy again. Infuriated by this blatant and unprovoked attack in international waters, the administration of President Lyndon B. Johnson on 5 August authorized attacks by US carrierborne aircraft against the bases used by the North Vietnamese craft.

This was not the end of the matter for on 7 August the Congress passed the Tonkin Resolution, authorizing the president to take 'all necessary measures to repel any armed attack' on the US armed forces and to take 'all necessary steps,

The first US combat troops arrive: men of the 3rd Marine Division land at Da Nang on 14 April 1965.

including the use of armed forces' to aid any country asking for support under the terms of the South-East Asia Collective Defence Treaty.

South Vietnam meanwhile lurched from crisis to worse crisis. In August and September the country was troubled by widespread rioting and demonstrations against the military regime, quelled temporarily only when Khanh promised an early return to civilian government. Khanh also survived a military revolt on 13 September and on 4 November a civilian government was installed under the leadership of Tran Van Huong: this may have pleased the civilians but was anathema to the military, who launched a military uprising on 19 December and installed a military council under Huong's nominal leadership. This regime was not destined for a long life and on 27 January 1965 Huong was deposed in favour of Khanh once more. Khanh was replaced on 21 February by Phan Huy Quat, the military man's desire to

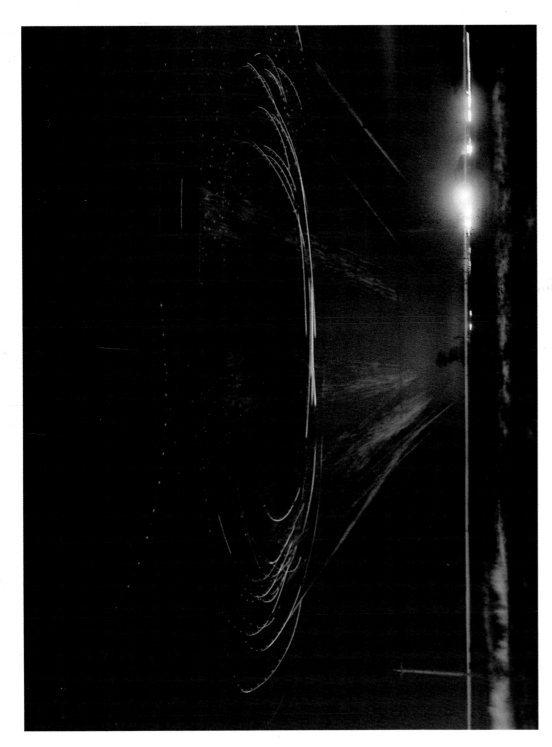

Above: One of the classic images of the Vietnam War as a Fairchild AC-119 circles and delivers a withering concentration of fire on suspected Viet Cong mortar positions in April 1969.

Right: A Sikorsky H-34 Seahorse helicopter ferries US Marines from the assault ship USS Princeton into South Vietnam during April 1966 as the build-up of US forces continued.

Above: The US Navy found hovercraft such as this PACV (Patrol Air Cushion Vehicle) of great tactical utility in the campaigns to find and destroy the Viet Cong base areas in the Mekong river delta during the Vietnam War.

Right: Men of the US 1st Marine Division in typical Vietnamese conditions during Operation 'Colorado' in South Vietnam during August 1966. The USMC's area was mainly in the north of the country.

Overleaf: US Marines in riverine action during Operation 'Lancaster' to the south-west of Con Thien. Deployed in the area of South Vietnam closest to North Vietnam and the Ho Chi Minh Trail, the Marines saw constant action.

Above: The Vietnam War saw the almost universal deployment of US tactical aircraft as low- and medium-level fighter-bombers. This is an F-100 Super Sabre unloading a GP bomb on suspected Viet Cong positions in 1965.

Left: UH-1H helicopters with AH-1G trailing return to Bu Dop Special Forces camp to refuel. Vietnam, May 1970.

Above: Typical of the Americans' mechanized approach to low-intensity war is the combination depicted here: a Hiller H-23 Raven scout helicopter carried on an armoured troop carrier used by the riverine forces.

Left: The Viet Cong fought with little in the way of battlefield communications, but the US technological approach is epitomized by this communications unit for radio and telephone links.

remain in the background as *de facto* head of government being overruled by military objections.

The final straw for the Americans had come on 7 February 1965, when the Viet Cong attacked the major air base at Pleiku at the upper end of the Ia Drang river valley in the highlands of central Vietnam. The attack killed eight Americans and wounded another 109 as well as destroying or damaging 20 aircraft, and Johnson felt that no longer could the USA take a back seat in this increasingly nasty war. American advisers had already been killed, but this overt attack on American personnel and *matériel* could not be ignored.

The situation called for US combat forces, the administration believed, and the families of all US personnel was evacuated from South Vietnam in preparation for what would inevitably be a singulary nasty war. HAWK surface-to-air missiles were brought in to protect US bases from an unimaginable air threat from North Vietnam, indicating that the US administration had a very real fear of Chinese or even Soviet interference.

In the short term Operation 'Rolling Thunder' was launched: supported by South Vietnamese

aircraft, US air power (both land- and sea-based) launched a limited but systematic campaign to destroy specific military targets in the south of North Vietnam, special care being taken to avoid civil areas or those northern targets whose destruction might spur the Chinese or Soviets to a response.

The first US combat unit to reach South Vietnam was a brigade of the US Marine Corps, which came ashore at Da Nang on 8 March. The brigade's task was to secure US installations (especially the vital air and naval base at Da Nang) and free South Vietnamese units for combat operations. More troops were quickly on the scene and by the middle of the year there were 25,000 US combat troops, as well as 50,000 other US personnel, in South Vietnam. On 15 June American combat troops entered action against the Viet Cong for the first time.

This would clearly be a considerable boost for the anti-communist effort but many sensible analysts thought that the USA had left it too late to intervene and that South Vietnam might fall to the communists by the end of 1964. Taylor and Westmoreland were united in

Over the years the US presence in Vietnam grew enormously, the Marines entrusted with the northern area often landing from the sea as a useful training exercise.

their effort to persuade Johnson that the only way to stave off his collapse was an increased threat to North Vietnam, which would then have to cease its support for the Viet Cong. Johnson was worried by the political implications of such a campaign, but after much deliberation decided to allow it to proceed.

The US administration was worried that a massive strategic bombing campaign close to the Chinese frontier might persuade China to a direct involvement and that the destruction of North Vietnam's economic and military infrastructure might spur the USSR to action, so that the northward extension of the current bombing effort was planned round a campaign of graduated intensity that excluded the North Vietnamese capital Hanoi, and its port, Haiphong. In this way, the Americans hoped, the North Vietnamese might be forced not into defeat, which was never an American objective, but into an abandonment of their support for the Viet Cong.

Left: The deltas of South Vietnam's rivers were a favourite Viet Cong haunt combated here by South Vietnamese marines on US patrol craft.

Bottom: Based on landing craft, these shallow-draught river assault craft feature gun turrets and overhead protection against grenades.

The pace of operations inevitably increased to match the US involvement in the war, but a measure of increased capability on the part of the South Vietnamese forces resulted from the restoration of what was, in comparative terms, a stable government. This resulted from a bloodless coup spurred by continuous feuding and rioting between South Vietnam's Roman Catholic and Buddhist factions between 12 and 19 June: Quat resigned and his government was replaced by a military regime headed by General Nguyen Van Thieu as president and Air Vice Marshal Nguyen Cao Ky as prime minister. The measure of political stability that began slowly to emerge from this event at last allowed the development and implementation of longer-term policies that at least offered the hope of a sustained defence against the communists.

The communist threat was now growing even more serious, for whereas the anti-communist forces had previously been faced by Viet Cong forces organized into conventional military formations but fielding only comparatively light weapons, they were now for the first time encountering inside South Vietnam elements of the North Vietnamese regular army, high-quality formations with some of the latest weapons supplied from the USSR. This posed sufficiently serious a threat for Westmoreland to demand the deployment of additional US combat forces and, after a fact-finding mission by the US Secretary of Defense Robert McNamara, Johnson announced that the US presence in South Vietnam was to be increased by an air-mobile division, supported if required by additional forces.

By the end of 1965 the US forces had fought their first battle with North Vietnamese regular troops (in the Ia Drang valley on 14 November) and attained a strength of 180,000 men. The availability of such forces, with the backing of considerable tactical air power from the US Air Force, US Marine Corps, and US Navy, began to dictate the operational deployment of forces that lasted essentially to the end of the USA's involvement in Vietnam: the US Marine Corps in the north, the US Army around Saigon and in the central provinces, and the South Vietnamese army in Mekong delta and southern provinces, where they were supplemented from late 1966 by specialized riverine forces of the American services.

The position remained comparatively stable up to the middle of 1966, largely as the communist forces adjusted themselves to the presence of the excellently equipped Americans and began to devise tactics to deal with the Americans' reliance on firepower and air-mobile tactics

over close engagement of the type in which the communists' superior motivation and tactical capabilities allowed them to prevail. By the middle of 1966 communist strength in South Vietnam had reached 225,000 men and it was clear that major military operations were required: the 'fire brigade' period had passed, and Westmoreland fully appreciated that the only realistic option for the anti-

communist cause was for the US forces to tackle the North Vietnamese and Viet Cong major formations, leaving the less capable South Vietnamese to undertake the task of 'pacifying' South Vietnam's rural areas.

A US Army helicopter prepares to touch down on a converted Armored Troop Carrier of the US Navy during riverine operations.

Below: A scene typical of the continual (and very heavily armed) search for Viet Cong hideouts in the river deltas.

This set the operational pattern for the rest of the war, a dismal series of campaigns with any type of front line and without any formal enemy. The communists relied heavily on their ability to fade into and out of the local population to engage the US and South Vietnamese forces wherever they could be found, with the latter seeking to use the advantages of air-mobility and air support to find and pin these elusive forces before they could disappear, and thus have the opportunity to bring their superior firepower to bear.

It was a war controlled down to a fairly low tactical level by the authorities in Washington and thus executive decisions were hopelessly out of date by the time they had reached commanders in South Vietnam. Strenuous efforts were made to reach the enemy in stronghold areas such as War Zone C along the Cambodian frontier and War Zone D around Bien Hoa to the north-east of Saigon, but these were as futile as the continuous sweeps through the heavily forested highland regions of the central provinces. The communists faded out of sight into the local populations after stashing their weapons or pulled back into Cambodia and Laos, which were forbidden to US troops as part of the US administration's effort to keep the war within Vietnam.

Higher command levels were totally out of touch with the realities of the war and took to assessing the progress of the anti-communist effort in terms of 'body counts', the numbers of villages 'pacified' and the miles of road, 'opened'. The system was entirely open to misinterpretation and exaggeration and was in any case completely irrelevant to the type of war being fought. Much success was claimed for the 'hearts and minds' policies of the Americans and South Vietnamese but the

Vietnam witnessed the emergence of the helicopter as vital to modern land operations in roles as diverse as attack and medevac (medical evacuation).

Above: Heavily equipped infantry of the US 1st Division disembark from their transport 'chopper' during an air-mobile operation.

Right: The Viet Cong could not match the Americans for equipment, but the country often favoured ambushes that pinned the Americans and cost them heavy casualties.

reality of the situation was that moral and physical control of the peasant communities stayed firmly in communist hands as a direct result of the anti-communist forces' almost incredibly heavy-handed approach, which also managed to alienate a large part of South Vietnam's city dwellers.

By the end of 1967 it was clear that North Vietnam was beginning to increase its direct presence in the northern provinces, and Westmoreland responded by bolstering the US Marine

formations in the theatre with US Army divisions from their zone further to the south. The nature of the communist effort began to become apparent when a US Marine Corps fire base at Khe Sanh, just to the south of the Demilitarized Zone, was invested by substantial North Vietnamese forces on 30 January 1968, the beginning of the Tet (lunar new year) festivities which had in earlier years been marked by an unofficial truce.

Left: The Viet Cong proved themselves masters of tunnelling and underground concealment, but the opposition sometimes found and destroyed such bunkers.

Below: US Marines round up Vietnamese women and children in one of their highly unpopular (and ultimately counter-productive) sweeps near the Demilitarized Zone.

Above: American M60 main battle tanks move up towards the former imperial city of Hue during the bitter fighting of February 1968.

Right: Men of the US 5th Marine Regiment gingerly lift 3.5-in rocket rounds to a commanding rooftop in the fighting for Hue.

This year was to be different: a countrywide offensive was launched by 84,000 communists against 125 locations, including Saigon, Hue, and other provincial capitals. Everywhere the communists made considerable gains, but only at considerable cost. The Americans and South Vietnamese responded with urgency, and within days all the efforts with the exception of those in Saigon and Hue had been crushed. The communists had lost 32,000 dead in comparison with 3,000 US and South Vietnamese dead, but the Tet Offensive had nonetheless been a major success for the communists: it brought home to the population of the USA the real nature of the war. The first expression of the communists' propaganda success in the Tet Offensive came when Westmoreland asked for additional troops to exploit what he saw as a communist reverse: Johnson refused the request, and in March Westmoreland was succeeded by General Creighton Abrams.

Meanwhile the siege of Khe Sanh was progressing, the communists being determined that this should be the Dien Bien Phu of the US involvement in the Vietnam War. But whereas the French had chosen the wrong site for their 'honeypot' and then lacked the air power to support and succour it, the Americans had all the air power that was needed. For 77 days the US Marines took all that the North Vietnamese

threw at them and returned it with interest. The communists called off the siege on 7 April and shortly after this the 6,000 Americans of the garrison abandoned Khe Sanh: it was an American victory whose potential importance had been lost to the modified swell of American public opinion even before the battle's end.

Johnson's political response to the failure of the communists' Tet

Offensive was to call a limit on the continuing bombing effort against North Vietnam in the hope of drawing the communists to the negotiating table. The North Vietnamese responded with some speed, and negotiation teams arrived in Paris during 1968 to

Supplies float down under their parachutes to the beleaguered US Marine garrison of the fire base at Khe Sanh.

131

Above: Part of the huge US investment in the Vietnam War went to the creation of the air bases that supported the air war over South Vietnam. This is an F-105 Thunderchief attack fighter.

Left: An undoubted success of the Vietnam War was the Sikorsky HH-53 combat rescue helicopter, which plucked many downed aircrew right out of the hands of the enemy.

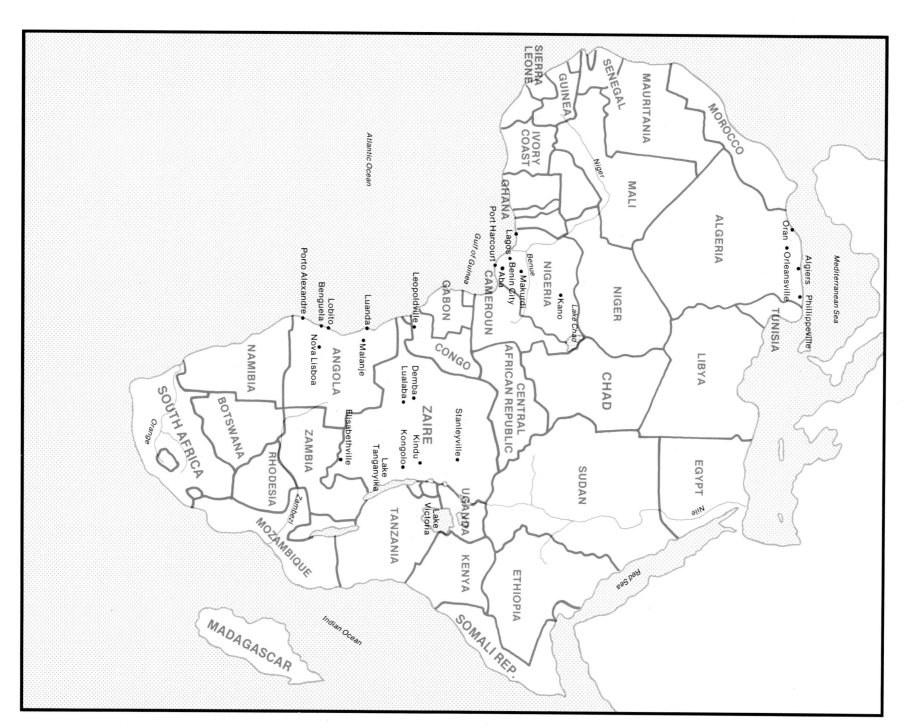

allow formal talks to begin on 1 January 1969. However, the non-negotiable North Vietnamese position was its intention of taking over in South Vietnam, and the communists refused to consider any alternatives offered by the Americans and South Vietnamese.

The US government came under increasingly severe public pressure during 1969, culminating in a series of massive anti-war demonstrations during November. The new president Richard M. Nixon decided that his best course was to extract the USA from the war, which was now absorbing some 539,000 American troops and vast quantities of *matériel*. But a unilateral abandonment of the South Vietnamese would have been political suicide and the administration opted for the combination of 'Vietnamization' and a gradual American

Below: A member of the Civil Irregular Defense Force leaves a UH-1D helicopter at the beginning of a search and destroy mission.

withdrawal. The Vietnamization programme was conceived to raise the combat capabilities and expertise of the South Vietnamese forces to the point at which they would no longer require US assistance in the fight against the communists, and it consisted of a huge retraining programme allied to the delivery of large amounts of

matériel. The burden of the war thus fell increasingly on the South Vietnamese as the Americans reduced their presence to 415,000 in 1970, 239,000 in 1971, and 47,000 in 1972.

The South Vietnamese were embroiled in extensive search and destroy operations throughout the war.

There was still much serious fighting during this period, the most infamous campaign being the American and South Vietnamese excursion into Cambodia between 1 May and 29 June 1970. A similar type of operation was undertaken by the South Vietnamese against Laos between 8 February and 25 March 1971 in an effort to disrupt the Ho Chi Minh Trail at its source end.

Seeing that the political wind in the USA was blowing increasingly in their favour, the communists were careful during the early 1970s not to respond in any

fashion that might provoke Nixon into revoking his plan. By 1972 the US withdrawal of its forces in South Vietnam was almost complete and the North Vietnamese decided to test the waters with a limited offensive designed in overt terms to gain territory, but in more important terms to test the commitment of the Americans to a continued withdrawal.

The offensive was undertaken from 30 March 1972, North Vietnamese regular forces crossing through the Demilitarized Zone to invade the northern provinces of

South Vietnamese troops are seen deep inside Laos in an invasion triggered by North Vietnam's use of the country as an access route to South Vietnam.

South Vietnam, while subsidiary thrusts were launched from Cambodia and Laos. The North Vietnamese used heavy armour and artillery, overrunning Quang Tri province in the far north before the South Vietnamese forces, supported by US air power, were able to remedy the situation. Nixon refused to countenance a reversal of the US withdrawal but

did go so far as to order an increase of the bombing effort against North Vietnam, including the mining of Haiphong harbour and the first use of Boeing B-52 strategic bombers against targets in the north.

The deteriorating situation in South Vietnam was signalled by the imposition of martial law on 10 May, just nine days after the North Vietnamese took Quang Tri. On 12 August the last US ground troops left South Vietnam, leaving 43,000 airmen to continue the prosecution of the bombing campaign against North Vietnam and the support of South Vietnamese field forces. Matters seemed for a time to be swinging slightly in favour of the South Vietnamese when Quang Tri was retaken on 15 September, but this gain was illusory rather than a genuine tactical or operational benefit.

Under the increasing pressure of the US bombing campaign, late in 1972 the North Vietnamese finally backed down from their demand that Thieu had to be removed as South Vietnamese president before any ceasefire agreement could be discussed, let alone signed, and in response the USA dropped its counter-demand that all North Vietnamese forces be pulled out of South Vietnam. Towards the end of the year North Vietnam and the USA were close to a preliminary agreement: but Thieu objected rightly to many of the promises made in South Vietnam's name by the Americans, and the US Air Force was ordered to mount a sustained 12-day blitz against North Vietnam in an effort to wring further concessions from the communists.

Top: Air power, both land- and sea-based, was an essential ingredient of the US recipe for defeating communist military efforts in South-east Asia. This is the USS Hancock.

Right: The US air forces were able to cause great logistical damage, but for political reasons were denied the chance of a 'knock out' blow against North Vietnam.

The North Vietnamese stood firm and on 23 January 1973 a ceasefire agreement was signed, to become effective on 28 January. There was an immediate flurry of operations in South Vietnam as the communists sought to gain as much ground as possible before the ceasefire came into effect. US operations against North Vietnam had ended on 15 January and the last US personnel were pulled out of South Vietnam on 29 March.

South Vietnam was now on its own: the US Congress enacted legislation forbidding any further US involvement in South-East Asia from 15 August 1973 and then cut back on military support for South Vietnam. A sporadic campaign was waged by the North Vietnamese from the moment the ceasefire came into effect and the US legislation confirmed the South Vietnam was now on its own. Rather than rush into large-scale military operations while negotiations between North Vietnam and South Vietnam were continuing (eventually to be

broken off in April 1974), the North Vietnamese stood back slightly to restore a measure of stability to their economy and prepare their plans for the final offensive, so that by the beginning of 1975 some 400,000 communist troops with all manner of heavy weapons were poised against 13 indifferent South Vietnamese divisions.

In January the North Vietnamese again tested the resolve of the USA, launching a major but limited offensive to take Phuoc Long province alongside the Cambodian frontier (including the important city of Phuoch Binh in the Fish Hook area) and, when the USA failed to take action the North Vietnamese set about implementing measures for the overrunning of South Vietnam. On 5 May 1975 major North Vietnamese offensives were opened in the central highlands and the northern provinces. Overmatched and outfought in these areas, the South Vietnamese forces began a retreat that turned

US Marines in action with a 105-mm light howitzer. Such weapons gave the Americans an edge in firepower but could not check the superior tactics of the North Vietnamese.

into a rout, allowing the North Vietnamese to push forward into many strategically important cities and areas without opposition. Thieu tried to rally his forces for a defence of Saigon and the southern regions of South Vietnam, but his demoralized and decimated forces were now faced by 20 North Vietnamese divisions and no effective defence was possible. On 21 April Thieu resigned and on 30 April his successor surrendered as North Vietnamese armour rolled into Saigon.

Saigon became Ho Chi Minh City, in honour of the North Vietnamese leader who had died 3 September 1969, and on 2 July 1976 the National Assembly voted for the reunification of the country's two halves as the Socialist Republic of Vietnam.

On 9 April 1965 a short but bloody little campaign started when Pakistani artillery shelled two Indian border posts to the south of Kanjarkot. For about two weeks heavy fighting continued until the advent of the monsoon brought about a forced ceasefire with the Pakistanis in the ascendant. British mediation was sought and on 1 July a formal ceasefire came into effect to re-establish the status quo as on 1 January of the same year. At the same time a tribunal was established to sort out the border dispute. At much the same time larger-scale but less defined fighting had broken out further to the north, and on 21 June the Indians complained to the United Nations that Pakistan had been responsible for 40 violations of the UN-mandated 1949 ceasefire line during the previous six days.

This was only a precursor to the undeclared war that broke out on 5 August when Pakistan launched a sizeable force of regular troops and irregular tribal forces against the Indian-held eastern portion of Kashmir, the fighting soon spreading south to include northern Punjab. The Pakistani irregulars made useful gains as the Indians rushed reinforcements to the front, and the start of conventional military operations was signalled by the attack launched by Pakistani regular forces against Chhamb on 14 August. By 23 August the Indians had marshalled their riposte and despatched columns across the ceasefire line at Kargil, Tithwal, and Uri, their objects being the penetration of Pakistani-held

Top: A jeep patrol moves out from Khalipur (near Jessore) in November 1971 in an effort to locate Pakistani forces facing the Indian II Corps.

Left: Indian infantry on the move in East Pakistan (Bangladesh), where the country dictates foot/air-mobile rather than armoured operations.

territory and the capture of the Poonch-Uri salient.

The Indian effort was moderately successful and on 28 August the Indians extended the front to take the Haji Pass. Pakistan responded with a substantial armoured counter-attack in the Chhamb sector, well supported by artillery. It was only after strenuous fighting that the Indians were able to check this advance, which was countered in turn by the Indians' Operation 'Grand Slam', a three-pronged armoured advance along the axis from Amritsar towards Lahore, launched on 6 September with the objectives firstly of drawing the Pakistani armour from the Chhamb sector and secondly of overwhelming them in a battle of attrition. The Indians extended their front further on 8 September, launching subsidiary attacks just to the south of the main sector at Sialkot, and considerably further to the south at Gadra with a view to advancing against Hyderabad. The armoured fighting was costly to each side and resulted in a tactical stalemate slightly favouring the Indians.

A UN ceasefire was ordered on 20 September and this came into effect three days later, though the Pakistanis kept up small-scale efforts to improve their positions over the next few days until the ceasefire co-ordination team, which arrived on 25 September, settled matters down. The ceasefire had ordered a retreat to the lines of 5 August, but the Indians were left in control of an important salient into Pakistan near Sialkot, and the Pakistanis with larger gains in Rajasthan and Kashmir. The Indians admitted to the loss of 2,200 dead, 7,635 wounded, and 1,500 missing, while Pakistani losses have not been revealed but are believed to have been similar. Each side lost about 200 tanks.

War between India and Pakistan flared again in 1971 and yet again the cause of the problem can be traced to the partition of 1947. In deciding the partition of

India at that time, the British found the major problem to be that of religion and Pakistan became the country of the Moslems. This meant that this new state, notionally a single political unit, was composed of West and East Pakistan, separated from each other by 1,000 miles (1600 km) of Hindu India. But the two wings of Pakistan were also completely different in terms of culture, economics, language, and race: East Pakistan generated some three-quarters of the complete country's foreign currency earnings, yet was controlled politically and militarily by West Pakistan. The local dislike of this control of East Pakistan by West Pakistan was exacerbated in practice by the fact that, though Pakistan was notionally a republic,

it was in fact a military dictator-ship. The result was inevitable: widespread rioting swept East Pakistan and when its leader Mujibur Rahman was arrested, the Awami League waited one more day before declaring East Pakistan to be the independent state of Bangladesh on 26 March 1971.

Just as inevitably, the reaction of the West Pakistani authorities was the despatch of the hard-line Lieutenant General Tikka Khan to crush the revolution in East Pakistan. Tikka Khan behaved with a ruthlessness that did nothing but harden local opinion against him and his forces. It is believed that perhaps 1 million

A Sikh soldier, backbone of the Indian army's combat strength.

civilians were killed in army rampages and, while much of East Pakistan's civil population fled to India, many other stayed behind to swell the ranks of the Mukti Bahini, the Awami League's resistance organization based on the 70,000 members of the Pakistani armed forces who had been recruited in East Pakistan and who had defected en masse.

By August the Indian state of West Bengal had been paralysed by the influx of some 6 million East Pakistani refugees and the Indian government decided to through its weight behind the Awami League's demand for an independent Bangladesh: the division of Pakistan into two smaller states was to India's decided advantage, for the military anti-Indian faction of West Pakistan would have its teeth well drawn by the

detachment of the economically more important East Pakistan.

Small-scale operations were not uncommon during October and November, however, for the Pakistani army was not averse to 'hot pursuit' of Mukti Bahini rebels fleeing into India. The Indians laid their plans with care, and on 3 December were faced with large-scale operations on two fronts, confident that they had read Pakistani intentions correctly. The course of events fully justified the Indian's confidence, for the Pakistani plan was a considerable effort in the west to draw off Indian forces that might otherwise be used in East Pakistan, thereby easing the task of Tikka Khan's forces in 'restoring order' and defeating Indian support for an independent Bangladesh.

At dawn on 3 December the Pakistanis launched air raids

In certain parts of the Indian subcontinent, pack animals are still as effective as wheeled transport.

against the Indians' ten most important airfields in the western theatre, attempting a pre-emptive strike to eliminate the air power that posed the greatest threat to their plans, but the Indians had anticipated this move and dispersed their aircraft to hardened shelters where they rode out the Pakistani storm with minimal losses. Soon after the air raiders had returned home, the Pakistanis launched their 12th and 23rd Infantry Divisions across the border in the area of Poonch, their objective a left hook through Kashmir towards Jammu and Chhamb. The Pakistanis made ground initially but the Indians slowly brought the advance to a halt by 6 December.

Confident in their assessment of Pakistani intentions, the Indians were able to start a major tactical air effort on 4 December and under this air umbrella Indian ground forces moved forward to take the Pakistani forward positions around Kahuta and in the Zoji Pass in Kashmir during 4 December. On the following day they advanced from Rajasthan against the Pakistani salient with its apex at Nagar Parkar. On 6 December the Indians switched their attention north again, occupying the Pakistani salient at Khem Karan north of Ferozepore.

The Pakistanis now tried to secure the operational initiative by taking the Chhamb salient on 7 December, but were driven out with 3,000 casualties in a major Indian effort that started on the following day and lasted until 14 December. A large armoured battle was fought on 15 and 16 December around Zafarwal and Pathankot just to the south of the Chhamb salient, the Pakistanis

Top: Western Bangladesh is one of the few areas of the country suitable for armour, and here the Indians deployed substantial armour.

Right: The Pakistani forces have been outnumbered, but hoped to divert sufficient Indian attention from the eastern sector to give their garrison in Bangladesh at least a chance.

losing a substantial number of tanks just before the Indian prime minister, Mrs Indira Gandhi, announced a unilateral ceasefire.

On the eastern front the Indians were greatly aided by the Mukti Bahini, who provided the Indians with excellent local knowledge and an unexcelled reconnaissance capability. Only one Indian airfield was attacked by the Pakistanis before the Indians moved against their forces in East Pakistan, crossing the frontier on 4 December and linking up with the Mukti Bahini on the following day.

On 6 December India recognized Bangladesh as an independent country and under

the overall command of General Jagjit Singh Aurora the Indian advances were carefully controlled as a series of exemplary concentric attacks by the Indian IV Corps from Tripura in the east, the 101st Communications Zone from Assam in the north, the Indian XXXIII Corps from Bihara in the north-west, and the Mukti Bahini and Indian II Corps from West Bengal in the south-west. By 14 December the Indians had taken most of East Pakistan, West Pakistani forces holding out only in Barisal, Chittagong, Dacca, Dinajpur, Khulna, Mainamati, and Rangpur. On 16 December General Niazi signed the Pakistani surrender,

though, the last fighting continued into the next day around Khulna and Sylhet.

The Indian campaign in East Pakistan remains a classic of its type: the country is dissected by rivers and marshes, and to cope with these physical barriers as well as the Pakistani forces the Indians adopted a masterly blend of amphibious, airborne, guerrilla, and conventional tactics to maintain the momentum that gave the Pakistanis no chance whatsoever.

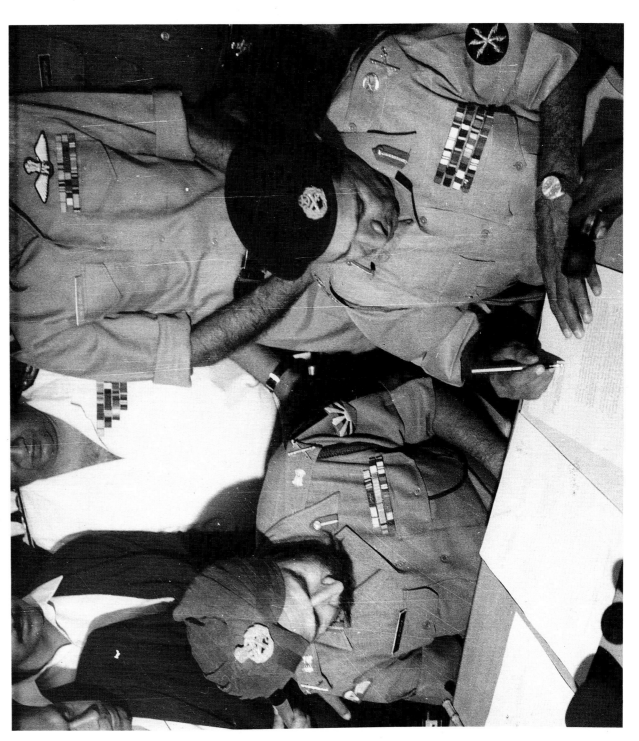

The West Pakistani surrender in East Pakistan is formalized.

AFRICAN WARS

THE ITALO-ABYSSINIAN WAR (1935-36)

In the late 1920s a treaty of friendship with Italy (signed on 2 August 1928 and intended to last for 20 years) gave Abyssinia a free zone in the Italian-controlled port of Assab, close to French Somaliland, in exchange for Italian rights to build certain roads in Abyssinia. Abyssinia was making a considerable effort to modernize itself during this period, and further evidence of this fact is the reorganization of the Abyssinian army along Western European lines, a formidable task undertaken from 1929 with the aid of a Belgian military mission. This reorganization was still being implemented when Abyssinian and Italian forces clashed at a road construction site on the border of Abyssinia and Italian Somaliland on 5 December 1935: this action at Ualual cost the Abyssinians 100 dead and the Italian colonial force about 30 dead.

The Abyssinians demanded an inquiry to establish the facts of the matter but the Italians went one step further and immediately demanded an apology and reparations. No immediate solution was forthcoming and a League of Nations arbitration during 1935 found itself unable to apportion blame for the incident. The League of Nations' finding (or rather lack of finding) was announced on 3 September and exactly one month later Italian troops invaded Abyssinia without any declaration of war. Well supported by artillery and aircraft,

the Italians pushed on rapidly and took Adowa on 6 October, the day before Italy was branded an aggressor by the League of Nations.

Italy had been preparing for this campaign during the previous two years and had built up in Eritrea and Italian Somaliland an excellent infrastructure of roads and bases, together with the ports through which supplies and men from Italy

could be fed up to the front. So while the League of Nations debated whether or not to impose international sanctions against Italy the Italian forces pushed steadily into the Abyssinian interior on two main axes (south

The SS Conte Biancamano is seen at Port Said in October 1935 with Italian troops destined for the war in Abyssinia.

The Ethiopians lacked the leadership, weapons and training to stem the modern forces fielded by an aggressive Italy.

The Abyssinian war was a classic juxtaposition of old and new, as these soldiers and tribesmen indicate.

from Eritrea and north-west from Italian Somaliland) towards the capital, Addis Ababa. On 8 November the Italians captured the fortress of Makalle and 10 days later the League of Nations announced the imposition of sanctions against Italy. Some 51 nations fell into line behind the resolution and embargoed the delivery of arms, credit, and raw materials to the fascist regime in Italy, but none saw fit to do anything as useful as embargo oil or close the Suez Canal to Italian shipping.

Between December 1935 and April 1936 there was a winter-imposed break in operations, though the Italians took advantage of the lull to reorganize their expeditionary force under the command of Marshal Pietro Badoglio. The weather allowed a resumption of operations in April and Badoglio advanced without effective hindrance, the courageous but woefully equipped and handled Ethiopian forces disintegrating in the face of constant Italian air attack in which poison gas was extensively used.

Addis Ababa fell to the Italians on 5 May 1936. Emperor Haile Selassie fled the country to seek international help and Abyssinian resistance crumbled entirely. On 9 May Abyssinia was annexed into Italian East Africa. Immediate recognition was afforded by Austria, Germany, and Hungary, with France and the UK following in 1937.

THE ALGERIAN REVOLUTION (1954-62)

In 1848 Algeria was declared part of metropolitan France thus encouraging the first great influx of French settlers or *colons*, later known somewhat derisively as *pieds noirs* (black feet).

Moslem (nationalist) fervour followed World War I, but was suppressed without undue difficulty, only to resurface after the liberation of France in 1944. On 8 May 1945, celebrated as VE-Day to commemorate the total surrender of Germany, Moslem extremists killed 103 Europeans at Setif between the Little Kabylia Mountains and the Hodna Mountains just inland from the Mediterranean coast on the east/west road. The pattern for future events was set by the European reaction, which took the form of 500 Moslems killed by the French army and possibly another 6,000 by the *pieds noirs*, members of settler families who knew no other home but felt constantly threatened by the vastly superior numbers of Moslem Arabs whose best lands had been expropriated by the initial settlers.

Throughout the world there was a steadily strengthening feeling against colonialism during the 1950s and Algeria was no

exception to this rule. The main centres of resistance to continued French rule were the Berbers from the Kabylia and Aures mountains, under the leadership of the CRUA (Comité Révolution-naire d'Unité de l'Action – Revolutionary Committee for Unity and Action). This thought it saw decisive signs of French weakness in French reverses in Indo-China and hastened its efforts to secure an Algerian uprising during 1954, when France's moral and physical strengths were expected to have reached their lowest ebbs.

The uprising was planned for 1 November 1954 under the leadership banner of the FLN (Front de Libération Nationale – National Liberation Front), to which the other main nationalist group, Ferhat Abbas's UDMA (Union Démocratique pour la Manifeste Algérien – Democratic Union for Algerian Destiny) allied itself in April 1956. Planning went ahead throughout the summer and autumn of 1954, but the uprising was a general failure that secured only limited success in the Kabylia and Aures mountains.

The French intelligence system

was moderately well aware of what was afoot and after the disasters of Indo-China the French were in fact determined that the same thing would not happen in Algeria which, after all, was part of metropolitan France. The French army acted swiftly against the FLN's military wing, the guerrilla bands that in August 1956 became the ALN (Armée de Libération Nationale – National Liberation Army) in the Soummam Valley conference that committed the FLN to a hard-line policy against the French and any Algerians resisting the 'blandish-ments' of the FLN: the preliminary uprising was therefore easily quelled. The leaders were not caught, however, and fled into the mountains to organize the guerrilla campaign which their initial failure had shown to be essential. The two most important leaders of the FLN were Ahmed Ben Bella and Belkacem Krim, whose initial move was to divide Algeria into six regions under a parallel system of *vilayas* and *mintaquas* for concerted military and political action respectively.

Right from the beginning of the campaign the FLN decided to inaugurate its own governmental apparatus to ensure that no one was left in doubt of the FLN's overall objectives. An important part of the FLN policy was therefore the establishment of a civil administration and it was notable from an early stage that the running of the *mintaquas* was often superior to local French administration.

Thus was the scene set for the Algerian Revolution, an immensely costly and protracted struggle whose main players were the Algerians Moslems, the *pieds*

French troops with Algerian dead and one prisoner after Operation 'Bigeaud' during 1956. Such sweeps did much to confirm the indigenous population's hatred of France.

A well-equipped Algerian unit receives its orders before moving out against the French.

noirs, the French government, and the French army – who generally stood between the *pieds noirs* and the French government but, as the war progressed, increasingly found that it had its own axe to grind. Against the guerrillas the army secured considerable early success, for the guerrillas had not yet learned their craft and the French were able to use their advanced technology (most notably helicopters and radios) to catch the guerrillas in the open. But in a sense these early successes later proved disastrous for the French: the Algerians who survived the early day proved themselves adept at learning guerrilla tactics the hard way, and soon began to

capture from the French the weapons that made them increasingly formidable in the field.

Other weapons were supplied via two other French colonies which, to the fury of the Algerians, secured their independence in March 1956 – Morocco and more importantly Tunisia. The latter also played host to guerrilla base and training camps until the French completed the Morice Line in September 1957. This line ran most of the length of the Algerian and Tunisian frontier in the form of an electrified barbed wire fence 8.2 ft (2.5 m) highly protected on each side by 55-yard (50-m) minefields and patrolled regularly.

The French also scored a notable success with the capture of Ben Bella and other FLN leaders in October 1956, when French special forces hijacked the airliner in which they were travelling to Tunis.

The revolution was soon confined to the rural areas, for the French acted with an effective ruthlessness in rooting out the revolutionaries and their bomb factories in the towns of the coastal cities so important to French and the *pieds noirs*. The most significant of these efforts

was the so-called 'Battle of Algiers', which started with a general strike and then raged from January to March 1957 after the brutal smashing of the strike. The French local commander was Brigadier General Jacques Massu, a determined and highly capable paratroop leader who acquired a fanatical local following in the French army and inspired an intense hatred from the Algerians.

But all was not going well for the French, for they were unable to extend their domination from the urban to the rural areas, and the FLN was capitalizing on the world reporting of atrocities by the French army. The FLN also committed a large number of atrocities, but managed generally to conceal or mitigate this fact while promoting world condemnation for the French. The war thus became

increasingly unpopular not only with most of the western world but also with the population of mainland France, which saw in the Algerian war just another massive drain on France's already strained economy. But French politicians were unable to come to terms with this fact, which was compounded by the discovery of large oil deposits in Algeria and by the particular problems of the *pieds noirs*. Calm analysis would have revealed that the only solution was independence for Algeria and the resettlement of the *pieds noirs*, but the politicians could admit no such thing even though matters were becoming increasingly bitter in Algeria, where relations between the *pieds noirs* and army had reached a low ebb during the latter's heavy-handed crushing of a European general strike in Algiers

during September 1957.

In January 1958 a French reconnaissance aircraft was shot down by fire from a Tunisian village and on 11 February the air force responded with a raid that killed 80 civilians. This event was extensively reported in the world media, increasing the odium in which French conduct was already wallowing. On 9 May the FLN 'executed' three captured French soldiers and local unrest with the conduct of operations spilled over into a *pied noir* occupation of French government building in Algiers. The army was also becoming increasingly disenchanted with the political control imposed on its efforts to

Some Algerians remained loyal to France, forming self-defence units to keep out the rebel forces and provide the French army with information.

deal with the revolution, and this fact found potent expression on 13 May 1958 when Massu led an officer uprising and formed a Committee of Public Safety to condemn the handling of the war by the French central government.

Coming after the disasters in Indo-China and the Suez campaign, this was the last straw that finally broke the back of the 4th Republic and nearly brought France to civil war. Public pressure resulted in the recall to power of General Charles de Gaulle on 1 June 1958 and the establishment of the 5th Republic, with De Gaulle as president from 21 December. De Gaulle brought to the French conception of the Algerian war a determined realism: he saw what had to be done, but realized that he would have to act with great guile to achieve the correct result without first being toppled by powerful factional interests.

De Gaulle's first step was to offer Algeria self-determination by

means of a referendum: this provoked total turmoil amongst the *pieds noirs*, and this was manipulated for its own ends by the OAS (Organisation de l'Armée Sécrète – Organization of the Secret Army), an extreme right-wing army faction opposed to De Gaulle and the further dissolution of France's overseas empire. De Gaulle also called for stronger and more effective measures against the FLN, resulting initially in Operation 'Binoculars' during July 1958: this was designed to crush some of the FLN heartland area, most notably those in the Kabylia mountains, and as part of the operation about 1 million Algerian civilians were rounded up into 'regroupment camps' while their home areas were razed to starve out the FLN.

De Gaulle visited Algeria in October 1958 and secured the dissolution of the Committee of Public Safety in favour of fully resumed French government and in a speech at Constantine he

announced French plans for the industrialization of Algeria as a means of boosting national wealth. This ploy was designed to weaken support for the FLN amongst less committed Algerians but was countered by the FLN's establishment of a GPRA (Gouvernement Provisoire de la République Algérienne – Provisional Government of the Algerian Republic) and a considerable resurgence of FLN terrorism in mainland France.

In Algeria Massu was replaced in December 1958 by General Maurice Challe as part of De Gaulle's effort to weaken control of the army by officers with strong personal followings and this process continued through 1959 as De Gaulle also prepared France for the shock of losing Algeria.

While his men relax and eat during operations in the Kabylla area, a commander radios in his position and information.

The course of De Gaulle's planning was becoming more plain by the end of 1959, and on 24 January 1960 the *pied noir* extremist faction, numbering some 30,000 in all under the leadership of Jo Ortiz and Pierre Lagaillarde, launched 'Barricades Week' in Algiers: Challe was under instructions to disperse the demonstrators, but was reluctant to use French troops against the *pieds noirs*, and was thus fortunate when heavy rain broke up the demonstration during 1 February. Challe was replaced in April.

Between 25 and 29 June preliminary talks were held between the French government and the GPRA at Melun, but these failed to reach any agreement. It was nevertheless an important first step towards the recognition of Algerian

independence, and in the autumn of 1960 the increasingly desperate OAS launched a concerted campaign of bombing attacks in Algeria and France. De Gaulle and the population of France were not to be swayed, however, and a referendum in January 1961 decided overwhelmingly in favour of Algerian self determination.

This was the last straw for the army, which started to plan a coup against De Gaulle and the 5th Republic: the coup was launched on 22 April under Generals Challe and Raoul Salan and was a complete failure everywhere except some points in Algeria: despite the backing of the foreign Legion and the French paratroop arm, which allowed the mutinous generals to hold Algiers for five days, the vast majority of France's soldiers heeded De Gaulle's pleas

to remain loyal and the coup collapsed on 26 April. The French opposition to De Gaulle was now confined largely to the OAS, which was determined to exact vengeance on the French president for his 'betrayal' of French interests in North Africa.

Limited operations against the FLN continued in 1961, being scaled down after the beginning of peace negotiations at Evian-les-Bains on 20 May. A formal ceasefire was brought into effect between 7 and 18 March 1962, and the Algerian Revolution was effectively over. On 3 July Algeria became an independent republic headed by Ben Bella.

French paratroops in control of Algiers during the April 1961 rebellion under Generals Salan, Challe, Jouhaud and Zeller.

THE CONGOLESE CIVIL WAR (1960-71)

Congolese troops and civilians at the detached post of Nya-Ngezi.

In 1908 the Congo Free State, personal possession of the Belgian monarch from 1879, became the Belgian Congo after a scandal about conditions in the region. The Belgian state, like the monarch before it, derived an enormous wealth from this fertile and mineral-rich possession. Little capital was returned to the Congo in any beneficial form, however, and this vast area remained one of the most backward in the world when granted republican independence on 30 June 1960 under the presidency of Joseph Kasavubu, head of the Bakoingo tribal grouping which controlled most of the western portion of the Congo.

Kasavubu was all too aware of the tribal, cultural, and linguistic differences that posed a threat to the new Congo Republic and saw a federal state at the best means of mitigating the factionalism so engendered. In an effort to secure a measure of national unity, Kasavubu therefore appointed the left-leaning Patrice Lumumba, head of the MNC (Mouvement National Congolais – Congolese National Movement), as his prime minister despite Lumumba's avowed intent to create a highly centralized Congo on dogmatic communist lines.

The legacy of earlier lack of concern by the Belgians almost immediately became apparent as the army and large numbers of civilians ran amok in an orgy of rioting, looting, murdering, and raping in a nationwide mutiny that started on 4 July. To compound the difficulties of the new republic these earlier disasters urged virtually all the remaining whites to abandon the country. As a result, most surviving administrative, medical, and technical capabilities went with them in an exodus that further complicated what was an already disastrous situation.

The remoter provinces descended into total disorder, the only core of discipline being in the mineral-rich southern province of Katanga, where some 10,000 Belgian troops controlled the areas containing the processing industries built with Belgian finance. These troops were flown in to protect the key cities of Elisabethville (now Lumumbashi), Luluabourg, and Matadi in response to a plan formulated by the Katangan leader, Moise Tshombe, in collaboration with Belgian and other European mining interests.

On 11 July Moise Tshombe refused to submit to the authority

of Lumumba, who demanded that Katanga expel the Belgian forces, and declared Katanga independent while requesting Belgium for additional forces. Belgium refused to supply these additional forces, and Tshombe began the process of hiring white mercenaries to safeguard his secessionist province. Lumumba prepared to invade Katanga, and fearing that Belgium was about to re-establish a colony in Katanga requested United Nations aid in support for his subjugation of the rebellious province.

On 14 July the United Nations Security Council approved the creation of a security force for the Congo (the first contingent, from Tunisia, arriving in the Congo during the following day as the advance guard of a force that eventually totalled 20,000 men), and by 31 July Belgium was complying with a United Nations request (on 22 July) to evacuate its forces with the exception of a small force in Katanga.

On 12 August UN Secretary General Dag Hammarskjold arrived at the airport of Elisabethville with 240 Swedish troops of the UN security force,

but was refused admission when he demanded that the last Belgian troops be withdrawn and replaced by UN forces. Lumumba denounced Hammarskjold for using white troops and also for refusing to place them under Lumumba's command. On 24 August the central province of Kasai followed Katanga's secessionist lead and launched a military rebellion under the Baluba chief, Albert Kalonji; Lumumba sent an expeditionary force up the Kasai river in response, but military operations were wholly inconclusive. On 30 August Belgium finally began to comply with the US resolution to pull out its last troops, though Hammarskjold had by now reached a truer appreciation of the local situation and asked that some Belgian forces should remain in Katanga under UN command.

But the situation began to become yet more complex on 14 September when Lumumba was overthrown and arrested by Colonel Joseph Mobutu, his army chief-of-staff, in the Congolese capital of Léopoldville (now Kinshasa.). Though Joseph Ileo was named prime minister, real control

was retained by Mobutu. Lumumba escaped and fled into hiding in the central Congo. On 20 September a virulent attack of Hammarskjold's policy on the Congo was made by the Soviet representative at the UN, Valentin Zorin, but the US voted overwhelmingly to support Hammarskjold.

Throughout October and November 1960 violence became endemic in the Congo as the various army factions became increasingly disorderly and at times clashed with the UN forces. Lumumba was rearrested on 1 December and flown back to Léopoldville. This prompted Lumumba's deputy, Antoine Gizenga, to declare the independence of Orientale province, with its capital at Stanleyville (now Kisangani), as a pro-communist state. Soviet aid began to flow into the area and this allowed Gizenga's forces to expand their control over most of the central and eastern parts of the Congo.

Congolese troops man a recoilless gun used as field artillery.

On 17 January 1961 Lumumba was moved to a 'more secure' prison in Katanga on the orders of Kasavubu, but on Tshombe's orders was murdered during 9 February. Increasing pressure was now being applied to compel the re-integration of Katanga and the rest of the Congo, and in response Tshombe ordered a mobilization of Katangan forces. Elsewhere in the Congo Gizenga was making good progress in his military operations and on 24 February his forces took Luluabourg, the capital of Kasai province. Ileo promptly requested US action against the secessionist (and also expansionist) regime based in Stanleyville.

Additional political moves were in hand, however, and after a conference at Tananarive in the Malagasy Republic, a new Congolese Federation was proclaimed by all the central government and regional leaders with the exception of Gizenga. On 17 April Kasavubu signed an agreement giving the UN forces the right to use force in their role of preventing a Congolese civil war, and after a unity conference in Léopoldville on 26 April Tshombe was arrested. After declaring that he would expedite the re-integration of Katanga into the Congolese Federation Tshombe was released on 2 June, but after reaching Elisabethville he repudiated this agreement as having been made under duress.

On 1 August the new Congolese parliament met, immediately electing Cyrille Adoula as prime minister and Gizenga as deputy prime minister. With a measure of internal accord evident throughout the rest of the Congo, the UN

As well as trying to stem the Congolese Civil War, the UN also sought to alleviate conditions with medical supplies.

forces now sought to compel Katanga back into the federation. The UN forces had been built up over previous weeks, and on 21 August the UN forces seized control of the main centres of communication in Elisabethville and other primary Katangan towns. At the same time the UN demanded that Tshombe begin to disband his mercenary forces, and though Tshombe reluctantly agreed to his move, he began secretly to prepare the defence of Elisabethville. On 13 September the US forces moved to secure control of Elisabethville but were unable to wrest control from Tshombe's forces.

152

A British mercenary in Stanleyville after the rescue mission. The local population wore white headbands to distinguish themselves from the rebels.

This was a highly significant political and psychological blow for the prestige of the UN and at the same time a considerable

propaganda and morale boost for the Katangan forces.

Hammarskjold arranged a meeting with Tshombe but while flying to the designated place was killed in an air crash near Ndola in Northern Rhodesia on 18 September. The Congolese forces decided to take a hand with an invasion of Katanga during November but were decisively

beaten by the Katangan forces. The UN forces finally secured Elisabethville on 18 December and Tshombe yet again agreed to re-integrate Katanga with the rest of the Congo. Yet again, however, Tshombe managed to avoid this unpalatable move and retained control of an autonomous Katanga.

In January 1962 disaffection spread once more as Gizenga attempted again to withdraw his Stanleyville area from the federation. Congolese forces rapidly regained control, Gizenga being arrested and sent into exile. For most of the year an uneasy peace followed this move, until the UN forces launched an offensive in Katanga on 29 December. The UN plan had been carefully prepared and proceeded smoothly: all Katangan resistance was overcome without difficulty, and Tshombe fled into exile on 15 January 1963 after agreeing to the re-integration of Katanga with the rest of the Congo.

A measure of long-term stability had apparently reached the Congo, and during the rest of 1963 and the first half of 1964 the UN forces were gradually reduced. There were many small pockets of trouble, mainly in the north-east of the country, but budgetary considerations forced the UN to allocate these to the Congolese forces after the last UN troops were withdrawn on 30 June 1964.

Yet the pockets of resistance proved more troublesome than the UN wanted to believe, for they were now receiving financial and military assistance from China for an effort that became increasingly unified under the leadership of Pierre Mulele: he was undoubtedly a natural leader and was able to exploit the people's genuine grievances against the authoritarianism of the central government and the considerable excesses of the Congolese army. The resultant fighting was particularly violent, Mulele's men

Indonesian troops prepare to board a UN transport 'plane at Mombasa before flying into the Congo.

Pro-Lumumba Congolese troops prepare for their invasion of Katanga after being airlifted into Bakwanga from Stanleyville.

calling themselves *simbas* (lions) to indicate their prowess in battle.

But while Mulele's forces began as hard-fighting and formidable men with good discipline, the course of the campaign witnessed a steady erosion of this discipline until the *simbas* were nothing but indiscriminate butchers of all who crossed their path. The *simbas* were eventually believed by themselves and by the men of the Congolese army to have magical powers, and the arrival of the *simbas* was generally reason enough for the Congolese soldiers to flee. In a desperate attempt to reimpose unity and capability Tshombe was recalled from exile and made prime minister on 9 July. Tshombe saw that, while the Congolese army was capable of dealing in part with the task, there were elements that might better be handled by less orthodox measures and thus he began once more to recruit mercenaries.

On 30 August the Congolese army retook Albertville (now Kalemie) on Lake Tanganyika from the rebels who had held it

for the last two months but in east and central Congo the communist-backed rebels began to make considerable gains during September and October despite strenuous government efforts. In Stanleyville the rebels were holding 2,000 white hostages under threat of instant massacre should the government forces approach Stanleyville, but the hostages were then rescued in an

extraordinary effort by the USA and Belgium. A full battalion of Belgian paratroops was carried in US Air Force transports via Ascension Island to take Stanleyville by coup de main after an air drop: some 80 hostages were killed by the *simbas* and another 40 wounded, but most

Part of the grim scene in Stanleyville after the massacres.

were retrieved by the paratroopers, who were supplemented later in the day by a government mercenary column headed by Colonel Mike Hoare.

There was an enormous outcry by African and communist countries against this example of 'white aggression', and the paratroops were pulled out before they could undertake other rescue missions planned for them: the result was that several hundred white hostages held in other towns were killed without mercy,

eliciting not the slightest response from the African and communist countries which had forced the Belgian withdrawal.

Better success attended the government's efforts in the first quarter of 1965 and by the end of March Hoare's mercenaries had retaken Aba, Arua, Faradje, Mahaji, and Watsa (in the region bordering Sudan and Uganda). Government control was steadily extended but on 25 November Tshombe was overthrown by Mobutu and removed to a prison

A key figure in the Congo's problems: Major Mike Hoare, leader of the mercenary force controlled by Tshombe.

in Algeria, where he died in 1969. During the first half of 1966 further consolidation by the government reduced unrest and by the end of July central government control was complete after a revolt by Katangan paramilitary police had been suppressed. In 1971 Mobutu changed the country's name to Zaire.

THE WARS OF LIBERATION FROM PORTUGAL (1961-75)

The smallest of the three Portuguese colonies in Africa was Portuguese Guinea, where the PAIGC (Partido Africano da Independencia de Guine e Cabo Verde – African Party for the Liberation of Guinea and the Cape Verde Islands) was formed in 1952 under the leadership of Amilcar Cabral. This was essentially an urban party with few connections in the rural areas, and its war of liberation for Portugal can be dated to 3 August 1959 when 50 strikers in the shipyards of Bissau were shot by Portuguese troops. This made it clear to Cabral that his movement could not survive as an urban organization and in 1960 he shifted his base to the Guinea republic and started to reorganize the PAIGC as a Maoist party, with its roots firmly embedded in the rural areas. Thereafter the revolution followed strictly Maoist lines and by 1963 the revolutionaries could claim that 'Guinea is a prison in which the Portuguese have sought shelter'.

Rural resistance grew steadily and the Portuguese found themselves powerless to resist the steady encroachment and development of the PAIGC. The situation was sufficiently crucial in 1968 for Antonio de Spinola to be appointed governor and commander-in-chief of Portuguese Guinea, and though some successes were achieved against the revolutionaries (often by airborne Groupes Especiales Paraquedistas and 'turned-round' guerrillas known as Flechas), the root causes of local disaffection were not considered or treated, with the result that the Portuguese found themselves increasingly isolated in towns and along the main lines of communication.

Some hope was offered to the Portuguese cause when Cabral was murdered by extremists within his own party during January 1973 (to be replaced by Aristide Pereira), but the lie was put to any suggestion that the PAIGC was mortally wounded when two Portuguese fighters were downed with Soviet-supplied missiles during March of the same year. In August Spinola returned to Portugal and on 24 September the PAIGC, by that time numbering perhaps 5,000 men, declared the independence of Guinea.

Just under one year later, on 10 September 1974, Portugal recognized the independence of its former colony as the state of Guinea-Bissau under the presidency of Louis Cabral, brother of Amilcar Cabral.

Further to the south lies Angola, an altogether larger Portuguese colony that came into being mainly to match Belgian and German developments to the north and south. The war for independence in Angola was an altogether more difficult matter than the campaign in Portuguese Guinea, for while there was general opposition to the authoritarian Portuguese administration, there was also considerable animosity between the three independence movements.

Like all other wars of independence, the conflict in Angola was widespread but small in overall scale, and those who suffered most were the civilians.

These were: the MPLA (Movimento Popular de Libertacão de Angola – Popular Movement for the Liberation of Angola – a 7,000-man Maoist organization led by the university-educated Dr. Agostinho Neto), the UPA (Union of the Population of Angola – an organization led by Holden Roberto, the brother-in-law of President Mobuto of Zaire) which in 1962 became the FNLA (National Front for the Liberation of Angola), and the UNITA (National Union for the Total Independence of Angola – a democratic organization led by the university-educated Dr. Jonas Savimbi).

A low level of resistance to the Portuguese had been evident for some time before the revolution can fairly be said to have started with an attack, during 3 February 1961, on the prison in Luanda where MPLA suspects were being held. While this was perhaps only a small beginning, altogether more significant was the UPA massacre of 7,000 blacks and several hundred whites in the Carmona district of Uige, the north-eastern province of Angola. The retribution for this action was swift and uncontrolled, blacks and whites seeking revenge in a series of attacks that cost perhaps 30,000 lives and caused another 300,000 people to flee mostly as refugees into neighbouring Zaire.

Sporadic fighting followed over the next 14 years without any readily discernible trend, the Portuguese being the common enemy but the three independence movements not infrequently fighting amongst themselves. The MPLA was generally supported by the USSR, the FNLA by the USA, and the UNITA initially by the Chinese. By 1972 the fighting raged over many parts of the colony but was generally unco-ordinated on the part of the independence movements. The Portuguese effort was masterminded by General José Bettancourt Rodriguez, an extremely capable officer who specialized in counter-insurgency warfare and was able to check the independence movements with 50,000 Portuguese and 10,000 black troops.

The Portuguese made extensive use of helicopters such as these Aerospatiale Alouettes for tactical mobility against the elusive freedom fighters.

The decisive moment arrived on 5 January 1975 when Neto, Roberto, and Savimbi met in Mombasa in Kenya to agree an overall strategy that would oust the Portuguese: in the north the weight was carried by the FNLA, with supplies arriving from Zaire; in the centre (along a narrow strip between Luanda on the coast and Henrique de Carvalho close to the Zairean and Zambian frontiers) the predominant force was the

MPLA, and in the south (below the Benguela Railway) the most important faction was the UNITA. Internecine quarrels were temporarily postponed so that unified pressure could be exerted against the Portuguese, who had hitherto relied on the independence movements' internal wrangling to prevent concerted action. The threat of such action was sufficient to persuade the Portuguese to announce, on 15

January 1975, that Angolan independence would be granted on 1 September of the same year.

From this time the fighting against the Portuguese tailed off as the independence movements geared themselves for the final solution of long-term disputes.

The leader of FRELIMO, Samora Machel, harangues some of his troops before a mission in Mozambique.

Mines are a favourite weapon of the freedom fighter, and the need to detect and clear such devices severely slowed down mechanized operations.

Some 300,000 whites left the country and by the time independence was formally granted on 11 September Angola was in a state of total disorder: on 7 August the FNLA had quit the January coalition, the UNITA following on 12 August. Already the MPLA had started to consolidate, however, with the arrival of Cuban and Soviet advisers from April. The scene was fully set for the Angolan Civil War, succeeding a costly independence war. The civil war continues though political moves towards peace started in 1988.

Over much the same period Mozambique won its independence from Portuguese rule by similar means, though in this country the independence struggle was dominated by a single faction, the 4,000-man FRELIMO (Frent de Libertacão de Moçambique – Front for the Liberation of Mozambique) headed by Dr. Eduardo Mondlane

from the time of its formation in 1962. Portugal was decisively hampered by having only limited manpower and financial resources to fight simultaneous campaigns on each side of southern Africa, while the FRELIMO had all the advantages of a friendly host country, Tanzania. Thus the FRELIMO headquarters were located in the Tanzanian capital, Dar es Salaam, while the main FRELIMO base and training area was located around Nachingwea in

southern Tanzania. Other African states in the region were not so generous, fearing that the Portuguese might cut their rail links to the sea at Beira and Lourenço Marques (now Maputo), but via the Tanzanian link the FRELIMO received generous Chinese supplies.

Mozambiquan Blacks protest about the continued presence of Portugal as the colonial power in one of the riots that preceded the war of liberation.

A FRELIMO column departs from its secret base for operations against the Portuguese.

The Mozambiquean war of independence began on 25 September 1964 when the FRELIMO launched a series of raids against Portuguese positions in the colony. Thereafter the campaign developed in a fashion typical of Maoist revolution, a slight hiatus in the FRELIMO effort following the assassination of Mondlane on 3 February 1969. In 1970 the leadership of FRELIMO was assumed by Samora Machel, a dedicated Marxist, and the pace of military events was increased as the party's strength within the rural communities of Mozambique increased.

The main effort was made close to the FRELIMO base areas in southern Tanzania and in 1970 and 1971 an intensive effort was made around the Cabora-Bassa dam on the Zambesi river, Portugal's single most important capital asset in Mozambique. During 1972, 1973, and 1974 the FRELIMO effort continued to gain strength and on 7 September 1974 the Portuguese foreign minister, Dr. Mario Soares, concluded an agreement with Machel in Lusaka, the capital of Zambia, for a ceasefire on 8 September and Mozambiquean independence on 25 July.

Rumours of the agreement had leaked out earlier in the month, leading to widespread rioting by whites and anti-FRELIMO blacks in Lourenco Marques, and in a backlash by pro-FRELIMO gangs some 9,500 people lost their lives. The campaign cost the Portuguese some 3,500 and the FRELIMO about 10,000 men, while civilian casualties were approximately 50,000.

A Portuguese-led column closes in on a suspect hamlet in one of the interminable search-and-destroy missions of the Angolan war.

THE NIGERIAN CIVIL WAR (1967-70)

Biafran recruits received a mere few weeks of extremely basic training before being moved to the front, where they had to obtain rifles from dead comrades.

Granted full independence in 1960, Nigeria had been a British colony whose origins can be traced to 1861 when Lagos was bought from a local chief. It was only in 1900 that Nigeria assumed its present boundaries when the Northern Nigerian Protectorate was brought fully under government control. In 1963 Nigeria recognized the differing needs and aspirations of its multi-faceted ethnic, religious, cultural, and linguistic make-up, and became a federal republic with considerable autonomy for its various regions. In January 1966, however, the civilian government was overthrown (by an army coup engineered by junior officers) and replaced by a military administration headed by General Ironsi.

A counter-coup in northern Nigeria was launched on 20 July and after the assassination of Ironsi a comparatively stable

administration was created under Major General Yakubu Gowan. Yet this apparent stability helped to conceal the national grievance against the Ibo tribe, whose members were generally felt to have gained more than an appropriate share of the very well paid governmental appointments. The coups had been accompanied by the massacre of many thousands of Ibos, especially in the Moslem north of the country, and a substantial number of other Ibos had returned to the tribal homeland in south-eastern Nigeria.

Gowan decided on a reorganization of Nigeria into four federal regions (Northern, Western, Mid-Western and Eastern), and then on 27 May 1967 into 12 states. At this point Lieutenant Colonel Odumegwu Ojukwu announced that the Eastern Region, of which he was

governor, was seceding from federal Nigeria as the independent Republic of Biafra. What Ojukwu sought to establish, in fact, was an Ibo nation out of the three south-eastern East Central, Rivers and South-Eastern states, with its capital at Owerri, its most important resource the oil town of Port Harcourt, and its boundaries running from Cameroun along the coast to the delta of the Niger river, up the river to a point north of Onitsha, and then east again via Nsukka to reach the Cameroun frontier east of Gakem. This basically rectangular state contained the Ibo heartlands and much of Nigeria's resources and most capable manpower.

Biafran reinforcements, somewhat better uniformed than most, arrive near the front at Onitsha.

Military operations were at first very small, being limited to probing attacks as the Biafrans prepared for the Nigerian onslaught and as the Nigerians gathered their forces. Biafran forces did push along the coast towards Lagos, which was also bombed by mercenary pilots, but the real object of the exercise was to establish the nerve of the Nigerian authorities rather than to capture the federal capital. Meanwhile the Nigerians were mustering their forces at Makurdi to the north of Biafra's northern frontier, and on 6 July 1967 these forces advanced on two axes towards Biafra: the right-hand Nigerian column advanced on Nsukka, which fell on 14 July, while the left-hand column made for Gakem, which was captured on 12 July.

The Biafrans responded not with a direct counter-attack but an effort to divert the Nigerians; on 9 July the Biafran forces moved west into Mid-Western state across the Niger, passing through Benin City to reach Ore just over the state boundary in Western state on 21 August. The Biafrans succeeded in their primary intention of diverting the Nigerians, four substantial forces were used to drive back the Biafran advance. Benin City was retaken by the Nigerians on 22 September, but the Nigerians were then repulsed three times as they tried to cross the Niger during October.

The Biafran army's heavier weapons were restricted to types such as this mortar, whose sight is being checked before it is brought into action.

The Nigerians then settled down to a blockade of Biafra, causing the starvation of many thousands of Ibos, most of them children. Amphibious landings had yielded two southern towns to the Nigerians (Bonny on the south of Port Harcourt on 26 July and Calabar on 18 October), effectively denying Biafra the opportunity of maritime supplies, and in the north the right-hand column's advance had reached Enugu by 4 October.

With the Biafrans weakened by their blockade, the Nigerians resumed their offensive between April and June 1968: the object was now to close the ring round the Biafrans with further advances on the two northern axes, and the development of two southern lodgements into advances against

Port Harcourt in the west and up Biafra's frontier with Cameroun in the east. This further isolated Biafra, making the air the only way to enter its shrinking 'frontiers': mercenary pilots to bring in weapons and other military supplies, but the airlift was wholly insufficient to allow the delivery of adequate food. The Biafrans claimed that Nigeria was undertaking the war in this manner as a deliberately genocidal effort against the Ibos, and the plight of Biafra certainly secured enormous sympathy in the West.

Throughout 1968 and 1969 logistical difficulties kept the Nigerians from finishing off a war that was effectively won, while the Biafrans struggled on against insuperable odds. Air supplies were still reaching the Biafrans,

As the war progressed, the Biafrans were overcome as much by exhaustion and starvation as by the efforts of the Nigerian federal forces.

and the Nigerians used their air power throughout 1968 and 1969 to attack Biafran airstrips and villages. The Biafrans were in desperate straits when the Nigerians launched their final offensive on 23 December 1969, two major thrusts being made from the south into the two surviving Biafran enclaves, one centred on Owerri and the other on Arochukwu further to the east. Owerri fell on 11 January, and the Biafran surrender was signed on 13 January at Amichi, in the extreme northern end of the western enclave.

Part II
MINOR WARS

EUROPEAN WARS

THE ITALO-TURKISH WAR (1911-12)

As a newer state which had been forced to consolidate its own internal position and structure before expanding its horizons to a colonial empire, Italy was slightly later than the other European countries in developing its interests in Africa. But across the Mediterranean Sea from Italy lay the decaying carcass of the Ottoman Empire's North African possessions, already the subject of intense French efforts at its western end (Tunisia, Algeria, and Morocco), and slightly smaller British effort at its eastern end (Egypt). In between lay Libya, and here Italy saw the possibility of securing the important

economic and political niche it desired in North Africa. On 29 September 1911, therefore, Italy declared war on Turkey.

In the shorter terms the Italians tried to distract the attention of the Turks from North Africa, its naval forces undertaking a bombardment of the Turkish base at Preveza on the eastern side of the Adriatic Sea in Epiros. For two days (29 and 30 September) the Italians maintained their effort, sinking several Turkish torpedo boats and effectively suggesting that the Italians were interested in a move east across the Adriatic rather than south across the Mediterranean. On 3 October the

Italian intentions became clearer when a sustained naval bombardment was started against the major city and port of Libya.

For three days the heavy bombardment of Tripoli continued, compelling the Turkish forces to evacuate the Libyan capital and leaving it open for the Italian invasion force that began to land on 5 October. Farther to the east another force had landed and

A Roman crowd watches the departure of Italian troops for the war in Libya. The crowd had anticipation of great things, which in fact could not be delivered by the army.

Italian cavalry proved useful in the coastal region of Libya for scouting, but could not penetrate far inland because the horses they used could not cope with the soft desert sand.

taken Tobruk on the previous day. These initial beach-heads were a naval responsibility but an Italian army expeditionary force under General Carlo Caneva arrived on 11 October to expand Italy's hold in their two areas as well as to occupy Benghazi, Derna, and Homs, thereby securing Italian control of Libya's littoral. In place the Turks resisted with considerable courage but

indifferent capability and the Italians were generally unmolested as they continued with their task of consolidating their initial lodgements.

For the rest of 1911 and the first half of 1912 there followed a military stalemate: the Turks were unable to respond militarily to the Italian invasion, but they inflamed the local Moslem population against the 'infidel' Italians so

successfully that Caneva thought it better not to essay further advances, concentrating his efforts instead on the complete consolidation of the Libyan coastal regions. Between 16 and 19 April

An Italian capital ship unleashes a salvo from her 305 mm main guns during the April 1912 bombardment of the Turkish defences in the Dardanelles.

1912 the Italians launched a naval feint off the Dardanelles, this persuading the Turks that the Italians intended to sail through to Constantinople and attack the capital of the Ottoman Empire. Widespread defensive measures were rushed through, but the Italians withdrew as the Turks succeeded in closing the straits.

The Italians' real interest in the area was the Dodecanese islands in the southern part of the Aegean Sea and in May 1912 the Italians took Rhodes and other islands without resistance. Then in July the Italians started finally to expand their holding in Libya, cautious but well planned moves steadily increasing the area of Italian conquest. The campaign culminated in decisive Turkish defeats at Derna and Sidi Bilal, and on 15 October the Treaty of Ouchy was signed to bring the war

to a close. Turkey faced a clear threat from the imminent Balkan wars far closer to home, and after two months of negotiations the treaty conceded Italy's possession of Libya and the islands already seized in the Aegean. Assessment of Italy's campaign was in general unfavourable, for against

indifferent opposition poorly led in areas far from home, the extraordinarily cautious Italians had been checked for a substantial period.

The signing of the Treaty of Ouchy that ended the Italo–Turkish War.

THE BALKAN WARS (1912–13)

Above: King Nicholas of Montenegro addresses his troops before their departure to the Balkan wars.

Right: Bulgarian troops on the move in the pass of Belogradchik on Bulgaria's western frontier.

The Balkan states of Bulgaria, Serbia, and Greece saw the Ottoman Empire's reserves in Libya as an excellent chance for them to enlarge their own countries at the expense of Turkey's European holdings, and also to eliminate Turkey as a European threat. The three countries formed the Balkan League during 1912, with Montenegro associated loosely with the three larger countries. The Balkan League reckoned it could put 310,000 men (180,000 Bulgars, 80,000 Serbs, and 50,000 Greeks) into the field against a Turkish strength of 240,000 men in Europe proper: the Turkish

disposition comprised 140,000 men in Macedonia and 100,000 men in Thrace.

The Balkan League rightly appreciated that Turkish reserves could sway the balance heavily in favour of the Ottoman cause should the war last long enough for these reserves to be mobilized and brought into the western part

of Asia Minor, but it thought that Greek naval control of the Aegean Sea was so dominant that the Turks would be unable to deliver large enough numbers of men to affect what was planned as a short campaign.

The Balkan League's pretext for the conflict eventually known as the First Balkan War was Turkish misrule and oppression in Macedonia and on 17 October 1912 the Balkan League launched simultaneous invasions of Turkey's surviving European possessions. In the north three Bulgarian armies under the overall command of General Radko Dimitriev invaded Thrace with Adrianople (now Edirne) as their main objective. Further to the south the Serbs and Greeks launched a concentrated effort against Macedonia, three Serbian armies under the overall command of General Radomir

Putnik striking south and one Greek army under Crown Prince Constantinos heading north to meet in the valley of the Vardar river with the Turkish forces trapped between them.

The Thracian sector saw comparatively unopposed Bulgarian advances on a broad front during the first five days of the war. But as the Bulgarian 1st, 2nd, and 3rd Armies advanced south they began to encounter strengthening Turkish resistance under Abdalla Pasha and between 22 and 25 October running battles were fought at Seliolu and Kirk Kilissa, the Turks being beaten in both battles but only after having checked the Bulgarians severely at Kirk Kilissa. Abdalla Pasha saw that he could not halt the Bulgarians so far to the north and thus fell back towards the 35-mile (55-km) line between Lule' Burgas

(now Luleburgaz) and Bunar Hisar (now Pinahisar) with his right flank protected by the mountains. The Bulgarian 2nd Army invested Adrianople and the other two armies wheeled east to engage Abdalla Pasha's force in its new positions.

The resulting Battle of Lule' Burgas was fought between 28 and 30 October. The Bulgarian attack started with a setpiece assault on the northern end of the line, where it was repulsed. Dimitriev then extended his assault to the south, the Bulgarians falling on the still over-extended Turks towards their left wing and finally compelling Abdalla Pasha to fall back once more, this time to the Chatalja (now Catalca) Line.

Medical services proved woefully deficient in the Balkan wars, and the wounded all too frequently died.

The shattered remnants of a Turkish position destroyed by a Bulgarian offensive.

This was designed to protect Constantinople and comprised a series of fixed fortifications between the Black Sea and the Sea of Marmora. On 17 November the Bulgarians made a highly determined but unsuccessful attempt to breach the Chatalja Line and exert additional pressure on Constantinople, and they continued their effort against these powerful defences until the ceasefire of 3 December (ignored by Greece and Montenegro) brought hostilities to a temporary end.

In Macedonia the operations against the Turks were a Serbian and Greek responsibility. The first Greek effort was a small offensive against Epiros on the extreme west of the Balkan League's front, but this was succeeded in short order by the main effort under Constantinos, an advance into the lower reaches of the Vardar valley from 20 October. On 23 October the Greeks engaged and decisively beat the Turks in the Battle of Elasson, forcing the Turks to fall back on Monastir. Constantinos refused to follow and so capitalize on his initial success, for the Bulgars had broken the previous arrangement and, supposedly to support the left flank of the Serbs, driven one division towards Salonika (now Thessaloniki), a major port desired by both Bulgaria and Greece.

The Greek effort was veered to the east by Constantinos, who was then unexpectedly checked at Venije Vardar by determined resistance on the part of an unexpectedly large Turkish force during 2 and 3 November. The Greek position was rendered somewhat parlous by the Turks' detailed defeat of the Greek left and right flanks at Kastoria and Banitsa, but Constantinos eventually broke through the Turkish centre at Venije Vardar on 5 November and advanced on

169

Salonika. The Turkish right flank, cut off to the north-west, pulled back towards Yannina (now Ioannina).

The Serbs had meanwhile been advancing south after starting their offensive on 20 October. The Turks hoped to check the Serbs at Kumanovo, but the Serbs broke this covering force on 24 October and pushed on to the Babuna Pass near Prilep. Here the Turks made a major effort and temporarily halted the Serbs, pulling back only when a double enveloping movement through the flanking hills threatened to cut off the Turks in Skoplje. The Turks saw the threat in sufficient time to react, and pulled back towards

Monastir, where hitherto separate forces were reunited to give the Turks a field strength of some 40,000 men. On 5 November the Battle of Monastir was fought, the Serbs starting with a divisional effort to secure the high ground dominating the Turkish left flank.

The Turks retook the high ground after boosting their left wing with troops from the centre of the front, virtually destroying the Serb division. But the weakened Turkish centre was then wholly incapable of sustaining a determined assault by the main body of Serbs. It had also become clear that the Greeks were advancing from the south, and the Turkish effort disintegrated with

the loss of some 20,000 men killed or captured.

The Greeks had meanwhile reached Salonika where on 9 November the garrison of 20,000 Turks surrendered as the Greeks were preparing for an all-out assault. The Bulgars arrived one day after the Greeks under Constantinos had occupied Salonika, and the dispute between the two allies for this city considerably soured relations between them. The Turks had

Artillery played a decisive part in opening the way for offensives, and also proved vital in the static warfare that dominated the closing stages of the Balkan wars.

Above: The victorious Montenegrins enter Scutari after its surrender by the Turks.

now lost the bulk of their previous possessions in Europe, the only remaining Turkish forces being to the west of Vardar being the garrisons of Yannina, besieged by the Greeks, and Scutari (now Shkoder), besieged by the Montenegrins. The other European powers were highly concerned about developments in the Balkans, and between 17 December 1912 and 13 January 1913 a peace conference convened in London: all parties were represented, but the combatants remained intractable and the conference collapsed.

The dire results of Turkish operations had led to considerable unrest in the western portion of the Ottoman Empire and on 23 January 1913 the Turkish administration in Constantinople was overthrown by the Young Turk nationalist party. Its leader, Enver Bey, denounced the ceasefire of 3 December, and hostilities were resumed. That this was a rash move by the new regime was soon proved by the Greek capture of Yannina and its 30,000-man garrison on 3 March,

the combined Bulgarian and Serbian capture of Adrianople and its 60,000-man garrison under Shukri Pasha on 26 March, and the capture of Scutari by the

Below: Like artillery, the machine-gun also played a dominant part in the Balkan wars and helped to halt mobile warfare in favour of semi-static operations.

Macedonia has many inhospitable features, and picks, shovels and hard work often turned these into useful defensive positions.

Montenegrins on 22 April, just six days after the supporting Serbs had fallen out with the Montenegrins and returned home.

This time the defeat of Turkish arms could not be ignored and on 30 May 1913 the Treaty of London brought the First Balkan War to an end: imposed by the great powers, this treaty deprived Turkey of all its European possessions but the Gallipoli and Chatalja peninsulas, but failed to apportion the spoils between the victors. This latter omission produced quarrels amongst the victorious allies about the division of Macedonia, with the Greeks and Serbs siding with each other

against the Bulgars. In addition, Montenegro was compelled to give up Scutari to newly independent Albania.

Thus the forced conclusion of the First Balkan War inevitably created the Second Balkan War. Bulgaria now fielded five armies and was determined to gain what it thought should be Bulgaria's rightful spoils. From west to east the Bulgarians arrayed their 1st Army between Vidin and Borkovitsa, their 5th Army to the south-east of Borkovitsa, their 3rd Army around Kyustendil, their 4th Army about Koccani and Radaviste (now Radovic), and their 2nd Army between Strumitsa (now Strumica) and Serres (now Serrai).

Against this the allies deployed the Serbian 2nd Army along the original Serb–Bulgar frontier, the Serbian 1st Army between Kumanova and Kriva Palanka, the Serbian 3rd Army along the Bregalnica river, and the Greek army between the lower Vardar and the mouth of the Struma river.

The Bulgarians did not bother with any declaration of war and on 30 May 1913 launched their 3rd and 4th Armies in a push towards the Vardar where they attacked the Serbians, together with an advance portion of the Greek army. The Bulgarians broke through the allied forward positions but, under the strategic leadership of Putnik, the allies had anticipated the Bulgarian effort and arranged their defences in depth to soak up the momentum of the Bulgarian advance. By 30 June the Bulgarians had been checked completely, and on 2 July the allies counter-attacked. The Serbian 3rd Army pinned the Bulgarians along the line of the upper Bregalnica, allowing the Serbian 1st Army to break through the Bulgarians' shallow defences and drive on towards Kyustendil. This Serbian advance

threatened to encircle a large part of the Bulgarian forces, and the Bulgars thus fell back to the north-east. The Greek army joined the offensive on 3 July, pushing back the Bulgarian 2nd Army and outflanking the Bulgarian left to allow an advance up the valley of the Struma.

The Bulgarians' position was precarious and became more so when a counter-move by the Bulgarian 3rd and 4th Armies against the Serbian 3rd Army was defeated on 10 July. These Bulgarian reverses were inevitably tempting to Bulgaria's other enemies in the region, and in July the Rumanians and Turks took a hand. Rumania declared war on

15 July and advanced against negligible opposition towards Sofia, the Bulgarian capital. At the same time the Turks also swept forward from the Chatalja Line and Bulair (now Bolayr) to retake Adrianople, lost to them in the First Balkan War. Bulgaria saw that the writing was on the wall and sued for peace in mid-July. Hostilities were ended by the Treaty of Bucharest on 10 August 1913, Bulgaria ceding all its gains in the First Balkan War.

Serbian soldiers keep abreast of developments, but like all soldiers they were right to be sceptical of the official line.

The Czech republic came into being on 14 November 1918 under the presidency of Jan Masaryk. The old provinces of Bohemia and Moravia had been military and industrial mainstays of the Austro-Hungarian empire and Czechoslovakia was thus well placed to defend its new-found independence. The first war in which the new republican found itself embroiled was an internal conflict against the ethnic Germans of Bohemia and Moravia, living in two major areas that declared themselves the Deutschböhmen and Sudentanland districts of Austria. The two regions were unconnected territorially with each other and did not border Austria, so this effort was speedily crushed by the Czech army after minimal bloodshed.

Czechoslovakia's first international war was thus that with Hungary, whose communist leadership sought to divert domestic attention and spread communism with its invasion of Slovakia, nominally under Hungarian rule but in the process of losing its purely Slovak regions to Czechoslovakia. The Hungarian invasion started on 28 March 1919

but Czech units were speedily despatched to Slovakia and after the Hungarians had been expelled during April 1919, Slovakia was fully incorporated into the new Czechoslovakia, declaring a short-lived Soviet republic on 16 June 1919.

A slightly longer-lived dispute was that with Poland for the Teschen (now Tesin) region of Moravia: in November 1918 the Poles had seized the area, being driven out in January 1919 by Czech army units. The two countries came close to war in May 1919, but the conflict remained sporadic as the Allies arbitrated the quarrel, in May 1920 deciding that Teschen should be divided between Czechoslovakia and Poland.

Hungary had been proclaimed an independent republic on 16 November 1919 when Graf Michael Karolyi emerged victorious from a brief revolution and became Hungary's first president. However, in March 1920 Karolyi's regime collapsed under external threat by Czechoslovakia and Allied threats designed to force Hungary's cession of border territories and was replaced by a communist

regime under Bela Kun, who had been sent into Hungary for just this purpose by Lenin. Shortly after this the Rumanians used the pretext of Hungary's desire to reclaim Transylvania as the reason for an invasion of Hungary on 10 April. The Hungarians fought with increasing skill and determination, but were unable to check the Rumanians (supported to the south by French and Yugoslav forces, who made small advances before halting on 28 April) before the Rumanians called a temporary halt on 20 July 1919.

Meanwhile in the Treaty of Trianon, signed on 4 June 1919, the Hungarians had accepted in full the provisions of the Treaties of Versailles and St Germain. Bela Kun fled on 1 August 1919, being replaced by the more moderate socialist administration of Gyula Peidl, but the Rumanians occupied Buda-Pest on 4 August, thereafter behaving in a completely disorderly fashion until their withdrawal from Hungary in November 1919.

Following this there was a period of internal disorder in Hungary until the assumption of power by Admiral Miklos Horthy on 1 March 1920.

THE GREEK CIVIL WAR (1943-49)

The need to support Italy in the Balkans was one of the reasons for the German invasion of Greece and Yugoslavia in April 1941, though greater strategic importance was attached to the need to secure the Axis powers' right flank before the invasion of the USSR in June 1941. Greece was in German hands by the end of April, but the growth of the Greek resistance movement in the months and years ahead showed that Germany most decidedly had not pacified the country.

Operations against the Germans were maintained, despite reprisals of a totally brutal nature, by the antartes (irregular units) which were controlled for the most part by the ELAS (National Popular Liberation Army), the military wing of the EAM (National Liberation Movement), itself the resistance wing of the KKE (Greek communist party).

From 1943, however, there was increasing friction between communists and anti-communist resistance forces, and despite the

efforts of British liaison officers these politically opposed guerrillas were soon more concerned with defeating each other than with combating the Germans. The Germans began to pull back from Greece as the Soviet advances through the Balkans threatened to cut them off, and ELAS prepared to assume the reins of power. However, the communists were beaten to the punch by the British, who re-established the legal administration of Greece and, in decisive fighting in the Athens and

British paratroops in Athens as part of the Allied effort to ensure the return of democratic government to Greece after the Germans pulled out.

Piraeus areas, effectively crushed the current operational strength of the ELAS between 3 December 1944 and 11 January 1945.

The British military victory did nothing to undo the political strength of the KKE in the country, and the ELAS remnants pulled back to recuperate in the mountains. The democratic government set about the process of re-forming the Greek army, and after a plebiscite the monarchy was restored on 1 September 1945 in the person of King Georgios II. By the early summer of 1946, however, the KKE felt that it was once more in a position to intervene militarily: the ELAS had been reconstituted as the DSE (Democratic Army of Greece), and its main strength under General 'Markos' Vaphiades was now available for operations against the Greek army in the Pindos mountains (forming the backbone

of mainland Greece to the west of the Plain of Thessaly), Macedonia, and Thrace.

These primary groupings had all the advantages of fighting from virtually inaccessible mountain strongholds that now had to operationally significant advantages of being backed against the friendly communist states of Bulgaria, Yugoslavia, and

Albania. The DSE was thus able to secure control over Greece's main border regions in the north, though extremely bitter fighting was reported in the lower reaches of the Axios river (as the Vardar is

The British effort to support the Greek resistance forces had grown considerably since 1940, and in 1944 uniforms were added to the list.

Greek infantry of the 25th Brigade in a forward position against the communist guerrillas near the Bulgarian frontier in 1948.

named after crossing the frontier from Yugoslavia into Greece) separating eastern Macedonia and Thrace from the rest of Greece. And while the DSE began to create the beginnings of a communist state in these northern regions, it kept the Greek government off balance with actions that were virtually sacrificial by the units located at the southern end of the Pindos mountains, the Peloponnesos, Evvoia, the western end of Crete, and the islands of Khios and

Lesbos. The UK was able to further a measure of support for the Greek government, but the insularity of the Attlee administration combined with Britain's desperate economic position to terminate this effort in the spring of 1947. A United Nations investigation had already condemned Albania, Yugoslavia, and Bulgaria for their support of the Greek communists and on 12 March 1947 the USA announced the Truman Doctrine of military and economic aid for both Greece

and Turkey to fight internal and external communist aggression.

US weapons and US training teams soon began to restore the initiative to the Greek army, which by the end of 1947 had restored democratic control to all of Greece with the exception of the areas bordering Greece's communist neighbours. Then on

176

1 January 1948 the Greek army relieved Konitsa, the important garrison close to the Albanian border that had long been under siege. The DSE forces fell back into Albania, regrouped and launched another offensive against Konitsa on 25 January, but were decisively beaten.

In June the Greek army started a major offensive designed to eliminate the DSE's last mountain strongholds, but this effort was only successful in part: heavy fighting continued for several months in the region around Mount Grammos to the north of Konitsa on the Albanian frontier.

However, from 28 June the position of the DSE had begun to worsen as a result of the rift between Yugoslavia and the USSR on that date. Yugoslavia was expelled from the Comintern, and rapidly began to scale down its support for the DSE. This effectively divided the Greek communist effort into two portions bolstered in the north-west by Albania and in the north-east by Bulgaria.

On 31 January 1949 Vaphiades was replaced as head of the DSE by General Nikos Zakhariadis, but this modification of the communist command structure could do little

to ameliorate the DES's position, which became impossible with the fall of Mount Grammos on 28 August 1949. The Greek Civil War ended on 16 October 1949. The communists had lost about 38,000 dead and 40,000 captured or surrendered, while the Greek army's losses have been quoted as 12,777 dead, 37,732 wounded, and 4,527 missing. Civilian deaths included 4,289 (including 165 priests) executed by the communists.

The nature of the terrain dictated the largely non-mechanized nature of the Greek Civil war.

MIDDLE AND NEAR EASTERN CONFLICTS

PALESTINE AND THE 1st ARAB-ISRAELI WAR (1920-49)

After World War I the Ottoman possessions between Syria and Egypt became the British mandated territory of Palestine. The Balfour Declaration of 1917 had promised the establishment of separate Arab and Jewish states in the region, and much effort had to be devoted to policing this volatile region as additional Jews arrived to bolster the number already in the area. There was considerable political disturbance during the early 1920s and in 1923 the UK split off the portion east of the

Jordan river as Trans-Jordan, a kingdom ruled by King Abdullah.

Nevertheless the disturbances continued in Palestine and between 1936 and 1939 there occurred a major Arab rebellion directed more at the Jews than the British. Considerable force had to be used to restore order and many thousands of lives were lost in the inter-communal fighting between the mainly urban Arabs and rural Jews. Although World War II reduced the level of hostility slightly, there were still frequent

From men such as this Ageyl bodyguard in World War I there evolved the Arab Legion, the most capable force pitted against the Israelis in the 1st Arab-Israeli War.

conflicts. From 1945 increasing numbers of European Jews began to arrive in Palestine and from this time onwards it was mainly the Zionist Jews who became responsible for the increasing violence in the area, directed equally against the Arabs and the British. The scale of the violence escalated steadily from 1945 to 1947, the more extreme Jews hoping in this way to cause a mass exodus of the Arabs and to force the British to pull out of the promised Jewish homeland that much more quickly.

On 29 November 1947 the General Assembly of the United Nations decided that the only feasible solution to the steadily worsening conflict between the Palestinian Arabs and the Jews was a partition of Palestine into separate Jewish and Palestinian states, effective from 1 October 1948. The Jews accepted the proposal, but the Palestinian Arabs and the Arab states supporting them adamantly refused to consider such a proposal, stating categorically that they would fight if the UN proposal was implemented.

Exasperated by the local situation and the terrorist methods of the Jews, the UK surrendered

its mandate of Palestine on 14 May 1948, and the Jewish homeland became independent as the state of Israel. It was immediately recognized by the USA and invaded by the Arab troops of Egypt, Iraq, Jordan, Lebanon, and Syria. The fact that the Arabs would undertake such an effort had been clear to the Jews for some years, and the small nation had prepared itself to resist such a move.

Despite their enormous numerical and *matériel* superiority over the Israelis, with the exception of Jordan's British-trained Arab Legion the Arab forces fared incredibly badly: from the north and north-east Iraqi, Lebanese, and Syrian forces invaded and were repulsed; from the east the Jordanians tried to isolate the Israeli positions in and around Jerusalem; and from the south-west the Egyptians invaded and were firmly repulsed. The

most important battle in this early stage of the war was for Jerusalem, which was held jointly by the Israelis and Jordanians. This Israeli garrison of the Old city surrendered to the Arab Legion after a bitter 11-day siege on 28 May, while the Arab Legion was driven from modern Jerusalem but managed to isolate the city from the rest of Israel.

Count Folke Bernadotte of Sweden was appointed as UN mediator on 20 May and on 11 June he managed to secure a four-week ceasefire, a UN ceasefire patrol arriving on 20 June. On 8 July the Arabs resumed their efforts with armoured offensives into northern and southern Israel as the Israelis strove desperately

A shipload of illegal Jewish immigrants to Palestine emphasize a banner designed to ease their arrival on the new Jewish homeland.

to relieve their isolated forces in Jerusalem. The main Arab threat was that of the Egyptian column directed against Tel Aviv, the Israeli capital, but on 13 July this was beaten back at about the time that land communications with Jerusalem were restored, and on 16 July the Jordanians secured a ceasefire in Jerusalem.

There were general ceasefires between 18 July and 15 August, and between October and December, but in general the Israelis had the strategic upper hand and advanced as when they pleased within the constraints of their limited logistic capabilities. On 3 January 1949 they launched a small but telling invasion of Egypt, calling it off on 5 January in response to repeated UN calls for an armistice. In the course of

this extraordinary war the Israelis had recaptured all the territory allocated to them by the UN, taken in the initial Arab advances, and then during their offensive phases taken the Palestinian pocket in northern Palestine adjacent to Lebanon, driven a corridor to Jerusalem through the Jordanian territories on the west bank of the Jordan, nibbled away other useful portions of the West Bank, and decisively reduced the Palestinian area in and to the south of the Gaza Strip adjacent to Egypt.

Between January and July negotiations were conducted on the island of Rhodes under UN auspices, resulting in armistices with Egypt on 23 February, Jordan on 3 April, and Syria on 20 July. No Arab country was willing to

end its formal state of war with Israel, however, and together with a massive exodus of Palestinian refugees from Israel this laid up greater trouble for the future. In May 1950 Egypt closed the Suez Canal to Israel, from 5 to 16 April 1953 there was a period of intense border hostilities with Syria and from 1953 to 1956 there were an increasing number of border incidents and Palestinian raids into Israel, resulting in heightened tension and Israeli counter-raids against the Palestinian camps and the growing Palestinian strength in Egypt, Jordan, Lebanon, and Syria.

Casualties are carried out of a hotel bombed by the Jewish underground in an effort to speed the British withdrawal from Palestine.

BULGARIA

Komotini

Xanthi

Drama

Aegean Sea

Naxos

Tinos

Andros

CRETE

Iraklion

Sea of Crete

Canea

Larissa

Corinth

Piraeus Athens

GREECE

Trikkala

Kalamai

Jannina

ALBANIA

Ionian Sea

YUGOSLAVIA

Split

Dubrovnik

BULGARIA

Burgas

Sofia

Plovdiv

Thessaloniki

Bitola

Skopje

Nis

Tirane

ALBANIA

GREECE

Aegean Sea

TURKEY

Rhodes

Dodecanese Islands

Greece

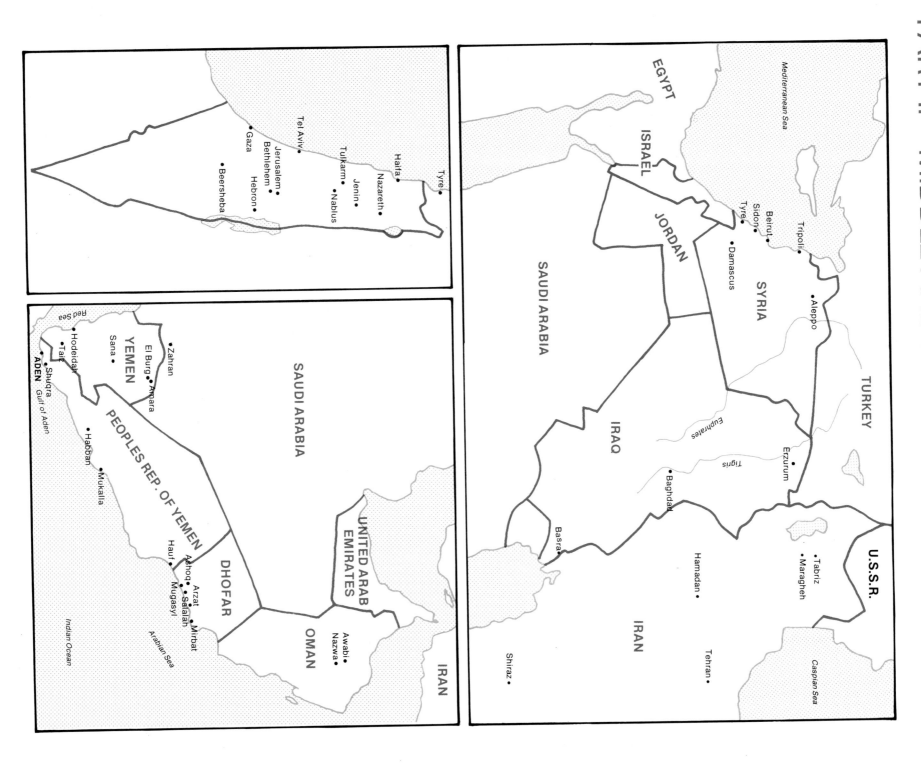

THE WAR IN DHOFAR (1962-75)

By the Treaty of Sib, signed in 1920, the Sultan of Oman was recognized as overlord to the various tribal chiefs of Oman, though the right of the inland tribes to choose their own *imam* (religious leader) was recognized at the same time.

In 1962 there broke out a major rebellion against the Sultan of Oman in the far south-western province of Dhofar. Many of the Omanis who had come into contact with the Western oil-drilling crews were beginning to realize that Oman in general, and Dhofar in particular, could enjoy greater material benefits than the sultan seemed prepared to allow from the country's increasing revenues.

On this basis of dissatisfaction Musallim bin Nuffl was able to build: Dhofar is a large area, though most of its population of 150,000 was clustered in the fertile and well-watered coastal strip which was connected to the sparse inland region to the north of the mountains by a single jeep road to Thumrayt, where it forked into mere tracks to Fasad in the north-west and to Dawqah and Muqshin in the north-east. For the first three years the rebellion secured only limited success, in 1965 redesignating itself the Dhofar Liberation Front and beginning to receive additional support from the communist forces in Aden, to the south-west of Dhafar.

But in 1967 the British pulled out of Aden, and the way was opened for the DLF to receive more substantial support from the Marxist People's Democratic Republic of the Yemen (South Yemen) as Aden had now become. In 1968 Nuffl was ousted and his place was taken by Ahmad al Ghassani as head of the PFLOAG (People's Front for the Liberation of the Occupied Arabian Gulf), an organization financed and supported by the USSR and China. By 1970 the PFLOAG had made considerable gains and controlled virtually all of Dhofar but the towns of Mirbat, Salalah, and Taqa.

The sultan was indeed a feudal overlord and this was recognized as the primary cause for complaint in most parts of Oman. On 23 July 1970 the sultan was deposed by his son, Qaboos bin Said, who immediately set about the modernization of the whole country while enlarging and revitalizing the armed forces with considerable British support. In the short term troops were brought in from India, Jordan, and Pakistan, and the gains of the PFLOAG were stopped almost immediately.

The fighting was protracted and costly before the campaign was declared officially closed on 11 December 1975. The Omani forces eventually scored a decisive success through interdiction of the PFLOAG's single line of communication from South Yemen, the use of helicopters for tactical mobility that could not be matched by the PFLOAG, and the resistance of most Moslems to the apparent blandishments of the Marxist creed. In addition there was the innate loyalty of the Dhofar tribes to a sultan who took immediate steps to develop the province with a steadily accelerating programme of modernization.

LEBANON AND THE 5th ARAB-ISRAELI WAR OR OPERATION 'PEACE FOR GALILEE' (1958-)

Lebanon became independent in 1946 when British and French troops were withdrawn. Though Lebanon had been a semi-autonomous region of the Ottoman Empire, after World War I the French created the modern Lebanon by combining the predominantly Christian area of Turkish Lebanon with the predominantly Moslem area farther north along the eastern littoral of the Mediterranean. This produced a somewhat artificial country with about equal numbers of Christian and Moslems, but the fact that the Christians held the economic and political upper hand inevitably produced friction between the two groupings, of whom the Moslems were supported by Syria. Between 1946 and 1958 a precarious peace was maintained, the most untoward incident being a quickly suppressed rebellion in July 1949.

By the late 1950s both the Christians and the Moslems were becoming weary of the Maronite Christian administration of President Camille Chamoun, who had fallen foul of both groupings for his support of France and the UK in the Suez campaign of 1956, and for the political manoeuvrings designed to extend his presidency beyond its legal term.

In May 1958 the Moslems of Tripoli rose against the Chamoun government, being joined rapidly by the Moslems of Beirut and Sidon, and by the Shi'a Moslems of the Baalbek region. Syrian forces occupied several border regions in support of the Moslems rebels, and Chamoun called for American military support to put down the rebellion.

US Marines landed in Beirut on 15 July as part of an American effort not so much to bolster Chamoun as to prevent a communist Arab take-over of Lebanon. The US troops stabilized the situation and curtailed the rebellion, allowing the withdrawal of the 14,300 Americans between 21 August and 25 October. Sporadic fighting continued over the first part of the American involvement, but the replacement of Chamoun by General Chehab during September marked the effective end of the Moslem rising.

There followed a period of peace and enormous economic growth before trouble again flared in April 1975, this time between the right-wing Christian Phalangist party and various left-wing Moslem groups. The superficial cause of the friction was again the Moslem's desire to share the economic and political power of the Christians, but the Christians were equally worried by the presence in the Moslem areas of some 200,000 Palestinian refugees, who formed virtually a state within the state, and whose raids into northern Israel led to retaliation that seemed to hit the Palestinians and Lebanese alike. Sectarian fighting began in Tripoli during March 1975, and by April had spread to densely populated Beirut.

On 15 May the government of Rashid Solh resigned, to be replaced by a military administration that lasted a mere three days. It was only on 30 June that President Franjieh was able to form a new administration under Rashid Karami. However, this government proved itself as powerless as its predecessors to end the fighting and the position was exacerbated from October when the Palestinian Liberation Organization, which had hitherto played a limited peacekeeping role between the two sides, swayed in

Top: US Marines storm ashore on a beach near Beirut as part of the 1958 landings to restore order to troubled Lebanon.

Left: The Israeli camp at Anjar in 1982: here were lodged many of the Palestinians whose raids into Israel prompted the invasion of Lebanon.

favour of the Moslems and entered the battle for control of Beirut. By January 1976 the war had settled to a pattern in which the Phalangists blockaded Moslem and Palestinian areas while the Moslems and, increasingly, the Palestinians, raided the largely Christian settlements on the coast.

Syria managed to impose a ceasefire on 22 January 1976, but on 13 March the fighting resumed. On 1 June the Syrians intervened militarily, advancing into the Bekaa valley against determined opposition from the Palestinians. Then on 21 October there came into effect a ceasefire agreed on 17 October at a meeting of Egyptian, Lebanese, Palestinian, Saudi Arabian, and Syrian leaders at Riyadh.

The ceasefire was policed by an Arab Deterrent Force comprising mainly Syrian troops. This ended a 19-month period of civil war that had cost 45,000 dead and 100,000 wounded as well as driving about 500,000 people to emigration.

The ceasefire could not last as the causes of friction remained unaltered and fighting again broke out during 1977, starting in February round Marjayoun just to the south of the Litani river in southern Lebanon. The fighting lasted all through the summer, the Christians being supported by Israeli armour and artillery. And in March the Druze leader Kamal Jumblatt was assassinated, prompting a series of Druze raids against Christian villages, in turn prompting Christian counter-raids.

The process continued and indeed increased during 1978: key features were: clashes between the Syrians and right-wing Lebanese during February; a full-scale Israeli invasion of southern Lebanon in March to destroy PLO bases (resulting in 1,000 dead, and the flight to the north of 200,000 Lebanese and 65,000 Palestinians); the separation of the Israelis and Lebanese by a United Nations force in late March; Syrian artillery bombardments of Beirut during July and August in response to the murder of the pro-Syrian son of ex-president Franjieh; and finally a Syrian-imposed ceasefire around Beirut in mid-August, leading to a slow but only partial withdrawal of Syrian troops around Beirut.

The same pattern of events was repeated in 1979 and 1980, the most notable alteration being the increasing presence of Israeli forces on the ground in southern Lebanon and in the air over central Lebanon in retaliation for PLO raids on Israel and in support of the pro-Israeli enclave of 'Free Lebanon' established along the Israeli frontier by Major Sa'ad Haddad.

Israeli forces on the move through southern Lebanon met increasingly severe resistance as they closed up on Beirut.

But by 1981 Israel was coming to the end of its patience with the PLO and with the Lebanese who allowed the PLO to operate from their country. During the second half of the year the Israelis planned Operation 'Peace for Galilee', a major effort into Lebanon designed to crush the PLO once and for all, and to force the Lebanese to expel the PLO. This 5th Arab–Israeli War was committed on 6 June 1982, with about nine divisions containing 90,000 troops and 1,300 tanks.

The offensive was generally condemned throughout the world, and this condemnation intensified as the offensive failed to make the same rapid progress as earlier

Israeli offensives. The campaign turned into a slogging match, and it was 15 September before the Israelis entered west Beirut. However, from 22 August the PLO had started to leave Lebanon in a process that continued to 1 October and effectively ended the PLO presence in Lebanon. British, French, Italian, and US peacekeeping contingents were delivered into Beirut, but these left quite quickly after the French and US contingents had suffered heavy casualties and after their governments had come to appreciate that the continuing internecine warfare between Christian and Moslem factions in Beirut was not amenable to

The already desperate situation in many Lebanese cities was compounded by the arrival of the Israelis and additional destruction.

international mediation efforts. The Israelis have also withdrawn, leaving the Syrians to impose a purely military solution to Beirut and other major centres. Sporadic fighting continues, together with a horrific toll of civilian victims or artillery fire, small arms fire, and devastating car bombs. The Syrians have managed to force a limited peace on the area, but there still appears to be no permanent solution in sight as the local militias seek superiority over each other.

THE WAR FOR KURDISH INDEPENDENCE (1961-)

The total number of Kurds is about 8.5 million and these semi-nomadic peoples occupy the area where Iran, Iraq, Syria, Turkey, and the USSR meet. In 1920 the Kurds were guaranteed self-determination by the Treaty of Sèvres, superseded in 1923 by the Treaty of Lausanne, but the governments under which the Kurds live have generally ignored these international agreements. The Kurds have long harboured a fierce determination to secure at least semi-autonomy if not a national homeland, and this resulted in numerous risings in the 1920s and 1930s.

In 1942 the Mullah Mustafa Barzani, leader of the Democratic Party of Kurdistan, secured a promise of autonomy from the Iraqi government, in whose country live some 1.5 million of the most militant Kurds. The Iraqi authorities immediately reneged on the deal and so provoked a two-year war that cost the Kurds heavy casualties. Barzani was forced to flee, eventually finding sanctuary in the USSR. After the death of King Faisal II in 1958, the new government of Brigadier Kassem allowed Barzani to return home. But relations soon soured, and by September 1961 the Kurds had secured a 250-miles (400-km) front between Zakho on the Iraqi/Turkish frontier and Sulaymaniyah on the Iraqi/Iranian frontier, the Iraqis responding with a major offensive, claimed as fully victorious for the Iraqis by 10 October.

Though the Kurds had lost 3,000 dead and 120,000 made homeless in the destruction of 270 villages and small towns, the front was still secure. A stalemate followed and after Colonel Aref replaced Kassem, who was shot on 8 February 1963, autonomy was again promised but then again denied to the Kurds. The war flared up again, the Iraqis fielding four divisions against an estimated 15,000 to 20,000 Kurds. The fighting was extremely bitter and Barzani later claimed that the Kurds had lost 167 villages. Yet the Kurds held their own and in November the Iraqis requested a ceasefire. Talks began in January 1964 and the agreement signed on 10 February formalized the ceasefire and promised both autonomy and amnesty for the Kurds, who were hardly confident of yet more Iraqi promises.

The nationalist demands of the Kurdish people have engendered powerful demands on manpower and emotion, and brought even children into the conflict.

On 3 April the Iraqis resumed the war, committing some 50,000 men on the 250-mile front between Zakho and Khanaqin on the Iraqi–Iranian frontier. The Kurds pulled back into the relative safety of the mountains, launching raids and ambushes as the government forces attempted to follow them. Another ceasefire was agreed on 29 June 1966 and yet again the Kurds prepared for an Iraqi offensive once they had recuperated. This offensive was delayed by the overthrow of the administration in favour of a regime headed by General Bakr, who undertook fresh but fruitless negotiations with the Kurds before launching his forces in another

offensive in October 1968. This failed to prosper and was called off, but the Iraqis made another effort in January 1969, some 60,000 men being launched on a 200-mile (320-km) front. Some gains were made by the Iraqis, who were then surprised by a Kurd counter-offensive that included an artillery bombardment of oil installations at Kirkuk.

By the time peace talks were resumed in January 1970, the front had swayed back and forward considerably, the Kurds alleging that the government forces had used napalm and nitric acid bombs against civilian areas. The agreement of 11 March ending this phase of the war again

guaranteed Kurdish autonomy. Some moves towards the implementation of the agreement were made, but the effort finally foundered on questions such as possession of Kirkuk and its oilfields, the government again launching its forces in an offensive on 12 March 1974: the offensive was launched close to Iraq's border with Turkey, but the Kurds soon seized the initiative and spread the campaign to the whole width of the front with Iraq, by 18 April reaching the plains only 70 miles (115 km) from Baghdad.

Equipped with elderly weapons, the Kurdish forces have fought with discipline and courage.

But between April and July the government got the better of the Kurdish offensive and in August launched their largest offensive of the war, including the forward deployment of at least 300 tanks. Some 130,000 Kurds fled into Iran but in early 1975 the Iraqis and Iranians concluded an agreement whereby the latter ceased support for the Kurds. Thus the government offensive of 7 March 1975 met only limited resistance.

In May 1976 the fighting broke out again, this time as a result of the Kurds' anger that refugees returning from Iran were forcibly resettled in southern Iraq as part of the government's policy of diluting Kurdish strength in the north. The fighting grew steadily more intense and in March 1977 the Iraqis undertook a major effort that continued into September 1980, when the outbreak of the Gulf War diverted Iraqi attention

The Kurds lack the logistic infrastructure for an advanced army, but have proved themselves well able to blunt the Iraqis' assaults.

to the Iranians. It is probable that the conclusion of the Gulf War (whenever that apparently unlikely event occurs) will see a resurgence of the Iraqi effort against the Kurds, who from February 1988 once again came under heavy attack.

THE WAR IN THE YEMEN (1962-69)

Yemen (often called North Yemen to differentiate it from South Yemen) became independent of the Ottoman Empire in 1918 and was ruled by the Imam Yahya from 1904 to 1948. Yahya was assassinated in 1948 and succeeded by his son the Imam Ahmed, who followed his father's feudal policies and maintained the exclusion of foreigners, but slowly inaugurated the process of bringing his country into the 20th century. Ahmed's son, the Crown Prince Mohammed al Badr was

sent to Cairo and there secured the despatch of an Egyptian military mission to retrain the Yemeni army on modern lines. This also allowed President Gamal Abdal Nasser to introduce Egyptian agents into this strategic country on the south-east coast of the Gulf of Suez.

These agents primed Yemeni revolutionaries for an overthrow of the regime and their chance came with the death of the Imam Ahmed on 18 September 1962. An attempt was made on al Badr's life

just eight days later in the palace at Sana, but the Yemeni ruler escaped to the north and the strongholds of the royalist faction. In the south the leader of the coup, Brigadier Abdullah Sallal, declared himself president of the new Yemeni republic. Egyptian support was rapidly forthcoming and by April 1963 Sallal's regime was bolstered by some 30,000 Egyptian troops, who controlled the coastal plain, south Yemen, and the main lines of communication from Sana.

The royalists held the mountain areas in north, east, and central Yemen, and received increasing support from Saudi Arabia, which was extremely worried about this Egyptian and communist penetration into the Arabian peninsula. The war was dominated by Egyptian air power but after the 'Six-Day War' of 1967 Egypt began to scale down its massive commitment in Yemen, which had peaked at 70,000 or more men, and the royalists began to hold their own and make limited advances. There followed a stalemate that continued even after the overthrow of Sallal in November 1967. In 1969 King Feisal of Saudi Arabia arranged a peace conference that resulted in the formation of a coalition government of pro-Western leanings.

Top: A Yemeni royalist truck column on parade, the flatbeds being used to mount weapons up to 75-mm calibre.

Right: Amir El Hassan, the Yemeni crown prince and prime minister (foreground), shows three of his men the intricacies of a Soviet 82-mm mortar captured from the Egyptians.

ASIAN CONFLICTS

THE BOXER REBELLION (1900-01)

In the closing stages of the 19th century the Great Powers made ruthless use of their military superiority over the Chinese to secure territorial concessions and economic advantages in the Chinese market. The effect was a marked increase in anti-foreign sentiment amongst the Chinese, the most fanatical of the anti-foreign organizations being the Society of Righteous Harmonious Fists (or Boxers, as they were known to Westerners). The immediate targets for the fury of the Boxers were Western missionaries and their converts, and all over China there were massacres of these hapless and defenceless people.

The powers complained to the government of the Dowager Empress Tzu Hsi, which claimed that it lacked the physical and moral capability to prevent these depradations, whereas in fact it was inciting and supporting the violence by all means at its disposal. Given the fact that the internal situation in China was becoming less and less stable, the powers began to build up a naval force at Tientsin, the port of Peking, during June 1900 and sent an allied force of 485 troops to bolster the legation guards in Peking.

In the first days of June the situation worsened still further, and on 10 June the allies, under the command of the British

A public execution during the Boxer Rebellion as a Chinese man is beheaded in front of European troops.

Admiral E. H. Seymour, sent a first relief force towards Peking. Some 2,000 men were despatched, but these met a vastly superior Chinese force at Yang T'su and returned to their ships off Tientsin by 26 June after suffering 300 casualties. On 17 June the Taku Forts guarding the entrance to the river at Tientsin had been captured after a naval bombardment, the Chinese having responded to an allied ultimatum by shelling the allied ships.

The situation at Peking became desperate on 20 June, when the Chinese mob murdered the German minister, Klemens Graf von Kettler, and invested the legation area. Extraordinary ingenuity and courage were used in the defence of the legations by the small allied forces available, and allied forces were despatched to Tientsin for a relief expedition. On 23 July Tientsin was taken by the expeditionary force of 5,000 men, who stormed the walls of the port city, and eventually the expeditionary force numbered 4,800 Russians, 3,000 British, 2,500 US, and 800 French troops within an overall strength of 18,700 men. No overall commander was appointed, decisions being reached by a consultative process.

This second relief expedition set off towards Peking on 4 August, moving along the line of the railway and river. The Chinese interposed a force of 10,000 men, but these were decisively beaten in the Battle of Yang T'sun on 5 and 6 August. The French contingent was detached at this position to guard the allied line of communication while the rest of the relief expedition pushed on through indifferent opposition to reach the walls of Peking on 13 August. The Russians, in the van, launched an immediate assault on the Tung Pien Gate, but were repulsed.

On 14 August a combined effort

This breach in the walls of Peking was made to allow a rail line to be run into the city during the China Relief Expedition's occupation.

LEST WE FORGET

A corner of the British legation in Peking after the end of the Boxer rebellion.

Field Marshal Alfred Alfred Graf von Waldersee.

secured Peking for the allies: the Japanese tried to storm Ch'i Hua Gate but failed, while the Russians and Americans took the Tung Pien Gate and the British waded under the wall by the Water Gate. The allies then drove through Peking to relieve the legation staffs, finally pinned in the British compound after their eight-week siege. The relief expedition also rescued the defenders of the P'ei Tang compound round the Roman Catholic cathedral, where 40 French and Italian marines had bolstered the defence based on some 3,000 Chinese Christians. With their primary task now

achieved, the relief expedition turned its attention to the Imperial City on 15 August: US artillery blew open the Ch'i Hua Gate, but rather than further slight the Chinese, the allies delayed their occupation of the city until 28 August. Other allied moves during this period were the Russian occupation of Manchuria between 4 September and 10 October, and between September 1900 and May 1901 a series of punitive forays in the region of Peking, most of them undertaken with extreme bloodiness by the German force that had arrived only on 12 September under the command of

The dowager empress had fled Peking before the arrival of the allies, and from Sian acceded on 26 December 1900 to all the allied demands, which were embodied in the Boxer Protocol signed on 12 September 1901: amongst other things this exacted a vast financial reparation from the Chinese and so laid up an additional source of Chinese resentment for the future.

FAR EASTERN WARS (1911-24)

Apart from the Far Eastern wars discussed above, the two main areas in which military operations were conducted in the period between 1900 and 1925 were the Philippines and the Dutch East Indies.

In August 1896 Emilio Aguinaldo led a Filipino insurrection against Spain, and the rebellion came to a peaceful conclusion when the Spaniards agreed to administrative and social reforms in exchange for the exile of Aguinaldo. Two years later, as part of the US effort against Spain in the Spanish-American War, Commodore George Dewy brought Aguinaldo back to the Philippines to raise a guerrilla force to fight against the Spanish. However, by the Treaty of Paris, signed on 10 December 1910, Spain sold the Philippines to the USA. Aguinaldo believed he had been tricked into supporting the

US effort with promises of Filipino independence and on 20 January 1899 proclaimed the independence of the Philippines and called on his countrymen to recognize the provisional government headed by Aguinaldo and to drive the Americans from the Philippines. Soon the US forces were closely invested in Manila, their single toehold in the Philippines since the end of the Spanish-American War.

The Filipino Insurrection formally began on 4 February 1899 when a US patrol was engaged in the outskirts of Manila. The insurrection rapidly spread through the islands of Luzon and the Visayas, the American counter-effort being controlled in the field by Major General Douglas MacArthur. Aguinaldo was captured by a ruse and this effectively broke the back of the insurrection in the northern islands

by 1902. The Moro campaign against the Moslems of the southern islands (most importantly Jolo and Mindoro) lasted through to 1905, and the Americans had to deploy 100,000 men to the islands. US losses were 4,243 killed and 2,818 wounded, while the Filipinos lost 16,000 killed and perhaps 100,000 dead of famine.

In the East Indies the Dutch fought a bitter and protracted series of campaigns to suppress rebellious local rulers and pirate fleets. The most serious of these lasted from 1873 to 1908 before the Dutch were finally able to overcome the Sultan of Atjeh in December 1907, allowing complete pacification of Sumatra in 1908.

US Marines in typical jungle conditions near Olongapo on a search and destroy mission against the Filipino insurrectionists.

Soviet troops in the fighting for Remizov Hill in the Khalkin-Gol fighting of August 1939.

Tension between Japan and the USSR remained high throughout the 1920s and early 1930s, the legacy of Russia's humiliation at the hands of the Japanese in 1904 and 1905. The situation was worsened by Japan's seizure of Manchuria (which became the puppet state of Manchukuo in 1932) and the fact that the border between the USSR and Japan was only poorly defined.

On 11 July 1938 severe fighting erupted between the Soviets and the Japanese in the area of Changkufeng Hill, near the mouth of the Tyumen river on the eastern border south-west of

Vladivostok. The Soviets had seized this tactically important point and fortified it and in protracted fighting the Japanese were unable to dislodge them before an armistice left the Soviets in possession on 10 August. This was not a reverse that the Japanese could accept, and in May 1939 the Japanese claimed areas of eastern Mongolia occupied by Soviet troops, and launched an offensive designed to take the Nomonhan area along the Khalkin river.

The weight and tactical surprise of the Japanese thrust caught the Soviets off balance, but the ground

they lost was regained during the summer, when three infantry divisions and five tank brigades (as well as a number of Mongolian units) were fed into the area under the command of General Georgi Zhukov: the Japanese were driven out of the disputed areas, suffering some 18,000 casualties before the fighting ended in August.

In June 1940 the two border disputes were settled by treaty.

195

THE WAR OF INDONESIAN INDEPENDENCE, THE INDONESIAN CIVIL WAR AND THE INDONESIAN CONFRONTATION (1945-66)

At the end of World War II the independence of the Dutch East Indies was declared as the Republic of Indonesia on 17 August. The authors of this

proposed independence were Dr. Achmed Sukarno and Mohammed Hatta, who had served in a puppet regime under Japanese rule during World War II and now hoped to

forestall the return of the Netherlands as colonial power. On 29 September, however, British and Indian troops arrived in Batavia (now Djakarta) to begin the process of disarming the Japanese and restoring the islands to the Dutch, whose first troops arrived on 3 October. This persuaded the Indonesian extremists to launch a 'war of liberation' and on 13 October the Indonesian People's Army declared war on the Dutch and, by implicit extension, on those aiding the Dutch.

On 6 November the Indonesians rejected a Dutch offer of dominion status and home rule for Indonesia. Severe fighting raged around the Indonesian capital, Surabaya, for about three weeks before it fell to the British on 29 November 1945, but thereafter the war took the more normal guerrilla pattern once the Indonesians had realized the futility of open battle with the superior weapons of the British, Indian, and Dutch troops. Throughout 1946 the Indonesians kept up the pressure with attacks on guard posts and convoys, and this seemed to be paying off as the British and Indians began to withdraw from the islands in the autumn of 1946. The last British and Indians left on 30 November, their presence having brought the Dutch the time to train and ship out an army that eventually totalled 130,000 men.

The pragmatic Dutch had already concluded, however, that the retention of the Dutch East Indies in their entirety was a task which was beyond the means of

President Sukarno of Indonesia, leader of the nationalist party that secured independence from the Netherlands.

the Netherlands and on 13 November 1946 the Cheribon Agreement recognized the supremacy of the Republic of Indonesia over Java, Madura, and Sumatra, including those areas currently held by the Dutch. On the same day the USA recognized Indonesia, but added the islands of Borneo (now Kalimantan), Celebes (now Sulawesi), Molucca, and Sunda to the area of the new republic. Local disagreement with the terms of the Cheribon arrangement was rife on both sides in the conflict, leading to frequent violations of the ceasefire and on 20 July a resumption of Dutch military operations in Java on the orders of the governor.

The Dutch ignored the United Nations ceasefire order on 4 August and retook most of eastern and central Java. On 19 December Dutch airborne troops took the Javanese capital, Jogiakarta, and by 25 December all of Java was in Dutch hands. Further hostilities followed as the UN attempted to secure a ceasefire and a transfer of sovereignty, the former finally being achieved on 7 May. On 2 November 1949 the Netherlands granted full sovereignty to the United States of Indonesia, and the Republic of Indonesia was declared on 15 August 1950. The war had cost the Dutch

A British patrol on one of the many waterways close to the Sarawak frontier from which the Indonesian forces operated in the 'Confrontation'.

some 25,000 casualties and the Indonesians about 80,000.

The new state now had to face a diverse but determined civil war, the main cause of grievance by the rebels being the government's concentration of effort and finance on Java. A Moslem organization, the Dar'ul Islam, soon made considerable gains, and by 1954 controlled most of western Java, central and southern Sulawesi, Borneo and parts of Sumatra. In February 1958 the rebels declared the Revolutionary Government of the Indonesian Republic, with its capital at Padang in Sumatra. The government forces were now stronger and more ably led, however, and a concerted offensive made considerable inroads into the rebel areas. A campaign of erosion yielded a steady trickle of successes, and by mid-1961 the government reckoned that there were only

17,000 rebels left, perhaps only half of them with weapons. An amnesty was offered, and between April and August most of the rebels surrendered.

Between 1957 and 1963 Indonesia operated a campaign of harassment against the Dutch in West New Guinea, which Indonesia claimed as the province of West Iran. Limited hostilities were undertaken between January

and August 1962, and on 15 August the Dutch agreed to the transfer of West New Guinea to Indonesia on 1 May 1963.

Indonesia still had designs on the portions of Borneo in British hands, but on 16 September 1963

The British made extensive use of helicopters such as this twin-rotor Belvedere to man, supply and reinforce jungle garrison positions.

Above: The Western response to the Boxer Rebellion was an allied effort: here Bengal lancers and German marines engage Chinese troops.

Right: German pioneers storm a defended pass during the Boxer Rebellion.

Preceding page: German sailors and marines storm the Taku Forts, barring the routes to Peking, during the Boxer Rebellion in 1900.

the colonies of Brunei, Sabah, and Sarawak were united with the Federation of Malaya to create the Federation of Malaysia.

Sukarno had already attempted to stir up trouble in Brunei (December 1962) in a rebellion by the North Kalimantan Liberation Army, but with British aid this had been quickly suppressed. This marked the beginning of the so-called Indonesian Confrontation, a small, nasty but undeclared war that lasted into 1966.

The campaign was fought as one of raid, counter-raid and ambush along the frontiers in Borneo (though on 17 August 1964 the Indonesians launched a small and wholly unsuccessful raid against the mainland coast of Malaysia), ending only when President Sukarno was overthrown by a military coup led by General Suharto in March 1966 after violent popular riots against the communists in Indonesia, which cost between 300,000 and 500,000 lives. The Indonesian Confrontation cost 114 British and Gurkha lives, while the Indonesians are thought to have lost about 600 dead.

The morale and performance of British patrols in the jungle were immeasurably improved by air-dropped supplies such as fresh meat.

KASHMIR (1947-49)

At the time of the partition of India in August 1947, the princely state of Kashmir was 80 per cent Moslem but ruled by a Hindu, Maharajah Sir Hari Singh. The Indian leader, Pandit Nehru, advised Singh to play for time, allowing tempers to cool before opting to take Kashmir into union with India. This was not to be as simple as Nehru had planned, for as Singh announced his decision on 26 October 1947, an armed rebellion broke out in Poonch. This was suppressed by Kashmir troops but the government of

Pakistan took the opportunity of local unrest to persuade the strongly Moslem hill tribes of the North-West Frontier region to invade Kashmir in support of their fellow Moslems.

By 24 October the hill tribes and Kashmiri rebels were within 18 miles (29 km) of the capitl, Srinagar, and Singh appealed to India from support. On 27 October Indian troops arrived just in time to save Srinagar. After this there followed some 14 months of undeclared war as Indian troops sought to secure Kashmir for India

against the efforts of the Kashmiri rebels, who were increasingly supported by regular units of the Pakistani army. The United Nations secured a ceasefire on 1 January 1949, and the ceasefire line has become the *de facto* frontier between India and Pakistan in this region.

On 27 January 1957 India annexed its portion of Kashmir, but the animosity that this created in Pakistan remains one of the main reasons for the continuing wars and tensions in this volatile area.

THE BURMESE CIVIL WAR (1948-)

On 4 January 1948 the Union of Burma secured its independence from the UK, and under the leadership of U Nu refused to join the British commonwealth. Almost immediately the country was plunged into civil war: by the end of March 1948 the Burma Communist party and the Communist party (Burma), known as the White Flag Communists and the Red Flag Communists respectively, had spread the area of their control from the delta of the Irrawaddy right up this mighty river to Mandalay. The government was able to respond but little because of the army's suspect loyalty, which had already resulted in mutinies by the garrison's of Mingaladon and Thayetmyo.

The problems of the govern-

ment were compounded by a major rising by the country's 2 million Karen tribesmen, living in comparatively small communities along Burma's eastern frontiers with Thailand and China. The rebellion started in August and by September the Karens had taken the southern region of the country around Thaton and Moulmein in the valley of the lower Salween river. By January 1949 the Karen rebellion had spread to Bassein, Insein, and Toungoo, by February to Maymyo and Meiktila, and by March to Mandalay. But the Karens appreciated that they could not hold this area, and from May pulled back into the valley of the Sittang river, where they claimed an independent Karen state, with its capital at Toungoo, during June.

During 1950 and 1951 the government made strenuous efforts against the communists and the Karens, reducing the area held by each grouping to a very considerable degree. Steady progress was made in the next seven years and after the offer of an amnesty on 31 July 1958 resistance declined rapidly. However, during the 1960s there was a resurgence in the fortunes of both groups, and the emergence of other revolutionary groups. The situation in Burma has remained one of constant civil war since that time, impossible to describe in a short compass.

A Burmese government soldier in action against a suspected rebel position. There appears to be no end to this incredibly protracted conflict.

Some indication of the opposition to the government is provided by a brief listing of the rebel groups: the Burma Communist party (12,000 regulars and 8,000 militia), the Kachin Liberation Army (5,000 men in four brigades), the Karen National Liberation Army (5,000 men in five brigades and three independent battalions), the Karenni Army (600 men in four 'brigades'), the Kawthoolei Moslem Liberation Front (linked to the Karens and incorporating

the Ommat Liberation Front and the Rohingya Patriotic Front, with unknown strength), the Kayan New Land Party (perhaps 100 men), the Mon State Army (perhaps 700 men), the Palung State Liberation Army (about 500 men), the Pa-O National Army (500 men), the Shan State Army (3,500) men, the Shan United Army (3,000 men), the Shan United Revolutionary Army (1,200 men) and the Wa National Army (300 men). These are all concerned with national identity

The body of a rebel lies beside a government soldier on the alert after the rebels have been ejected from a factory they were looting.

with their home areas, the smaller parties being loosely federated under the National Democratic Front. Finally there are the well equipped and ruthless para-military forces of the opium and heroin gangs operating in the so-called 'Golden Triangle' covering the junction of Burma, Laos, and Thailand.

THE MALAYAN EMERGENCY (1948-60)

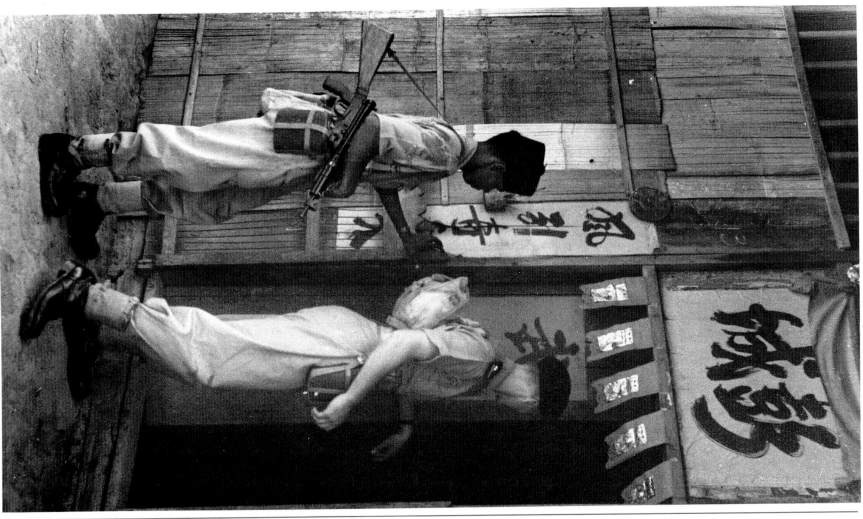

Members of the Malay Special Police prepare to enter a building as part of a co-operative action with the armed forces in a search for terrorists.

After their occupation of Malaya in late 1941 and early 1942, the Japanese treated the Malays with a comparatively lenient severity, but the Chinese with the utmost brutality, and this was largely instrumental for the development in the Malayan jungles of the MPAJA (Malayan People's Anti-Japanese Army) under communist leadership but with British backing. The Old Comrades' Association of the MPAJA formed the basis for the MRLA (Malayan Races Liberation Army), a Chinese communist guerrilla and terrorist organization which returned to the jungles after the failure of Malaya's ethnic Chinese to prevent the formation of the Federation of Malaya on 1 February 1948.

The federation was based largely on the desires and practices of the majority Malays, and after the failure of their political effort to secure a greater voice in local affairs for themselves, the Chinese extremists opted for violence as a last resort: they could call on an active strength of some 5,000 and the overall strategy of the campaign was to disrupt the Malayan economy as a means of forcing the British hand while developing a classical infrastructure based in Malaya's rural areas.

The MRLA's campaign of terrorism began during February and the sale of the potential threat was recognized by the British declaration of a state of emergency on 16 June, immediately after the murder of three British rubber plantation managers near Sungei Siput in Perak state. Even at this stage of the campaign the government forces had a considerable numerical advantage over the

MRLA, with 11 battalions of infantry (6 Gurkha, 3 British and 2 Malay) available for operations. The government forces were generally better equipped than their opponents, but this superiority was not as marked as it could have been, for the communists had carefully (and very farsightedly) stashed their British-supplied weapons at the end of World War II.

For the first two years of the emergency the government was content to keep the communist insurgents in check while preparing its plans and securing the right intelligence network against the communists, who were

hampered by their inability to melt into the rural background of Malay villages. In April 1950 Lieutenant General Sir Harold Briggs was appointed director of operations, and he soon evolved the basis of the most successful anti-guerrilla campaign yet seen.

The MRLA was undertaking some 400 terrorist incidents per month, with its most prolific efforts in the north around Betong, and on the island of Penang and the mainland coastal region opposite it; in the centre around Cameron Highlands and Raub; and in the south around Kuala Lumpur, Tasek Bera, and Kluang. Briggs could eventually call on

Men of the Royal West Kent Regiment keep in contact with Base HQ by means of radio while on patrol in Malaya.

45,000 troops (22 battalions), 67,000 police, and 325,000 home guard troops, but refused to be drawn by the illusory advantages of mass against so elusive a foe. The 'Briggs Plan' called for the resettlement of large numbers of villagers in the so-called New Villages on land made available by the Malayan princes and provided with modern conveniences, much improved teaching/medical facilities, and administrative centres. The last two were used to create a steadily evolving psychological barrier against the blandishments of the guerrillas, an effort aided by the payment of lavish bounties for information about the guerrillas, and a high level of protection against any possible counter-moves by the guerrillas. All this slowly weaned the villagers from the guerrillas,

isolating the latter in an increasingly deserted land without ready sources of supply.

In February 1952 General Sir Gerald Templer was appointed British high commissioner and commander-in-chief, and he saw that the time was now ripe to exploit the weakness created in the MRLA's capabilities by the

'Briggs Plan' and a careful air interdiction campaign by the Royal Air Force. On 7 February 1952 the government forces went over to

Suspected terrorists were held in rehabilitation camps such as this centre near Penang. These camps achieved considerable success in 'turning' the terrorists.

the offensive, using small groups of highly trained men on search and destroy missions given un-excelled mobility by helicopter lift supplemented by the paradropping of supplies.

The government patrols were thus able to maintain their pursuit of communist groups even as the latter became exhausted and fell back towards their safe areas. At the same time Templer unleashed a powerful psychological effort against the guerrillas: millions of leaflets were dropped to encourage their surrender, the

government forces were imbued with the overwhelming sense of victory, and the Malays were turned yet further against the guerrillas by Templer's repeated avowal that the only thing standing between Malaya and full independence was the MRLA.

From this time onwards the capabilities of the MRLA were eroded steadily, a fact signalled by the removal of the communist high command from Malaya to Indonesia in February 1954. On 31 August 1957 Malaya achieved full independence as a constitutional

The Malay population were of great assistance to the authorities in locating and capturing terrorists.

monarchy within the British commonwealth, and by this time MRLA strength had dropped to a mere 1,700 men, generally pinned into inhospitable areas and in very poor physical shape. On 31 July the emergency was declared officially over: the government forces had lost 2,384 dead and 2,400 wounded, while the MRLA had lost 6,705 dead, 1,286 wounded, and 2,696 surrendered.

THE CHINESE CONQUEST OF TIBET (1950-51)

Although nominally under Chinese sovereignty, Tibet in fact became autonomous in 1912 within the British sphere of influence. The situation in this theocratic state remained little altered for the next 35 years, though the rise of the communists in China during the mid-1940s gave cause for concern. On 24 November 1949 there came from Peiping a radio call for the communist 'liberation' of Tibet from the rule of the Dalai Lama. The demand was made by the Panchen Lama, who had left the country to solicit communist aid and found ready acceptance in a country which had long owned Tibet.

On 1 January 1950 the new communist government of China indicated its intention to honour the Panchen Lama's request and on 7 October of the same year Chinese troops crossed the frontier in an invasion of eastern Tibet. Chamdo was soon occupied against determined but indifferent opposition from units of the 10,000-man Tibetan army, which was equipped only with small arms, and after negotiating the 16,700-ft (5090-m) Shargung Pass

and the 17,100-ft (5212-m) Tro Pass, the Chinese debouched into central Tibet and by the end of November had secured the country.

Tibet's appeal to the United Nations on 10 November proved fruitless and the 15-year-old Dalai Lama fled on the 21 December to set up his government at Yatung, just over the frontier from Bhutan. On 17 August 1951 the Chinese brought him back to Lhasa to head a puppet regime. There was enormous civil unrest throughout Tibet and it was 26 October 1951 before the Chinese thought it wise to introduce their main occupying force and garrison into Lhasa.

The Chinese dogmatically attempted to destroy the theocratic Tibetan state, killing the monks, destroying monasteries, and using the Tibetans as forced labour for the opening of better communications with the main body of China, and this stirred enormous resentment throughout the country. In the spring and summer there was widespread rebellion, ruthlessly and bloodily suppressed by the Chinese, the anti-communist effort being resurrected in March 1956 when

the Golok tribe of Kham in eastern Tibet rose and inflicted severe casualties on the Chinese, including the total destruction of one garrison of 900 men. The Chinese responded with air attacks against the Tibetans' villages, causing considerable casualties. Unrest continued on a sporadic basis for the next three years, but between 10 and 27 March 1959 the unrest flared into a major rebellion that was again put down by the Chinese with great loss of life.

The Dalai Lama fled to India where he was granted asylum and publicized his claims that the Chinese had killed 65,000 Tibetans, removed 10,000 children to China for forcible indoctrination, and moved 5 million Chinese into Tibet in an effort to dilute the country's national strength.

In 1965 Tibet was formally absorbed into China, but unrest has continued unabated. In the mid-1980s the liberalization of China spread to Tibet in modest fashion, but this failed to quell internal dissent which was expressed in widespread rioting during 1987.

THE LAOTIAN CIVIL WAR (1953-73)

Laos was declared a French protectorate in 1893 and its present frontiers were fully defined for the first time only in 1907. After they had occupied France's territories in Indo-China, the Japanese declared Laos independent (though it remained under full control of the Japanese), and with the Japanese surrender

Least known of the South-East Asian wars, the Laotian conflict was fought sporadically with very limited means.

PART II   ASIAN CONFLICTS

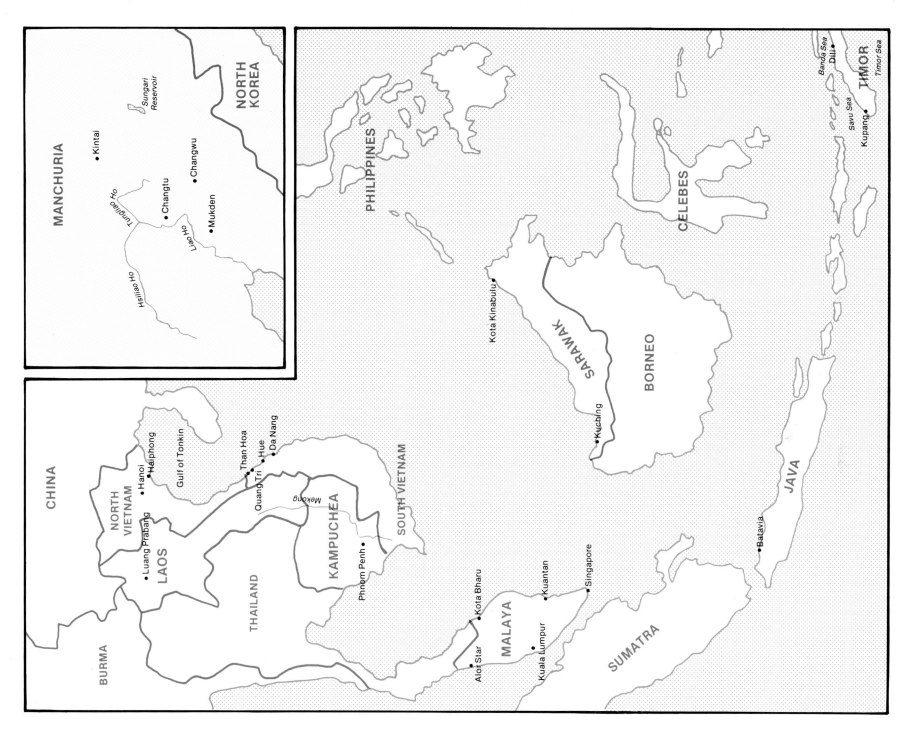

MANCHURIA

Kintai

Sungari Reservoir

NORTH KOREA

Tungliao Ho

Changtu

Changwu

Liao Ho

Mukden

Hsiliao Ho

CHINA

BURMA

NORTH VIETNAM

Hanoi

Haiphong

Gulf of Tonkin

LAOS

Luang Prabang

Than Hoa

Hue

Da Nang

Quang Tri

THAILAND

Mekong

KAMPUCHEA

Phnom Penh

SOUTH VIETNAM

Kota Bharu

Alor Star

MALAYA

Kuantan

Kuala Lumpur

Singapore

SUMATRA

PHILIPPINES

Kota Kinabulu

SARAWAK

Kuching

BORNEO

CELEBES

JAVA

Batavia

Banda Sea

Dili

Savu Sea

TIMOR

Kupang

Timor Sea

Above: Vietnamese troops move up towards the front during the short but bloody Sino-Vietnamese war.

Left: One of the main assets enjoyed by the Vietnamese in the Sino-Vietnamese War was a wealth of operational and combat experience at all levels.

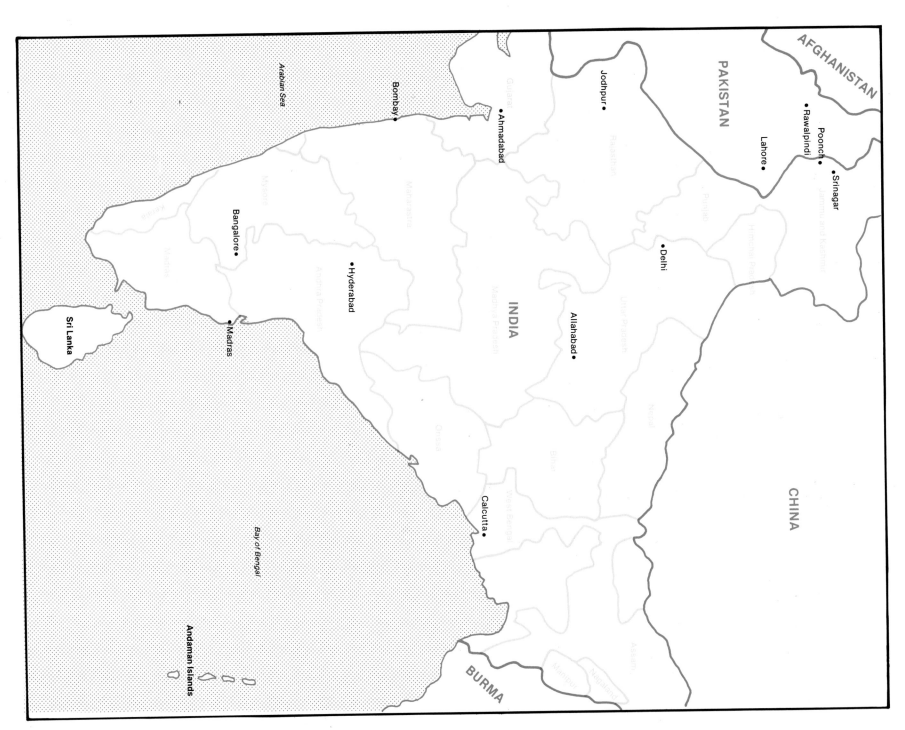

PART II ASIAN CONFLICTS (continued)

in 1945 the Lao Issara movement reasserted its claim to Laotian independence. However, with the re-arrival of the French in 1946 this movement collapsed, its leaders fleeing to Thailand.

On 19 July 1949 France declared Laos an independent state within the French Union and eventually allowed the Lao Issari leaders to return home, though the most important of these, Prince Souphanouvong, and his immediate followers opted to remain in exile and work for full Laotian independence.

Souphanouvong created the Pathet Lao (Lao State) communist movement, which soon allied itself with the comparable Vietminh movement fighting from

Pathet Lao troops in one of the defensive positions around the city of Phoukout, held by the communists.

Vietnamese independence. During April 1953 the increasingly powerful Vietminh invaded Laos with the support of the Pathet Lao, capturing the abandoned French base of Xieng Khouang on 20 April as a first step towards Luang Prabang, seat of the neutral administration of Prince Souvanna Phouma, Souphanouvong's half brother. This effectively launched a 20-year civil war in which the three main protagonists were the neutral government, the Pathet Lao, and the right-wing military under a succession of leaders of whom the most important was General Phoumi Nosavan.

Early in May 1953 the Vietminh began to pull out of Laos, leaving the fighting to the three Laotian parties, of which the neutralists (often but not always supported by the army) were supported by France and later by the USA.

Laotian independence was fully recognized from 22 October 1953, and after the Geneva accord of 21 July 1954 France withdrew its troops. Fighting continued on an almost uninterrupted basis over the following years, principally on the Plain of Jars in the north centre of the country. From 1967, however, there was increasing North Vietnamese involvement on the side of the Pathet Lao as the pace of the Vietnam War increased and southern Laos became increasingly important as a supply route (the Ho Chi Minh Trail) for the communist forces in South Vietnam.

In October 1972 the Pathet Lao and the government opened talks in Vientiane, but by the time the ceasefire agreement was signed in February 1973 the Pathet Lao had made further important advances to control most of the country's strategic areas. With the fall of South Vietnam in April 1975 the communists were able to increase their pressure on the government, and soon assumed total control of the country. In December 1974 Souphanouvong was declared president, and communist control was complete.

THE INDO-CHINESE BORDER WAR (1962)

Much of the frontier between China and India lies in the inaccessible Himalayas and for this reason considerable stretches of the border between these two huge countries have never been fully defined. On independence India merely adopted the frontier claimed by the British, though the Chinese claimed that this frontier had in fact never been formalized in any way. Thus there were several areas of dispute, most notably in the north-east of Kashmir (the Aksai Chin and points as far south as the Shipki Pass and Nilang), and in the south-east in the area of the Indians' North-East Frontier Agency (between Bhutan and Burma along the British-fixed MacMahon Line).

In 1951 the prime minister of China, Chou En-lai, offered talks to settle the boundary question, but the Indian prime minister, Pandit Nehru, refused and in 1954 announced that India had unilaterally fixed the frontiers. There matters rested uneasily but in 1956 and 1957 China built a road through the Aksai Chin to link Tibet with Sinkiang, the Indians not becoming aware of the fact until the Chinese announced the completion of the project in September 1957.

This prompted an Indian protest and Chinese counter-protest as tensions rose. Nehru thought his forces could beat the Chinese without difficulty and therefore made no secret of the movement towards the frontier region of substantial Indian reinforcements, and the Chinese became increasingly exasperated with the Indians, especially after the latter had given asylum to the Dalai Lama after his flight from Tibet.

The first overt hostilities occurred on 28 August 1959, when there were exchanges of fire in the west at the Kongko Pass in Ladakh, and in the east near Longju. Further exchanges of fire followed on 10 June 1960 and, despite the advice of his military commanders to the contrary, Nehru insisted on the creation of some 40 advanced positions in the regions claimed by the Chinese. In June 1962 India protested at Chinese incursions into Ladakh, while the Chinese countered with protests of Indian incursions into Sinkiang. Matters were clearly approaching boiling point and further pointers were provided by the Chinese seizure of an Indian position on the Galwan river on 10 July, and by exchanges of fire in the Chip Chap valley and near Lake Panggong 11 days later.

The inevitable war broke out on 20 October when Chinese troops launched two substantial offensives 1,000 miles (1600 km) apart in the main disputed regions. The Indians could stem neither advance, that in the east proving highly successful and destroying all Indian resistance north of the valley of the Brahmaputra river. By 21 November the Chinese had secured the regions they wanted and announced a unilateral ceasefire followed by a withdrawal to points 12.5 miles (20 km) behind the front of 7 November.

The Chinese have never revealed their losses but the severity of the fighting is indicated by those of the Indians: 1,400 killed, 1,700 wounded, and 4,000 taken prisoner. It was a salutary lesson to the Indians and led to wholesale reforms of the Indian forces. There have been a number of border incidents since that time but India has essayed no major effort.

A Chinese soldier on guard at one of the many points along the hotly disputed Sino–Soviet frontier.

During the 19th century a steadily weakening China was forced by an increasingly strong Russia to accede to three treaties considered wholly unjust by the Chinese of the time and still disavowed by the communist regime in China. The 1858 treaty cost China the territory in the great bend of the Amur river, the 1860 treaty the territory to the east of the Ussuri river, and the 1864 treaty large portions of western Sinkiang around Alma Ata and Bakhti as far west as Lake Balkash.

Deteriorating relations between China and the USSR led to a resurgence of animosity about these border regions and on 2 March 1969 a small but intense battle was fought for possession of an uninhabited island in the Ussuri, known to the Soviets as Damansky Island and to the Chinese as Chen Pao Island. In May the fighting spread to the Bakhti area between Sinkiang and Kazakhstan.

The scale of events is indicated in a Chinese complaint to the United Nations on 19 August, alleging that the Soviets had been responsible for 429 border violations in June and July, countered on 10 September by a Soviet allegation of 488 Chinese border violations between June and mid-August.

Between 1977 and 1980 there were several other border clashes, but none of these attained the severity of the 1969 fighting. Talks to resolve the problem have been held intermittently since 1969, but no real progress has been evident.

THE KAMPUCHEAN WAR (1978-)

By 1973 a stalemate was evident in Cambodia, now generally known by its Khmer name Kampuchea: most of the region to the east of the Mekong river was in North Vietnamese hands, together with some of the areas in the extreme south of the country; and the rest of the country, including most of the major towns, was still held by the government headed by General Lon Nol. North Vietnam was supporting the Khmer Rouge revolutionary party seeking to overthrow Lon Nol, who enjoyed US financial and *matériel* support.

However, the North Vietnamese victory over South Vietnam in April 1975 allowed the diversion of greater support to the Khmer Rouge at a time when the US disenchantment with its adventure in South-East Asia was curtailing its support for the government, whose general inefficiency and corruption also severely hampered the efforts of its forces to check the Khmer Rouge. The Cambodian capital, Phnom Penh, fell to the Khmer Rouge on 17 April 1975 after the government's main supply route up the Mekong had been cut during February, and the

new Khmer Rouge administration of Pol Pot soon gained control of most of Cambodia.

The Khmer Rouge operated on the crudest of Marxist principles and there followed the complete ruralization of the country: the entire population of Phnom Penh and other urban areas was driven into the country and it is estimated that between April 1975 and

Khmer Rouge soldiers, armed with Chinese-made copies of Soviet weapons, man an outpost on the Mekong river outside Phnom Penh.

Manning the heavy machine-gun on a government patrol boat attacking a Khmer Rouge position on Anloung Chen island in the Mekong river.

January 1979 something like two or three million Cambodians (perhaps half of the country's entire population) were killed or otherwise died as the Khmer Rouge savagely implemented its policies. The Vietnamese disapproved of this, wishing to extend their own brand of communism to the west but instead seeing the creation of what was rapidly becoming a fundamentalist communist desert.

On 25 December 1978 substantial Vietnamese forces invaded Cambodia, sweeping aside the Khmer Rouge, who had only light weapons with which to face the Vietnamese forces' heavy equipment including armour and artillery. On 7 January 1979 Phnom Penh fell to the Vietnamese, who installed a puppet regime under Heng Samrin over the People's Republic of Kampuchea. The country was once again plunged into civil war, with the Khmer Rouge reverting to their guerrilla origins in an effort to stem and reverse the increasing power of the puppet regime and its Vietnamese masters. The war has continued unabated since that time, causing an enormous flood of refugees over Kampuchea's northern and western frontiers with Thailand.

The political situation remains very complex despite a recent reduction in Vietnamese force

strengths and there are fears that the pressure of the Vietnamese and Kampucheans against the Khmer Rouge may eventually cause the war to spill over into Thailand, where the refugee camps along the frontier regions provide a ready base organization for the Khmer Rouge. Already there have been border incidents, including artillery bombardments and air raids, but the Thai government has chosen to maintain a low profile in an effort to ameliorate the situation.

THE SINO-VIETNAMESE WAR (1979)

A Chinese prisoner of war under Vietnamese guard during the Sino-Vietnamese border war.

The Khmer Rouge enjoyed the full support of the Chinese government, which was incensed at Vietnam's involvement in what it considered its own puppet in the region. On 17 February 1979, therefore, Chinese forces launched an offensive into northern Vietnam along six main axes: from east to west these were directed against Mon Cay, Dong Dang, Cao Bang, Ha Giang, Lao Kay, and Lai Chau, along the whole length of the Sino-Vietnamese frontier. China had massed some 200,000 troops for the operation, which initially used only about 80,000 of them; the Vietnamese defence rested in the hands of about 50,000 regulars and 50,000 local militiamen.

China expected a comparatively simple victory, but had failed to appreciate the full capabilities and determination of Vietnam's

combat-experienced regulars, who were well supplied with heavy weapons of the latest types. Thus the Chinese advances were stalled on 18 February after progressing an average of about 6 miles (10 km) into Vietnam. Fighting for several towns continued, but the Chinese local command decided to pause while waiting for reinforcements to come up. By 24 February the full 200,000 men were available to the Chinese, who resumed the advance. There was very heavy fighting at Lang Son on the rail line south-west of Hanoi and on 5 March the Chinese announced that their forces were pulling back to the frontier after attaining 'the goals set for them'.

It was not to be that easy, however, for the Vietnamese harassed the retreating Chinese with great skill and it was 17

March before the Chinese authorities were able to confirm the complete evacuation of all Chinese forces. Both sides claimed victory: the Chinese said that they had suffered 20,000 casualties but inflicted 50,000, while the Vietnamese baldly announced the destruction of 280 Chinese tanks and the infliction of 62,500 casualties on the Chinese. There seems little doubt that the Chinese figures are more accurate and, while the Vietnamese may justly claim to have won a number of tactical victories, the Chinese achieved their operational aims in razing the provincial capitals of Cam Duong, Cao Bang, Lang Son, and Lao Kay as a lesson to the Vietnamese.

AFRICAN CONFLICTS

COLONIAL WARS IN AFRICA (1900-31)

From 1900 there was resistance to the colonial powers from the indigenous peoples; this resistance took the form of risings against the established power or continued indigenous resistance against further development of the colonial powers' holdings. From the Horn of Africa clockwise round the continent the most significant of these campaigns were:

- the war against the British and Italians in Somaliland (waged by the 'Mad Mullah', Sayyid Muhammed ben Abdullah, between 1891 and his death in 1920);
- the Gusii revolts against the British in south-west Kenya in 1905 and 1908;
- the Tutsi and Hutu revolts against the Germans and British in German East Africa (later Tanganyika) between 1911 and 1917;
- the Maji-Maji revolt against the Germans in the southern part of German East Africa from 1905 to 1907;
- Chilembwe's rebellion against the British and Portuguese in Nyasaland and Portuguese East Africa (later Mozambique) in 1915;
- the Madagascan revolt against the French between 1898 and 1904;
- the Zula revolt in Natal against the British in 1906;
- the Herero and Hottentot revolts against the Germans in German South-West Africa (now Namibia) between 1904 and 1906;
- the Angolan rebellions against the Portuguese in 1913;
- the revolts against the French

in the French Congo during 1905;
- the Anyang revolt against the Germans in the Cameroons in 1904;
- the revolt under Rabih Zobeir against the French in that part of French West Africa which is now Chad between 1897 and 1900;
- the French conquest of Wadai (eastern Chad and central Sudan) between 1909 and 1911;
- the completion of the British seizure of northern Nigeria between 1900 and 1903;
- the Ashanti rebellion against the British in the Gold Coast (now Ghana) during 1900;
- the French conquest of Mauritania between 1908 and 1909;
- the Jelaz incident against the French in northern Tunisia in 1911;
- the rising against the French in southern Tunisia during 1915;
- the Sanusi war against Italy in Libya between 1912 and 1931;
- and the Denshawai incident against the British in Egypt during 1906.

After World War I the colonial troubles of sub-Saharan Africa subsided for the most part. The colonial powers (minus Germany, whose holdings had been re-allocated to the victorious allies) had consolidated their territories and were now extending their administrative and judicial systems to create considerable stability in the region. The main area of conflict was thus North Africa where, as noted above, the Italians were fighting a seemingly endless war against the Sanusi tribesmen of Libya and where the French and Spaniards eventually joined

forces to eliminate the troublesome Riffs of western Algeria and Morocco.

Between 1900 and 1906 there had been great inter-colonial friction about Morocco, the differences being largely patched by the Algeciras Conference that took place between January 1906 and April 1907 to mediate the demands of the British, French, Germans, Italians, and Spanish. On 20 July 1907 there was serious unrest and rioting in Casablanca and once they had quelled this with a naval bombardment the French extended their hold on Morocco to include the country's Atlantic coast.

But rapidly reaching proportions sufficient to eclipse the rivalries of the colonial powers was the threat posed by Riffian nationalism and between July and September 1909 Riff tribesmen launched a series of attacks against Spanish positions around Melilla. The Spaniards managed to check these initial efforts and in April 1911 the French came under attack, responding by occupying the city of Fez. On 30 March 1912 the Treaty of Fez established a French protectorate over Morocco, carefully nurtured by General Louis Lyautey with the express purpose of mitigating the effects of French occupation and so promoting local popularity for the French.

The Riffs therefore turned their attentions against the Spanish possessions on the southern shore of the Mediterranean. In the west the bandit leader Raisuli constantly harassed the Spaniards' forward positions and by 1920 was moving forward against Tetuan, while in the east the Riffs under

Abdel Krim were succeeding in raising local hostility to the Spaniards in the area of Melilla. Raisuli was brought under control by the sensible efforts of General Damaso Berenguer but Krim was faced by the considerably less capable General Fernandes Silvestre.

Moving against Krim with a force of some 20,000 men, Silvestre was pushing into the Riff mountains during July 1921 when he was met at Anual by the garrison of a Spanish frontier position, fleeing from the Riff advance after hearing of the Riffs' capture of the position closest to them. As the two Spanish forces met, Krim's men opened fire from both flanks and drove the Spaniards into a panic-struck rout in which some 12,000 men were killed and several thousands more captured. Spain's positions in the area collapsed and the Riffians advanced to pen the Spanish into the fortified area centred on Melilla and Tetuan.

This caused the collapse of the Spanish administration and while the Spaniards were still in total disarray Krim prepared to launch his 20,000 men, well equipped with captured Spanish weapons, against the French in Morocco to complete the 'Republic of the Riff' he had recently proclaimed.

Krim was a leader of great tactical perception and his forces were launched with great secrecy through the mountains along the Franco-Spanish frontier to take, on 12 April 1925, 43 of the 66 blockhouses guarding the border between Taza and Fez. Lyautey had only small military assets in the French protectorate but these he used with great skill to slow the Riff advance and finally to check it within sight of Fez. This bought the time for diplomacy to work and on 26 July the French and Spanish buried their former quarrel about supremacy over Morocco to conclude an agreement of co-operation against the Riffs.

France increased its forces in Morocco to 150,000 and Spain marshalled an expeditionary force of 50,000 men under General José Sanjurjo. The carefully planned offensive got under way on 8 September when the Spanish expedition was landed in the Bay of Alhucemas under cover of a joint Franco-Spanish naval squadron, thereupon advancing to the capture of Ajdir by 2 October. This gave the two forces the starting points for a vast pincer movement designed to trap the Riffs between overwhelmingly superior allied forces and capture the Riff capital, Targuist.

The allied offensive got moving with a Spanish advance straight south and a French advance, in six columns under the field command of Marshal Henri Petain, to the east. Lyautey retired on 24 September, being replaced as governor of Morocco by Petain, who handed field command to General Boichut. Until the arrival of winter the French drove the Riffs back towards the slower-moving Spanish, the allies pausing during the winter but resuming the offensive in the spring to force Krim's surrender on 26 May 1926 as Targuist was taken.

THE KENYAN EMERGENCY (1952-60)

Men of the Kenya police interrogate Mau Mau suspects in a scene of unlikely tranquillity during November 1952.

The coastal strip of what is now Kenya was leased from the Sultan of Zanzibar in 1885 and became the East African Protectorate in 1896. Thereafter the colonial size of the protectorate grew steadily to reach the present boundaries and in 1920 the region became the crown colony of Kenya. Large numbers of Kenyans served in the British forces during World War II and after the war returned home with an increasing dissatisfaction about their lot. This unrest grew steadily in the period between 1945 and 1952, largely amongst the Kikuyu tribal group. On 9

PART II   AFRICAN CONFLICTS

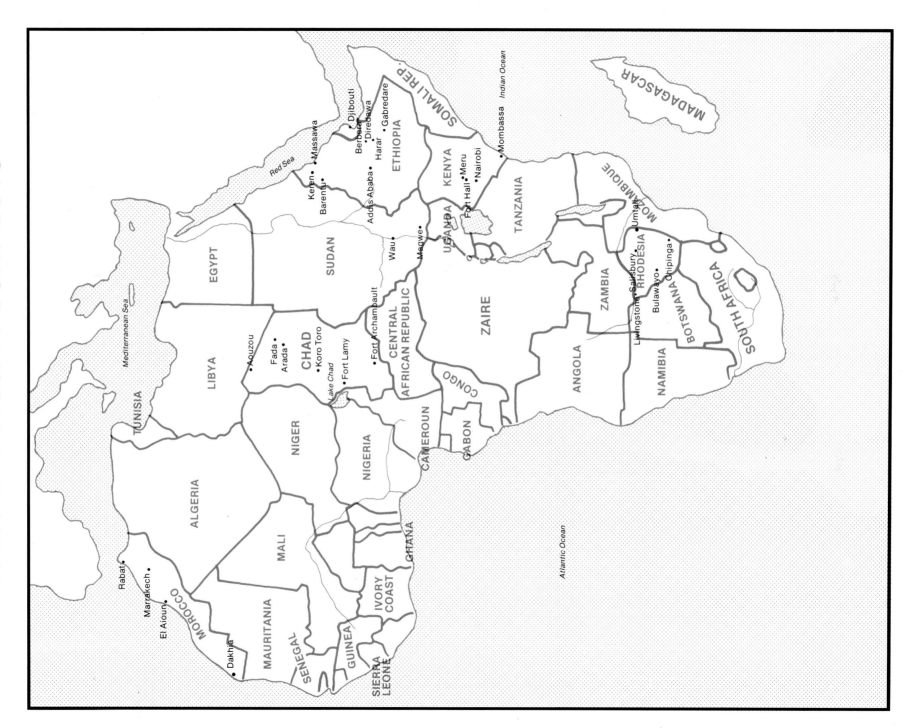

222

Above: France has maintained a policy of consistent support for her ex-colonies, as typified by this mechanized column of French troops seen in 1984 near Mossovo in war-torn Chad.

Right: Local experience and determination count as much as weaponry in Chad, though there is no shortage of lighter weapons supplied from Eastern- and Western-bloc sources.

In a government-sponsored programme, a witch doctor cleanses two ex-Mau Mau men of the oath they made to this secret and extremely dangerous society.

October 1952 the pro-British Chief Waruhiu of the Kikuyu was murdered by the Mau Mau, a Kikuyu secret society of the utmost brutality based largely on ritual, magic, and barbarity, and on 20 October a state of emergency was decreed.

Terrorism and guerrilla warfare spread rapidly from the Kikuyu homelands in the Aberdare mountains to the north-west of the capital, Nairobi, being directed at all Europeans (especially the vulnerable settlers) and any

Africans who supported them. Immediately after the outbreak of hostilities the UK reinforced its military presence in Kenya, and between January and May 1953 military and punitive measures were instituted, the first to contain the Mau Mau rebellion in south-western Kenya and the second to remove all leaders suspected of Mau Mau involvement. The most important of these was Jomo Kenyatta, who was given a seven-year sentence in October 1953.

The military measures were

controlled by General Sir George Erskine, heading the East African Command that encompassed Kenya, Tanganyika, and Uganda. Initially success against the Mau Mau was limited, largely because Erskine adopted inappropriate 'European' tactics: nevertheless on 15 June 1953 an operation in the

Aberdare Forest resulted in the killing of 125 terrorists, increasing to more than 1,000 the number of Mau Mau activists killed since the beginning of the emergency. The tactics evolved in the Malayan emergency were rapidly adapted for the Kenyan situation and greater success began to attend British operations as the Mau Mau found themselves isolated physically and psychologically. Between February and June 1955 the British launched their decisive campaign, some 10,000 troops

being used in the Aberdare and Mount Kenya areas to disperse the last concentration of about 4,000 guerrillas. From 2 September 1956 the numbers of British troops in Kenya were scaled down, though sporadic fighting continued into 1956 and the emergency was not declared over until January 1960. Mau Mau casualties amounted to 10,527 killed and 1,538 surrendered, while another 24,000 had been captured or detained as suspects. Other casualties amounted to 1,826 African

civilians killed and 918 wounded, 534 African soldiers killed and 465 wounded, 32 European civilians killed and 26 wounded, 63 European soldiers killed and 102 wounded, and finally 3 Asian soldiers killed, 26 Asian civilians killed and 12 civilians wounded.

Constant contacts were maintained with villagers in an effort to maintain an accurate intelligence picture of Mau Mau movements, strengths and likely intentions.

THE SUDANESE CIVIL WARS (1955-)

After the 1885 death of the Mahdi, who had led Sudan into a revolt against the Egyptians and British in 1883, this early war of independence was carried forward by the Khalifa Abdullah, who was finally defeated in the Battles of the Atbara River (April 1898) and Omdurman (September 1898). This paved the way for the signature, on 19 January 1899, of an Anglo-Egyptian agreement that Sudan would be jointly administered henceforth as the Anglo-Egyptian Sudan. On 12 February 1953 Sudan was granted self-government and on 1 January 1956 full independence was declared – on 16 August of the previous year the Sudanese government had demanded the withdrawal of the last 900 British and 500 Egyptian troops by 12 November. Part of the British overall policy in Sudan had been to keep separate the Arabs of the north and the Africans of the south. But this led in July 1953 to the beginning of the protracted 17-year First Sudanese Civil War

when the southerners were allocated only six out of the 600 most senior posts in the government of the country as it approached full independence. The problem was at first confined to rioting in southern towns, but on 18 August southern troops mutinied in Torit and there then flared up a widespread progrom of northerners in the southern region.

From this time onwards the civil war became increasingly bitter, the northerners exacting an extremely heavy and indeed protracted price from the southerners as the price for these early riots and killings. The worst period of government repression coincided with the rule of Lieutenant General Ibrahim Abboud who led a military coup on 17 November 1958. The southerners created the Anya-Nya (venom of the viper) resistance organization, but its guerrilla forces could never halt the superior military of the north, who enjoyed the support of Soviet air power after the arrival of the pro-

communist regime of Gaafer Mohamed Numeiri in the May 1969 elections that followed a military coup. The First Sudanese Civil War was finally brought to an inconclusive end during 1972 after the intervention of the World Council of Churches and Emperor Haile Selassie of Ethiopia.

As part of the settlement of the war, greater economic support was furnished to the south, and the Anya-Nya was absorbed into the Sudanese army. But in September 1983 Numeiry imposed Moslem law over the whole Sudan, including the predominantly Christian and animistic south, and this paved the way for the outbreak of the Second Sudanese Civil War, currently most violent in the Upper Nile and Bahr el Bhazai regions of southern Sudan. The local resistance is centred on the Anya-Nya II guerrilla movement, the most extreme of the organizations loosely grouped under the banner of the 12,500-man Sudanese People's Liberation Army.

THE RHODESIAN CIVIL WAR (1964-80)

In 1889 the British South Africa Company, headed by Cecil Rhodes, was chartered to develop 'North and South Zambesia'. In 1896 the area was renamed Rhodesia and in 1911 was split into Northern Rhodesia and Southern Rhodesia. There followed considerable white immigration to Southern Rhodesia, which in 1922 became in effect a dominion though still technically a colony. The UK realized the importance of trying to create a strong and viable political and economic entity in this area and in 1953 created the Federation of Rhodesia and Nyasaland, comprising Northern Rhodesia, Southern Rhodesia, and

A C-47 transport 'plane of the Rhodesian air force brings in supplies to a long-range patrol of the defence forces fighting the insurgents in the Zambezi valley.

Nyasaland. However, the resistance of whites in Southern Rhodesia to the nationalist aspirations of the blacks doomed the federation, which was dissolved in 1963 into a white-controlled Southern Rhodesia and the two independent black states of Malawi (Nyasaland) and Zambia (Northern Rhodesia).

As the UK was still apparently determined to impose majority black rule on Southern Rhodesia, Prime Minister Ian Smith in November 1965 declared Southern Rhodesia to be the independent state of Rhodesia. The subsequent shape of local history had already been created, however by the presence of two major black opposition groupings in the form of the ZAPU (Zimbabwe African People's Union, established by Joshua Nkomo in 1961 and operating its own Zimbabwe People's Revolutionary Army

drawn mainly from the Ndebele-oriented tribes) and the ZANU (Zimbabwe African National Union, an offshoot of the ZAPU established in 1963 by Ndabaningi Sithole and Dr. Robert Mugabe, and operating its own Zimbabwe National Liberation Army drawn mainly from the Shona-oriented tribes).

The ZIPRA's most useful foreign support came from the Soviets, while that of the ZANLA came mainly from the Chinese, though a large quantity of Soviet weaponry was supplied via the Organization of African Unity. The first guerrilla incursions across the Zambesi river were made in 1964, and in April of the same year Smith banned both the ZAPU and

One of the most effective of the defence force units was Grey's Scouts, a mounted organization using personal kit and weapons.

ZANU, which moved their headquarters to Zambia. There followed a classic guerrilla campaign, in which the ZIPRA and ZAPLA forces sometimes co-operated but mostly worked in parallel, against Rhodesia's isolated white communities, key economic locations, and lines of communication.

Rhodesia operated a small but highly effective air force which played a major part in reconnaissance and interdiction, but the main weight of the defensive war fell on the

Rhodesian army (Rhodesian Security Force), comprising the 8 all-white battalions of the Rhodesia Regiment, the 1,000 men of the all-white elite Rhodesian Light Infantry, the white-officered Rhodesian African Rifles, the 180 whites of the Special Air Service, and the 1,000 men of the Selous Scouts. The last comprised both blacks and whites, all very highly trained to operate in small groups for deep reconnaissance and strike.

The black states on Rhodesia's eastern, northern, and western frontiers supported the ZIPRA and ZANLA forces, while considerable assistance was provided to the white regime by South Africa.

The British attempted to blockade the East African coast to prevent the arrival of weapons and supplies for Rhodesia, and also to cut off Rhodesia's exports as dictated by the United Nations' embargo, but this effort was notably unsuccessful.

In the war inside Rhodesia the white forces were well able to hold their own in the early part of the war, aided in part by the increasing distrust of each other entertained by the ZAPU and ZANU, nominally joined under Bishop Abel Muzorewa's African National Council from 1971.

Men of the Zimbabwe African People's Union at a training camp near the Rhodesian border.

However, from mid-1977 the efficiency of the ZIPRA and ZANLA began to improve, allowing them to operate with increasing effect over all parts of Rhodesia after the creation of the joint ZAPU and ZANU Patriotic Front in September 1976. From this time Smith's administration was fighting a rearguard battle, and in April 1979 Smith stood down in favour of Muzorewa, the country's first black prime minister.

This was unacceptable to the Patriotic Front, however, and the war continued until the British in November 1979 put forward proposals for a ceasefire and on 6 December appointed Lord Soames governor to supervise the change of power.

In January 1980 12,000 ZANLA and 4,000 ZIPRA guerrillas came out of the bush to surrender their arms to the multinational Commonwealth Monitoring Force

Men of the African National Council, the interim administration which was established by Rhodesia but was unacceptable to the ZANU and ZAPU organizations.

and the Rhodesian Civil War was effectively over. In March Mugabe became prime minister and on 18 April the independence of the Republic of Zimbabwe was proclaimed.

THE CHADIAN CIVIL WAR 1968-   )

A comparatively remote area to the north-west of Nigeria, Chad was proclaimed a French protectorate in September 1900 and in July 1908 was incorporated in French Equatorial Africa. On 1 January 1959 Chad achieved autonomy within the French Union and finally became fully independent on 11 August 1960. As with Sudan, there was an uneasy situation in Chad because of the country's ethnic blend of Moslem Arabs in the north with Christian and animist blacks in the south, though in the Chadian situation it was the blacks of the south who held the reins of power.

In 1966 and 1967 there was a border dispute with Sudan, with more than 200 people being killed during the course of this low-intensity squabble. Of much longer-term importance for the region, however, was the outbreak of a civil war in 1968, when Arab northerners of the FROLINAT (Front de Libération Nationale du Tchad – Chad National Liberation Front) besieged a number of government garrisons. The Chadian authorities appealed for French assistance but, unwilling to become involved in a civil war, the French offered only air support. This was sufficient to allow the government forces to reassert themselves, but in March 1969 French assistance was again required when the forces of President François Tombalbaye proved incapable of restoring order in the course of nationwide civil disturbance. About 2,500 French troops became involved. Several Frenchmen lost their lives and this led to considerable public disquiet in France. Assistance to Chad was therefore officially terminated in September 1972 after 50 Frenchmen and perhaps 3,000 Chadians had been killed, though a large number of French troops and technical advisers remained in Chad.

After leading his country to independence Tombalbaye was assassinated on 13 April 1975 and the short interregnum that followed was ended in May by the formation of a military regime

Men of Hussein (or Hissene) Habre's Popular forces of North Chad are seen in the area of the Tibesti mountains on the border with Libya.

under Brigadier Felix Malloum. The new regime had to face greater problems than had its predecessor, for to the north the fundamentalist Moslem state of Libya, under its communist leader Colonel Muammar Ghadaffi, was trying to seize the 'Aouzou Strip'. Lying to the north of the Tibesti mountains on the Chadian–Libyan frontier and containing vast mineral deposits, this strip had been temporarily ceded between 1935 and 1938 by France to Italy, the colonial power in Libya then.

Libya now saw this as the legal pretext to reoccupy the strip. After seizing the strip unilaterally, together with the towns of Aouzou, Gezenti, and Ouri, the Libyans saw that their occupation could be eased by civil war in Chad and therefore started developing and supporting the Toubou rebel movement, which took the Chadian town of Bardai in the Tibesti mountains in July 1977. A ceasefire was signed in Khartoum during January 1978 but failed to halt the fighting despite the fact that on 29 August the Toubou leader, Hussein Habre, was appointed Chadian prime minister.

The division between the two parties had been papered over rather than bridged, however, and in February 1979 the alliance fell apart when President Halloum ordered an attack on Habre's residence by the police in N'Djamena (previously Fort Lamy), the Chadian capital. There followed severe fighting between the ANT (Armée Nationale de Tchad – Chadian National Army, loyal to Halloum), and the FAN (Forces Armées de Nord – Armed Forces of the North, loyal to Habre). The local problem soon spread to most of Chad, three-quarters of which was still controlled by the FROLINAT. France again intervened, this time with a paratroop force on the side of Habre, and a truce was arranged between the ANT and FAN.

The complexity of the situation is attested to by the agreement reached in the Nigerian capital, Lagos, during March 1979: 11 separate factions were represented, and the result was an interim government of national unity under Goukouni Oueddei. The impossible situation could not and did not survive for long and in March 1980 civil war again flared over about three-quarters of the country, this time between Habre's FAN and Goukouni's FAP (Forces Armées Populaires – Popular Armed Forces). Advantage of this disorder was taken by Colonel Wadal Kamougue, vice president of the transitional government, to establish his own small state in the south with its capital at Moundou.

The severity of the fighting is

The assault force receives final instructions before the attack on Faya-Largeau in February 1978.

proved by the fact that 70,000 refugees entered Cameroun, and many others fled to the Central African Republic, Niger, Nigeria, and Sudan. France refused to become embroiled in so confused a situation and pulled out its forces during May. By June Habre's forces had advanced far enough to the north to take the strategic town of Faya-Largeau and Goukouni responded by signing a treaty with Libya. This supplied additional equipment and men to

Goukouni, who went over to the offensive and took N'Djamena in December.

Just a few days later Habre's last stronghold, Abeche in the east of the country, fell to Goukouni's forces. Libyan forces effectively controlled the country for most of 1981 until withdrawn, at Goukouni's request, in November. Habre had meanwhile been biding his time in Sudan, building up his forces and laying his plans. In November 1981 he took advantage

of the Libyans' withdrawal to launch his invasion from Sudan, rapidly taking all important towns in eastern Chad, thereafter pushing on to Faya-Largeau, Massakory, Mao, Ati, Massaguet, and, on 7 June 1982, N'Djamena once more.

In August 1980 Goukouni Oueddei ordered out the French, and N'djamena became a battleground as all Chadian factions flooded the capital with troops.

Goukouni was forced out of office to become, once more, a guerrilla in the Tibesti region while Habre ceased being a rebel leader and assumed power in the capital, again with French assistance. At this point Ghadaffi chose to play a more decisive role in supporting Goukouni, and Habre's regime had therefore to rely on French and, increasingly, US assistance. In June 1983 the

fighting became very severe and in the following two months Faya-Largeau changed hands three times, ending in possession of the rebels.

Both sides have maintained the efforts since that time, the fighting between 1984 and 1986 has periodically been severe though fairly static. French air power has been decisive for the government, which sprang a considerable

surprise on the world during 1987 by taking Faya-Largeau and then, in a surprise move, retaking the Aouzou Strip from an apparently demoralized and completely inefficient Libyan garrison force. Libya claims to have abandoned

Oueddei's troops prepare for their invasion of northern Chad in 1982 with advanced weapons supplied from Libya.

its interest in the strip, but this seems unlikely when there may be every likelihood of regaining it during the continuing civil war, which pitches Habré's government forces against some 10,000 rebels: in the north are the mainly Arab forces of the Armée de Liberation Nationale (Army of National Liberation, the military wing of the Gouvernement d'Union Nationale du Tchad – Government for National Union in Chad), the FAP, the CDR (Conseil Démocratique de la Révolution – Democratic Council of the Revolution), and the FROLINAT; and in the south are the mainly black forces of the FAT (Forces Armées de Tchad, an organization or rebel Chadian army personnel), the FAC (Front d'Action Commune – Front for Communal Action), the MPLT (Mouvement

Oueddei's troops were prepared for French air attack with guns such as the 23-mm ZU-23-2 twin cannon (foreground) and 14.5-mm ZPU-4 quadruple machine-gun.

Populaire pour la Libération du Tchad – Popular Movement for the Liberation of Chad), the UND (Union Nationale Démocratique – National Democratic Union) and seven smaller groupings.

THE WAR FOR THE INDEPENDENCE OF NAMIBIA (1966-)

Colonized by the Germans between 1884 and 1890, German South-West Africa was overrun by South African troops in 1915 and after World War I became a South African-mandated territory. After World War II South Africa refused to hand South-West Africa over to the trusteeship of the United Nations, successor organization to the League of Nations, and continued to maintain its previous relationship with the area. In 1968 the UN declared that South-West Africa should become independent as Namibia, but South Africa has in fact only allowed a token autonomy to South-West Africa.

African aspirations to full independence rest with the SWAPO (South-West African

People's Organization), created in 1966 by Sam Nujoma and subsequently supported with finance, weapons, and base areas by the USSR and Angola. Since 1966 the SWAPO's military wing, the People's Liberation Army of Namibia, had undertaken a limited guerrilla and terrorist campaign from its bases in southern Angola. The SWAPO strength of about 9,000 is drawn mainly from the tribes of Ovamboland in northern Namibia, but only 1,500 of these are deployed against the South Africans in Namibia, the remaining 7,500 paying the organization's base fees by supporting the government in its war with the UNITA guerrilla movement.

South Africa provides enormous physical support for the South-West Africa Territory Force in the campaign against the SWAPO guerrillas, who have been unable to secure significant gains in Namibia as a result largely of the South African forces' excellent anti-guerrilla tactics, which have frequently involved incursions by air and ground forces deep into Angola to attack SWAPO base areas, and to keep this black organization and its Cuban or Soviet advisers off balance.

A South African mounted patrol is seen on a search and destroy patrol against SWAPO guerrillas in South-West Africa (Namibia).

THE WAR FOR THE INDEPENDENCE OF ERITREA (1970-)

Colonized by the Italians in 1882 but seized by the British in 1941, Eritrea was federated to Ethiopia in 1952 but annexed completely into that country in 1962. This incensed the highly independent Eritreans and in 1963 the Eritrean Liberation Front was created as the controlling organization to regain Eritrean independence. Some initial successes were achieved against the Ethiopians, but the independence effort was rapidly diluted by the factionalism of the ELF, which soon split into the Marxist-oriented Eritrean People's Liberation Force, the ELF Popular Liberation Forces, the Tigre People's Liberation Front, and the Ethiopian Democratic Union.

Thus the chance of early victory was lost, and in 1970 the Ethiopians declared martial law over Eritrea after the ELF had assassinated Major General Teshome Erghetu. In 1974 Emperor Haile Selassie was overthrown in a Marxist revolution that brought Colonel Mengistu Haile-Mariam to power. The Eritreans made extensive use of the chaos accompanying the change of regime to make another bid for complete Eritrean autonomy; Asmara was almost taken but factionalism again reared its head and the chance was lost.

The government has tried all types of tactics in its effort to crush the Eritrean independence factions, ranging from the use of peasant armies to starvation via Soviet-flown air attacks, but all have failed and the war continues unabated despite Ethiopia's desperate plight in the mid- and late 1980s as a result of drought, the ensuing famine, and the

extraordinary economics of the government.

This and some smaller liberation wars continue in Ethiopia, the rebel forces being mainly the 6,500 men of the ELF People's Liberation Force (operating as 14 'brigades'), the 5,000 men of the People's Liberation Front Revolutionary Guard, the 13,000

men of the Eritrean People's Liberation Front, the 600 men of the Oromo Liberation Front, and the 5,000 men of the Tigre People's Liberation Front.

ELF forces move cautiously towards the town of Kerkebet in the government-controlled Agordat region of Ethiopia.

ELF guerrillas at their Mongatil training camp in Agordat, Soviet-made weapons well in evidence.

235

The Spanish Sahara was colonized in 1884 as Río de Oro, but in the wave of European decolonization in the 1950s and 1960s was slated for independence. The region was claimed both by Morocco to the north and by Mauritania to the east and south. Algeria favoured a Saharan entity independent of both these states and therefore supported the Popular Front for the Liberation of Saguia el Hamra and Río de Oro (generally known as the Polisario), most powerful of the several independence movements of the area. Morocco supported the FLU (Liberation and Unity Front) while the Spanish backed the moderate PUNS (Sahrawi National United Party) for an independent state under local rather than exterior control.

In this highly confused situation the Spanish were hamstrung, the United Nations calling for a plebiscite and the International Court of Justice rejecting all Moroccan and Mauritanian claims to the area. In 1975 Spain announced its determination to pull out as rapidly as possible, and King Hassan of Morocco organized a 'peace march' of 350,000 Moroccans over the border into the northern reaches of Western Sahara, calling them back only under intense international pressure three days later on 9 November. In February 1976 Spain handed control of Western Sahara jointly to Morocco and Mauritania, which occupied the northern and southern halves of the country respectively, while on 26 February the Polisario declared its Saharan Arab Democratic Republic.

The scene was set for a difficult and continuing struggle for control of Western Sahara: Mauritania and Morocco were pitted against

The flag and men of the Algerian-backed Polisario.

236

concentrating its efforts on securing its holding in the northern part of Western Sahara (behind a vast and monumentally expensive line of fixed fortifications shielding the huge phosphate-mining operations around Bu Craa) and the Polisario striking at Moroccan targets in Western Sahara and southern Morocco with the aid of bases in Algeria and Mauritania.

This seems to be another of the modern wars without an apparent end, the Polisario being able to maintain its limited effort with Algerian support, and Morocco appearing willing to support the military effort in the region. The Polisario currently fields some 15,000 men and operates an increasingly sophisticated array of weapons that at times has cost the Moroccans dearly in aircraft and the other trappings of modern war.

Ethiopian troops near Kebri Dahar in the Ogaden region during September 1977.

Occupying the Horn of Africa, the Somali Democratic Republic came into being on 1 July 1960 from the former British Somaliland Protectorate (dating from 1884) and the former Italian colony of Somaliland (dating from 1886 but under British occupation from 1941 and British trusteeship from 1950). Somalia sees its historical purpose as providing a homeland for ethnic Somalis, including those

of Djibouti, Ethiopia, and Kenya.

In 1962 the UK established a commission that confined the desire of the Shifta people of northern Kenya for union with an independent Somalia, but rather than affront the black government that was about to take power in an independent Kenya, this desire was refused and, after breaking off relations with the UK, Somalia turned to the communist world for

arms and financial support. Somalia was already supporting the limited revolt of the Somali tribesmen in the Ogaden, Ethiopia's easternmost province, and also encouraged the disaffection of the Shifta nomads.

each other and the Algerian-backed Polisario fought both. The campaign proved too much for Mauritania's manpower reserves and finances, and in August 1979 Mauritania handed over its holding in the south to the Polisario, which immediately came under sole and intense military pressure from Morocco.

Since that time the war has continued unabated, Morocco

In 1967 Djibouti opted to maintain its links with France and President Kenyatta reduced the intensity of operations in northern Kenya by offering the Shiftas an amnesty. Thus the Somali effort was increasingly concentrated on the tribes of the Ogaden, especially after the installation of a military-backed revolutionary council as government of Somalia in October 1969.

In 1974 the Western Somalia Liberation Front was formed with the intention of integrating the eastern third of Ethiopia into Somalia. A sporadic guerrilla campaign between the 6,000 men

of the WSLF turned into full-scale war in 1977. There was clearly a large extent of direct Somali involvement in this campaign, which secured great success and cut Addis Ababa's rail link with the coast. Both Ethiopia and Somalia were receiving Soviet aid and the anomaly of the situation was resolved from November when the Somalis ordered out all Soviets and Cubans in anger at the former's massive resupply effort for the Ethiopians.

In February and March 1978 the revived Ethiopians went over to the offensive and recovered much of their losses in the

Ogaden rebels pose with an American-made 0.5-in machine-gun captured from Ethiopian forces.

previous year. The Somalis had anticipated this move and in February had overtly committed their troops for the first time. But under Soviet leadership and with a new generation of Soviet-supplied weapons, the Ethiopians proved more than a match for the Somalis and their rebel allies, and the Somalis were ejected from Ogaden by 9 March. This did not mark the end of the war, however, for the WSLF is still fighting a small-scale guerrilla campaign in Ogaden.

PART II   AMERICAN CONFLICTS

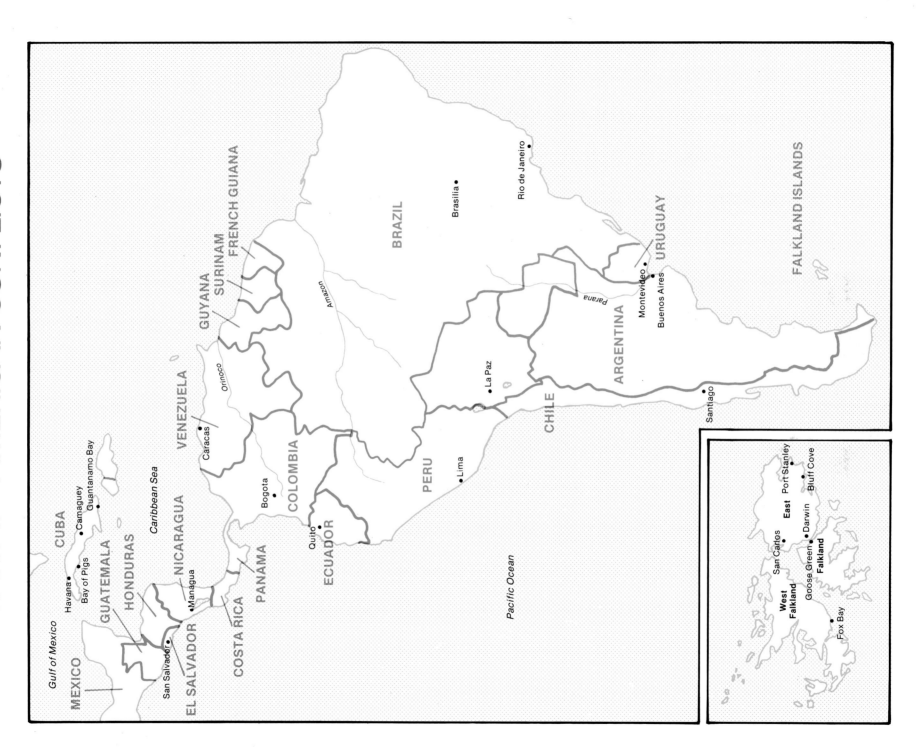

MEXICO

Gulf of Mexico

CUBA

Havana •
Camaguey •
Bay of Pigs • Guantanamo Bay

Caribbean Sea

GUATEMALA

HONDURAS

NICARAGUA
• Managua

EL SALVADOR
San Salvador •

COSTA RICA

PANAMA

VENEZUELA
Caracas •

COLOMBIA
Bogota •

ECUADOR
Quito •

Orinoco

GUYANA

SURINAM

FRENCH GUIANA

Amazon

PERU
Lima •

La Paz •

BRAZIL
Brasilia •

Rio de Janeiro •

Parana

ARGENTINA

URUGUAY
Montevideo •
Buenos Aires •

CHILE
Santiago •

Pacific Ocean

FALKLAND ISLANDS

West
Falkland

San Carlos •

East
Falkland

Port Stanley •
Bluff Cove •

Goose Green •
Falkland

Darwin •

Fox Bay •

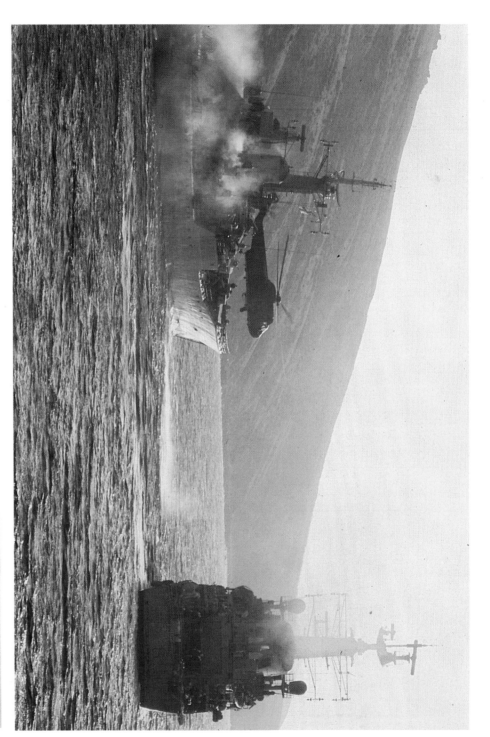

Above: Following an Argentine air attack, the frigate HMS Plymouth is seen in flames with HMS Avenger in close attendance during this episode on 8 June 1982 during the Falklands War.

Right: Poorly led and ultimately demoralized after being cut off from reinforcement and supply, the Argentines were finally able to offer only modest resistance to the British recapture of the Falklands.

AMERICAN CONFLICTS

CENTRAL AND SOUTH AMERICAN WARS (1900-41)

North America has been generally peaceful during the 20th century, though Central and South America have been a ferment of internal and external unrest throughout the period. In Mexico the overthrow of President Diaz on 25 May 1911 was followed by a succession of revolutions and squabbles between rival leaders, most notably Francisco Madera who was defeated and killed in February 1913, Victoriano Huerta whose regime was not recognized by the USA, and Venustiano Carranza.

In April 1914 the Huertists arrested a number of US sailors in Tampco and in response the USA occupied Vera Cruz between 25 April and 25 November 1914. In August 1914 Carranza became president of Mexico, but was opposed in the north by Francisco Villa, generally known as Pancho Villa. Defeated in his attempt to secure the presidency by General Alvaro Obregon, Villa launched a major raid across the border into the American state of New Mexico during March 1916. The Americans decided to bolster their garrisons along the frontier with Mexico, a task that eventually absorbed 158,000 men, and also to commit a punitive expedition into northern Mexico.

This expedition was commanded by Brigadier General John J. Pershing and the 10,000 US troops crossed the border on 15 March 1916 with Carranza's tentative approval. Several inclusive skirmishes were fought, some of them with government troops, but Villa refused to be brought to action and the Mexican authorities became increasingly restive with the presence of the US force, which was finally withdrawn on 5 February 1917.

In April 1920 Carranza was overthrown in a military rebellion headed by Generals Obregon, Adolfo de la Huerta, and Plutarco Calles, and, after a brief period of

US Marines in action during the occupation of Santo Domingo in the Dominican Republic during 1916.

renewed civil war in which Villa was defeated and surrendered, Obregon was declared president in September 1920. There followed a period of reconciliation and stability for Mexico.

Other Central American countries suffered a more tumultuous history in the period. On 3 November 1903, for example, there was a revolution in the Colombian province of Panama when the Colombian authorities refused to sell the isthmus of Panama to the USA for the proposed Panama Canal. US warships effectively prevented Colombian recapture of the area and on 6 November the USA recognized the independence of Panama, just 12 days later signing the treaty whereby the Panama Canal Zone was granted to the USA.

Between February and November 1907 war flared between Honduras and Nicaragua, the former being defeated and occupied by the Nicaraguans. In 1909 Honduras was racked by civil war when ex-president Manuel Bonilla rose against the government of President Miguel Danila. The war see-sawed until February 1911 when an armistice was agreed and in October Bonilla became president of a country that continued to suffer considerable internal unrest. US Marines had to be landed in January 1912 to protect US property in Honduras. Six months later civil war broke out in Nicaragua and again US Marines were landed, this time to stop the fighting and oversee elections.

A similar process was followed in the Caribbean, where US forces were used to quell trouble in Cuba (between February and March 1917), the Dominican Republic (May 1916, with the US Marines finally withdrawn in 1924), and Haiti (July 1915, with the US Marines remaining on the island to create and train a local police force). South America was comparatively quiet apart from revolutions or civil wars in Brazil (1924), Colombia (1900–3), Ecuador (1924–5) and Peru (1914).

The 1930s were generally quiet in Central and South America and the same pattern followed in the

Air supply was used by the US Marine Corps to maintain the momentum in its 1930 operations in Nicaragua by dropping food, medicines, and other supplies.

1940s when several of the countries of the region declared war on Germany and Japan. Mexico and Brazil contributed small combat forces but the main effort of Central and South America was passive, though food and bases were provided to the more active Allies.

From 1945 to 1965 Central America, the Caribbean, and South America reverted to their historical tendencies, with coup, counter-coup and border wars only slowly dying away as the countries of the region began to accept a less violent (but only slightly less violent) manner of solving their problems. Increasingly, however, the traditional antagonism between militarism and democracy has been superseded by the fight between communism and democracy, the latter often finding itself uneasily in bed with the militarism it had previously fought.

Tensions remain high in and between a number of South American states but the emphasis has shifted north to Central America, where communism has made considerable inroads, first in Cuba and then in Nicaragua, and threatens further progress in this region of small and almost incredibly volatile states. The major occurrences in Central and South America are extremely difficult to describe in a short compass, but are here sketched in alphabetical order of country.

In ARGENTINA there was considerable political unrest during

and after the overthrow of the administration of Juan Peron in 1956, there following a series of unstable military and civil regimes much beset by left-wing terrorists and right-wing death squads. In October 1983 Raoul Alfonsin was elected president and seems to have put Argentina back on to an basically democratic course.
In BOLIVIA there was a major revolution in 1946, President Villaroel being lynched. In 1952 a revolution by the MNR (National Revolutionary Movement) cost additional lives and ended with the presidency of Victor Paz Estenssoro from 1957. In 1967 a

communist revolution was started by Ernesto Guevara (Che Guevara) but this was poorly planned and led, and thus failed. In BRAZIL considerable urban terrorism has been undertaken since 1945 by the communist MR-8 movement, but from the early 1970s right-wing death squads have suppressed the communist effort and themselves become a major threat to Brazilian stability.

Troops loyal to President Alfonsin of Argentina prepare for possible action against rebellious units. Divided loyalties have often adversely affected the Argentine army.

In CHILE the 1970 elections produced the world's first democratically elected Marxist government under Dr. Salvador Allende, but this was overthrown (and Allende killed) in a military coup during September 1973 that led to the current military administration of General Augusto Pinochet.

In COLOMBIA a major civil war was fought between conservative and liberal factions in the period from 1948 to 1958, it being estimated that some 200,000 people lost their lives. The civil war was effectively ended by General Rojas Pinilla but the extremist elements became guerrillas in the FARC (Revolutionary Armed Forces) movement, supplemented from the mid-1970s by the M19 urban terrorist organization.

In COSTA RICA there was a civil war between March and April 1948, resulting in victory for the rebels, and in the aftermath of this conflict there were two abortive invasions by right-wing Costa Ricans from Nicaragua, the first in December 1948 and the second in January 1955.

In EL SALVADOR the country's withdrawal from Honduras after the Football War of 1969 led to widespread unrest as the country sought to assimilate the 300,000 Salvadoreans expelled from Honduras. A popular coup in 1978 installed a joint civil–military

Chilean troops have played a decisive part in maintaining the authoritarian position of President Pinochet.

Right: *Men of a Salvadorean government battalion take a rest during operations in Morazan province against the communist rebels.*

Bottom: *The hooded leaders of the Guatemalan labour party sit in front of the party's banner to display weapons captured from the government forces.*

administration, but this has been sorely beset by a force of some 6,000 FMLN Marxist guerrillas who took the offensive against the government in 1980. Some 40,000 lives have been lost, the majority of them to government reprisals and right-wing death squads, and the war continues to the present. In GUATEMALA right-wing forces led by Colonel Carlos Castillo Armas invaded the country from Honduras in June 1954 and ousted the communist President Arbenz.

In HONDURAS there were two wars in this period: the Honduras–Nicaragua Border War of 1957 in which Honduras retained the disputed town of Gracias a Dios, and the Football War of July 1969, a draw fought ostensibly because

of El Salvador's defeat of Honduras in the world cup football competition but over the underlying cause of Honduran annoyance with the presence of large numbers of Salvadorean unskilled labourers in Honduras.

In NICARAGUA the dictatorial family regime of President Anastasio Somoza was finally overthrown in July 1979 after a protracted effort (since September 1978) by the communist Frente Sandinista de Liberación Nacional (Sandinistan Front for National Liberation). The communist government installed under Dr. Daniel Ortega has since been beset by internal revolt (the Indians of the Moskito coast) and external threat (the Contra right-wing movement operating largely from Honduras and Costa Rica with American

support). The Contras are based on Somoza's national guard and are currently trying to overthrow the communist regime in a long-lasting war.

In PERU there was considerable Indian unrest in the 1950s and in 1965 the MIR (Movement of the Revolutionary Left) was suppressed by the army. Since the late 1970s the main threat to the government has been the Maoist Sendero Luminoso (shining path) movement.

In URUGUAY the main resistance to the government between 1963 and

1973 was the pro-Chinese Tupamero movement, but this was broken by a strong government full military backing.

In VENEZUELA there were four coups between 1945 and 1961, but then greater problems were caused up to 1964 by the communist FALN (National Liberation Armed Forces).

Managua suffered considerable casualties when President Somoza ordered his own Nicaraguan air force to bomb the forces attacking his palace in 1979.

THE CUBAN CIVIL WAR (1953-61)

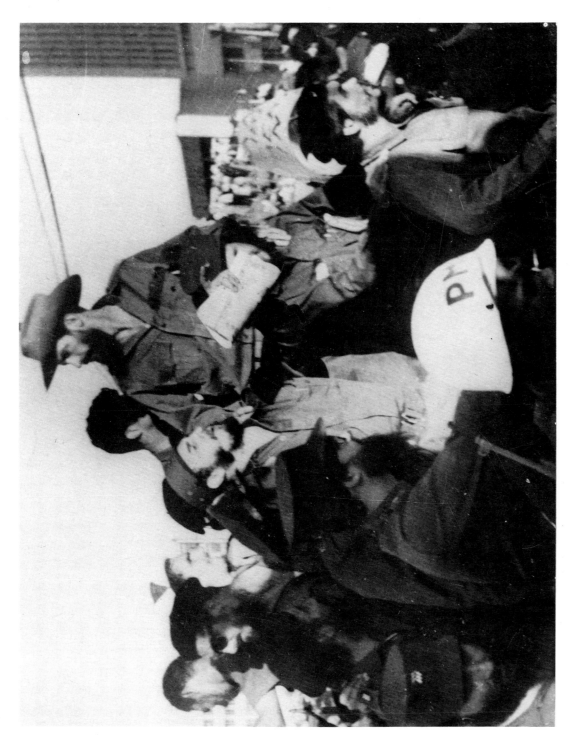

Fidel Castro enters Havana in triumph at the end of the Cuban revolution.

After the Spanish–American War of 1898 Cuba in 1901 became an independent republic under US protection. In 1940 Fulgencio Batista became president, rapidly turning Cuba into a state notable all over the world for its corruption and total inefficiency. With these two failings went an authoritarianism that secured the country's hatred for Batista.

In July 1953 communist risings were led in Santiago and Bayamo by the brothers Fidel and Raul Castro but were quickly suppressed. Fidel Castro was later freed and departed to Mexico, where he set about building up the organization and forces for a more effective revolution, which

started inauspiciously with a defeated landing in Oriente province on 30 November 1956. The government thought that Castro had been killed, whereas he had escaped into the Sierra Maestra mountains to build up a popular following. This was easily secured and from October 1958 Castro took the offensive against Batista, moving out of the Sierra Maestra area and increasing his support constantly as he advanced towards Havana.

Batista fled and on 8 January 1959 Castro entered Havana, establishing the communist regime that has lasted to the present day as a staunch ally of the USSR on the USA's southern doorstep. The

USA recognized Castro's government in January 1959 but broke off relations in January 1961 just before the catastrophic Bay of Pigs incident when Cuban counter-revolutionaries (with Central Intelligence Agency backing) were captured as they attempted a landing on 15 May 1961. Castro declared Cuba to be a socialist nation on 1 May 1961, and after the Cuban Missile Crisis of late 1962 the USA decided to call off any overt attempts to overthrow the Castro regime.

THE FALKLANDS WAR (1982)

The most 'conventional' military operations to have taken place in the Americas during recent times have been the Falklands War, occasioned by the Argentine occupation of the Falklands on 2 April 1982 as part of its effort to secure what Argentina claims as the Malvinas. The Argentines' military government thought that the British would not fight to resecure a comparatively small group of islands so far from the UK but was wildly far off the mark.

It took determined effort to create a task force for operations in the South Atlantic under Rear Admiral 'Sandy' Woodward with his land forces commanded by Major General Jeremy Moore but the first elements of this considerable expedition sailed on 5 April.

On 25 April Royal Marines retook South Georgia island, a dependency of the Falklands, and the tempo of operations around the Falklands increased with Argentine garrisons being overrun as part of the build-up to an assault on Port Stanley, the Argentines' main base in the islands. The converging columns had just secured jumping-off points for the final attack on 13 June when Menendez surrendered his forces and the campaign was brought to a victorious British conclusion.

Water, on the west side of East Falkland island, during 21 May. Once the British had consolidated this beach-head, infantry columns were despatched south-east and south across the island, small Argentine air attacks on the ships of the task force. Several ships were lost by the British but considerable damage was inflicted on the Argentines' air strength, and the islands were effectively cut off from the mainland. Under the command of Brigadier General Mario Menendez the Argentine occupation force now realized that it would have to fight for its existence when British forces started to land at San Carlos Water, on the west side of East Falkland island, during 21 May.

British troops come ashore during the 1982 landing at San Carlos that led to the defeat of the Argentine forces in the Falklands.

THE US INVASION OF GRENADA (1983)

A US Marine Corps UH-46 assault helicopter lifts off after landing an assault force in the US invasion of Grenada during 1983.

Lying in a strategically important position in the Leeward group of islands in the eastern Caribbean, Grenada became independent of the UK in 1974 and was then run by the corrupt but anti-communist Sir Eric Geary until the latter's overthrow in March 1979 by the communist Maurice Bishop. Shortly after this the Soviet and Cuban involvement in the island began to grow and from December 1979 Cuban construction brigades arrived to start the building of a new airport at Point Salines in the extreme south of the island.

The Grenadan government averred that this was to encourage tourism but the USA became increasingly worried that its real function would be as a staging post on Cuba's air bridge to its various support and advisory groups in Africa, and as a base for Soviet maritime patrol aircraft. In an effort to placate the Americans Bishop travelled to Washington in June 1983 but on his return was seized and executed by the hardliners in his own government, which was then taken over by General Hudson Austin.

Alarmed by this increasingly revolutionary trend in Grenada, the Organization of Eastern Caribbean States asked the USA to intervene and on 25 October 1983 US Marine Corps forces assaulted the island under the command of Admiral Wesley McDonald. Token contingents from the Caribbean states were also used and by 27 October the US presence had increased to 5,000 US Army paratroopers, 500 Marines, and 500 US Rangers. Local and Cuban resistance was tough and though the Americans secured the island without undue difficulty, it took them several days to find and overcome the smaller pockets of resistance.

INDEX